SUFI WISDOM SERIES

UNIVERSE RISING

BY
SHAYKH MUHAMMAD HISHAM KABBANI

EDITED BY MARC BOOTMAN

Discourses delivered by permission of his master
Mawlana Shaykh Muhammad Nazim Adil Al-Haqqani,
World Leader of the Most Distinguished
Naqshbandi Sufi Order

February 2006 -June 2006
Detroit, London, Oakland, Palo Alto, Washington

INSTITUTE FOR SPIRITUAL AND CULTURAL ADVANCEMENT

ISBN: 978-1-930409-48-4

Library of Congress Cataloging-in-Publication Data

TBD

Published and Distributed by:
Institute for Spiritual and Cultural Advancement
17195 Silver Parkway, #201 Fenton, MI 48430 USA
Tel: (888) 278-6624
Fax:(810) 815-0518
Email: staff@islamicsupremecouncil.org
Web: http://www.islamicsupremecouncil.org

Shaykh Muhammad Nazim Adil al-Haqqani (right), world leader of the most distinguished Naqshbandi-Haqqani Sufi Order, with his representative, and author of this book, Shaykh Muhammad Hisham Kabbani.

These are the portents of God which We recite unto you (O Muhammad) with truth, and Lo! you are of the number of (Our) messengers; Some of these messengers have We endowed more highly than others: among them were such as were spoken to by God and some He has raised yet higher.'

Holy Qur'an: The Heifer, 2:253

TABLE OF CONTENTS

EDITOR'S NOTES

This book consists of the teachings of Mawlana Shaykh Hisham Kabbani the authorized representative in the West of Mawlana Shaykh Nazim al-Qubrusi al-Haqqani ق. Mawlana Shaykh Nazim ق is Grandshaykh of the Most Distinguished Naqshbandi *Tariqat*, he holds the attention and love of millions of followers around the world. Our only hope is that they both be pleased with this work.

These are associations and Friday Prayer sermons given mainly in California in the late winter and spring of 2006. We present them largely in the same format in which they were given in order to preserve the spirit and charm of their transmission to all humanity. Wherever we could, we gave the date and place of each association (*suhba*).

As this book was designed to be accessible to non-Muslims, we have taken out many Arabic words and the original Arabic Quranic and hadith (traditions of the Holy Prophet Muhammad ﷺ) language, leaving only the English translation. Some limited use of Arabic words remains—for instance "*Sayyidina*" for "Our master." Where Arabic words are important to and explained by the substance of the text, they have been retained.

Since the original material was an oral transmission, extensive liberties were taken with the structure of the talks: there are some revisions of language that make it more readable in written form, and the addition of scientific and religious references were added where necessary. However, we have tried our best to retain the full flavor and essence of Shaykh Hisham's talks. We take full responsibility for these changes, and ask our shaykh's and our reader's forgiveness for any errors in the final text.

Citations from the Quran are footnoted with the chapter (*surah*) and verse number (e.g. 25:20) for easy look-up. The Traditions of the Holy Prophet ﷺ which have been placed in the text are referenced.

For people knowledgeable about Arabic and Islam: we apologize for the vastly simplified transliteration style used in the body of this. Our experience has been that transliteration symbols, when unfamiliar, make for heavy and difficult reading. Since this book is designed to be inviting and accessible to people without extensive knowledge of Arabic or Islam, we have completely omitted the diacritic marks. We ask for your patience with this compromise between accuracy and accessibility.

We use the personal pronouns "he" and "him" when speaking about a person who may be male or female—"he" is less awkward than the other solutions to this problem. We do not wish to offend women who read the book; this decision is only to improve flow of the text.

The following symbols are universally recognized by Muslims and have been respectfully included in this work:

The symbol ﷾ represents *subhaanahu wa ta'ala*, (may His Glory be Exalted) praise customarily recited after reading or pronouncing the name "Allah" and any of the Islamic names of God.

The symbol ﷺ represents *sall-Allahu 'alayhi wa sallam* (God's blessings and greetings of peace be upon him), which is customarily recited after reading or pronouncing the holy name of Prophet Muhammad.

The symbol ﷺ represents 'alayhi 's-salam (peace be upon him/her), which is customarily recited after reading or pronouncing the holy names of the other prophets, family members of Prophet Muhammad, the pure and virtuous women in Islam, and the angels.

The symbol ؞ represents radi-Allahu 'anh (may God be pleased with him/her), which is customarily recited after reading or pronouncing the holy names of companions of the Prophet.

The symbol ق represents qaddas-Allahu sirrah (may God sanctify his secret), which is customarily recited after reading or pronouncing the name of a saint.

ABOUT THE AUTHOR

Shaykh Muhammad Hisham Kabbani is a world-renowned author and religious scholar. He has devoted his life to the promotion of the traditional Islamic principles of peace, tolerance, love, compassion and brotherhood, while opposing extremism in all its forms. The shaykh is a member of a respected family of traditional Islamic scholars, which includes the former head of the Association of Muslim Scholars of Lebanon and the present Grand Mufti[1] of Lebanon.

In the U.S., Shaykh Kabbani serves as Chairman, Islamic Supreme Council of America; Founder, Naqshbandi Sufi Order of America; Advisor, World Organization for Resource Development and Education; Chairman, As-Sunnah Foundation of America; Chairman, Kamilat Muslim Women's Organization; and, Founder and President, The Muslim Magazine.

Shaykh Kabbani is highly trained, both as a Western scientist and as a classical Islamic scholar. He received a bachelor's degree in chemistry and studied medicine. In addition, he also holds a degree in Islamic Divine Law, and under the tutelage of Shaykh 'Abd Allah Daghestani ق, license to teach, guide and counsel religious students in Islamic spirituality from Shaykh Muhammad Nazim 'Adil al-Qubrusi al-Haqqani an-Naqshbandi ق, the world leader of the Naqshbandi-Haqqani Sufi Order.

His books include: *A Spiritual Commentary on the Chapter of Sincerity* (2006), *Sufi Science of Self-Realization* (Fons Vitae, 2005),

---

[1] The highest Islamic religious authority in the country.

Keys to the Divine Kingdom (2005); *Classical Islam and the Naqshbandi Sufi Order* (2004); *The Naqshbandi Sufi Tradition Guidebook* (2004); *The Approach of Armageddon? An Islamic Perspective* (2003); *Encyclopedia of Muhammad's Women Companions and the Traditions They Related* (1998, with Dr. Laleh Bakhtiar); *Encyclopedia of Islamic Doctrine* (7 vols. 1998); *Angels Unveiled* (1996); *The Naqshbandi Sufi Way* (1995); *Remembrance of God Liturgy of the Sufi Naqshbandi Masters* (1994).

In his long-standing endeavor to promote better understanding of classical Islam, Shaykh Kabbani has hosted two international conferences in the United States, both of which drew scholars from throughout the Muslim world. As a resounding voice for traditional Islam, his counsel is sought by journalists, academics and government leaders.

INTRODUCTION

Awliya teach us that Prophet Muhammad ﷺ is in continuous ascension towards the Divine. His uplifting is outside of time and space. It began before the beginning and will proceed to the end. He rises in every direction through creation as it emerges new and fresh in each instant. God, the Exalted, creates continuously and the Prophet ﷺ witnesses each new Divine Attribute as it emerges, develops, and replicates in all its aspects.

The implications are vast. While modern day physicists struggle to identify natural laws and universal constants, arguing about the Big Bang versus continuous creation, the Prophet ﷺ is witness to the ever-growing creation as it emerges from the unknown. He comprehends the knowledge that flows forth from this process and shares this bounty with the saints who follow in his path. These saints, or *awliya*, shine like polished jewels in our midst.

In this book, a compilation of talks given by Mawlana Shaykh Hisham Kabbani in 2006, a clear indication is given of the connection that the Prophetic Essence has to the process of creation. The connection for us today is immediate and vital: there are living saints who form a line of communication back through time to the Prophet ﷺ. In fact, these talks were inspired by such a one, Shaykh Hisham Kabbani's ق master, Mawlana Shaykh Nazim Haqqani ق. The saints live among us, we need only listen.

Marc Bootman

THE GREAT ASCENSION

In the name of God, the Beneficent, the Merciful.

Glory to He Who did take His servant for a Journey by night from the Sacred Mosque to the farthest Mosque, whose precincts We did bless,- in order that We might show him some of Our Signs: for surely He is the Hearing, the Seeing.[2]

God has revealed this as the first verse of the Holy Qur'an's chapter al-Isra, The Night Journey, which is also known as The Children of Israel, or the Chapter of Glorfication (*subhaan*). In it God mentioned the night journey, (*al-isra*), in which He called the Prophet Muhammad ﷺ to His Divine Presence.

As God began the Holy Qur'an in the Opening chapter al-Fatiha, with the words *"Alhamdulillah—Praise be to God,"* He similarly opens Surat al-Isra, the chapter of the Night Journey, with "Glory to Me, the One who brought the Prophet on the Night Journey calling him to My Divine Presence."

Reaching beyond comprehension of the human mind, God is not just reminding us about this event. Rather, He is glorifying Himself in regards to it, whereby He transported the Prophet ﷺ almost instantaneously from Mecca to Masjid al-Aqsa followed by the Prophet's ﷺ Ascension, traversing in an incredibly short span of time the worldly domain of this universe and beyond, transcending the laws of physics.

---

[2] Suratu 'l-Isra, (The Night Journey), 17:1.

1

There is no scientific, worldly way to comprehend how the Prophet ﷺ moved across the globe and was then carried to Allah's Divine Presence: such a journey is beyond the scope of imagination. Therefore Allah glorifies Himself saying, "Yes it happened! Glory to Me Who can do this! I am beyond these laws and systems. I am the Creator of all systems."

Angelic Preparation for the Miraculous Journey

Malik bin Anas ﷺ related that the Prophet ﷺ said, "I was lying in the Hijr (of the Sacred Mosque of Mecca) when someone [the archangel Gabriel ﷺ] came to me and cut open my chest from throat to belly. He removed my heart and cleaned it with the water of the well of Zamzam before putting it back in its place. Then he brought me a white creature called al-Buraq by whose means I was lifted."

Another narration relates that the two archangels "Gabriel and Mika'il ﷺ came to the Prophet ﷺ when he was laying down in al-Hijr [of the Sacred Mosque in Mecca] and carried him to the well of Zamzam. They laid him down on his back and Gabriel ﷺ opened his chest from top to bottom, despite which there was no bleeding. He said to Mika'il ﷺ, 'Get me water from Zamzam,' which he did. Gabriel ﷺ took the Prophet's ﷺ heart and washed it thrice before putting it back. He filled it with faith and wisdom. Then he closed his chest and they took him out from the door of the masjid to where the Buraq was waiting."

Archangel Gabriel could have removed the Prophet's ﷺ heart miraculously by means of a small opening or without opening his chest at all. Yet we see in this Tradition of the Prophet ﷺ a hint of how to perform open heart surgery. This same technique of opening the entire chest cavity is used by heart surgeons today.

Perfection of Servanthood

How did God describe the one whom He brought on the Night Journey? He describes him ﷺ as "His servant" — 'abdih. Abu Qasim Sulayman al-Ansari said that when the Prophet ﷺ reached the highest levels and most distinguished stations. God revealed to him, "With what shall I honor you?" The Prophet said, "By relating me to You through servanthood ('ubudiyya)." This is why God revealed this verse of the Holy Qur'an honoring the Prophet ﷺ by the title "His servant" when describing the Night Journey. God did not grant such an honor to Moses ﷺ. Rather He said, *"And when Moses came to Our appointed tryst..."*[3] referring to Moses ﷺ by his name. Instead of saying, "Glory be to Him Who made Muhammad to go..."

God honored the Prophet ﷺ by referring to him as 'abdihi — His servant. Another subtle inference from God's use of the term 'abdihi — His servant (a construct in the absent form or third person) is the meaning that, 'He called the Prophet ﷺ to a void where there was nothing except His Own Presence.' More miraculous than calling the Prophet ﷺ to His Presence was His bringing the Prophet's ﷺ body and soul, which exist in time and place, to where there is no time and place, no 'where' and no 'when'. God brought His sincere servant, our master Muhammad ﷺ, from a physical form of this worldly life to the completely abstract Divine Presence.

States of Proximity to the Divine Presence

The verse goes on to describe the Prophet's movement through countless stations. Having perfected his character through constant worship, 'ubudiyya, the Sacred Mosque, or Holy Sanctuary, is here an indication of the Prophet's ﷺ having already

---

[3] Suratu 'l-'Araaf, (The Heights), 7:143.

3

been elevated beyond all sin. God's description of the Prophet ﷺ as "'*abd*"—servant—precedes His mention of the two mosques: the Sacred Mosque (Masjid al-Haraam) and the Far Distant Mosque (Masjid al-Aqsa). God did not say His Servant was taken "from Mecca," rather He said, "from the Sacred Mosque," Masjid al-Haraam. "Sacred" means inviolable, no sin being permitted within its precincts, nor backbiting, cheating, or lying. There one must be ever mindful of God's ﷻ Presence.

Masjid al-Haraam, represents here a station where those sins which signify the animal life can never be committed. 'Aqsa' in Arabic means 'the Farthest'. Thus Masjid al-Aqsa here is named as the farthest mosque in relation to Masjid al-Haraam and symbolizes the spiritual realm. The literal meaning is, 'He brought His servant from Masjid al-Haraam to the mosque at the farthest end.' Symbolically, God brought the Prophet away from that which is forbidden things of this earthly life, *haraam*, to the place furthest away from it—*al-Aqsa*. The furthermost point from the animalistic life is the spiritual dimension.

The contrast between these 'stations' is further demonstrated by the famous stone at each of these holy sites. In Masjid al-Haraam, the Sacred Mosque in Mecca, the Black Stone is governed by physical constraints, held up in an encasement, having fallen from heaven and become darkened by the sins of humanity. At Masjid al-Aqsa the holy stone marking where the Prophet ﷺ ascended to the heavens is miraculously suspended in the air, disregarding the physical law of gravity, seeking to leave the earthly pull of gravity to soar towards the Divine Presence.

The subtle meaning derived from the order of the words here is that Allah's one true servant, the Prophet Muhammad ﷺ, began from station of '*ubudiyya*, servanthood, for which he was created. This allowed him to begin from the station of perfected and flawless character ('*ismat*), shunning the forbidden and the love of

4

this worldly life (*al-haraam*) and move from there to the farthest station, the highest rank of all creation, as indicated by the station of the farthest mosque, *al-aqsa*.

Stages of Sufism

In the Science of Purification of the Self, *tasawwuf*, these stages are termed *Shari'ah, tariqat* and *haqiqat*. The first corresponds to the realm of physical discipline, whence the seeker moves on the path, *tariqat*, with the vehicle of *'ubudiyya*, worship, and thence ascends to the station of *haqiqat*, reality, in which all falsehood vanishes and the Lordship of God is made eminently manifest to the servant.

Allah brought Prophet Muhammad ﷺ to Masjid al-Aqsa in Palestine from which most of the prophets hail. There he ﷺ found all of the prophets gathered, and they prayed in congregation behind him ﷺ. From there Allah raised him to the heavens, as if saying, "O My prophets! I did not raise anyone from Masjid al-Aqsa as I am raising Muhammad ﷺ." This was in order to demonstrate to them Prophet Muhammad's ﷺ ascendancy— unlike any one of them, he was not restricted by the laws of this universe.

Risen by Night, Illuminating Like the Full Moon

Allah then lifted him from the Sacred Mosque in Jerusalem, Masjid al-Aqsa by means of the Ascension (*mi'raaj*), to His Divine Presence. Why did God use the words, "*laylan*—by night"? Why didn't He say, "*naharan*—by day"? "*Laylan*" here illustrates the darkness of this world; it becomes illumined only by the bright moon of the Prophet ﷺ rising to brighten every darkness. "*Glorified be He Who carried His servant by night...*" Look at every word of this holy verse. First God praised Himself in the third person, in absence. God then miraculously moved the Prophet from Mecca to Masjid al-Aqsa (*asra*). Then He referred to the Prophet as *'abd*, servant, distinguishing him through that elevated title as being related to the spiritual life, not the animal life. The message of Prophet Muhammad ﷺ completed and perfected both the physical discipline and jurisprudence (*Shari'ah*) of Moses and the spirituality (*rawhaaniyya*) of Jesus ﷺ. The *Shari'ah* of Moses ﷺ relates to the worldly life and the spirituality of Jesus ﷺ relates to the heavenly life. By passing from the worldly life, represented by the Night Journey, to heavenly life, represented by the Ascension, the Prophet ﷺ was carried on these two wings. No prophet was carried in both these dimensions except our master Muhammad ﷺ.

Prophetic Conveyances

One of the great scholars of Qur'anic exegesis, al-'Ala'ee said:

On the Night of Ascension the Prophet used five different vehicles. The first was the Buraq, a winged creature which carried him from Mecca to Masjid al-Aqsa. The second was the Ascension by which the Prophet ﷺ reached the sky of this world, *as-sama ad-dunya*. There are two explanations for Mi'raaj: one that the Buraq carried the Prophet ﷺ up and the second that a ladder descended and raised the Prophet ﷺ very rapidly. The third vehicle was the wings of angels taking the Prophet ﷺ up to the seventh heaven. The fourth were the wings of Gabriel ﷺ from the seventh heaven to the Furthermost Lote Tree, *sidrat al-muntahaa*. The fifth vehicle was the carpet (*ar-rafraf*) to the station of *"two bows-length—qaaba qawsayn."*[4] Similarly, the Prophet ﷺ stopped in ten different stations: seven heavens and the eighth at the Furthermost Lote Tree, *sidrat al-muntahaa*. The

---

[4] Suratu 'n-Najm, (The Star), 53:9.

ninth is where he heard the sound of the angels' pens writing the actions of human beings and the tenth level was at the Throne. And God knows best."

Miraculous Aspects of the Night Journey and Ascension

All these miraculous events took place on the night of the Night Journey and Ascension, Laylat al-Isra wal-Mi'raaj. The many hadiths detailing the events of the Night Journey were authenticated by numerous *huffaazh* (hadith masters) such as Ibn Shihaab, Thaabit al-Banaani, and Qataada. God supports His prophets with miracles (*mu'jizaat*) to be able to transcend the laws of physics and the constraints of our human realities. If Allah grants a miracle we should not view it as something improbable, otherwise we will be like scientists who cannot understand anything beyond what they perceive.

Scholars differ as to what night this great journey occurred on. Imam Nawawi said that it took place in Rajab. In Nawawi's *ar-Rawdah*, he states it occurred ten years and three months after the beginning of the Prophecy, while in *Fatawa* he states it was five or six years after the onset of revelation. Whatever the case, all scholars concur that the Night Journey and Ascension took place both in body and spirit.

Abraham's Vision and the Spiritual Dimension

God said in the Holy Qur'an:

> *So also did We show Abraham the kingdom of the heavens and the earth that he might have certitude.*"[5]

Allah showed the kingdom of heavens and earth to Prophet Abraham ﷺ, by opening his spiritual vision (*baseera*) to see the wonders of the universe from where he was on earth. Allah

---

[5] Suratu 'l-An'am, (Cattle), 6: 75-79.

showed him what is beyond the laws of the physical universe through the eyes of his heart. Yet immediately after this verse God has shown Abraham ﷺ the glories behind the physical universe:

> *When the night covered him over he saw a star. He said,*
> *"This is my Lord."*[6]

In the following verses Abraham ﷺ similarly "mistakes" the moon and sun for his Lord:

> *When he saw the moon rising in splendor he said, 'This*
> *is my Lord." But when the moon set he said, "Unless my*
> *Lord guides me I shall surely be among those who go*
> *astray." When he saw the sun rising in splendor he said,*
> *'This is my Lord."*[7]

These verses regarding the stars, moon, and sun are directed to the non-believers. God showed Abraham ﷺ the Truth and he had reached certitude of faith.

As a prophet he was also free of sin, and thus could not have considered other than Allah as his Lord. However, Abraham's ﷺ duty was to convey a heavenly message. Seeking to bring everyone under God's mercy, Abraham ﷺ attempted to teach his people in a way that would not cause them to reject his message. Wisely using a process of elimination, he demonstrated to them that a spiritual dimension exists. He eliminated the star (something small); then the moon; then the sun (the biggest heavenly body). Abraham ﷺ then reaffirms his true belief in Allah and his turning away from worldly distractions saying:

> *But when the sun set he said, "O my people, I am*
> *innocent and free from the sin of you ascribing partners*
> *to God. For me I have set my face firmly and truly*

---

[6] Suratu 'l-An'am, (Cattle), 6:77.
[7] Suratu 'l-An'am, (Cattle), 6:78.

*towards the One Who created the heavens and the earth,
and I am not one who ascribes partners to God."*[8]

The meaning of this demonstration: don't chase the things of this worldly life, but seek the spiritual dimension which transcends the laws of the physical universe.

In our time, materialistic scientists and certain narrow-minded Islamic sects try to negate spirituality, the fourth dimension, which Allah showed to Abraham ﷺ. Those rejecting the spiritual dimension of Islam are falling into the same trap as the people of Abraham. The Prophet ﷺ said, "what I fear most for my community is the hidden *shirk* (associating partners to God)."[9] Hidden *shirk* is for a person to be prideful of himself, most easily manifest in rejecting the words of others.

The Distinction of Prophet Muhammad's Ascension

Prophet Abraham ﷺ was shown the kingdom, *malakoot*, of heavens and earth. Prophet Moses ﷺ did not see this kingdom. However he was able to hear God and speak with God from Mount Sinai, thus being known as Kalimullah (the one who spoke with God directly). Although Abraham ﷺ was granted the ability to see in spiritual dimensions, and Moses ﷺ was granted to hear God directly, both of these great prophets' bodies remained on earth, subject to its physical laws. Prophet Abraham's ﷺ vision and Prophet Moses' ﷺ hearing went beyond the physical by means of the power of the soul, but their bodies did not move beyond the physical world.

However, Allah caused Prophet Muhammad ﷺ to move in spiritual dimensions with his body in complete freedom from physical laws. Allah called the Prophet *"to show him from Our*

---

[8] Suratu 'l-An'am, (Cattle), 6:79.
[9] Ahmad, at-Tabarani, and al-Bayhaqi.

signs...[10]" God showed Abraham the kingdom of this universe, but He moved the Prophet ﷺ in body and spirit beyond the physical laws of this universe to show him 'Our signs'—*ayaatina*. This possessive form relating the Signs as belonging to God directly, indicates the greater honor and knowledge bestowed on the Prophet ﷺ. The kingdom of heavens and earth shown to Prophet Abraham ﷺ was the workings of this physical universe and did not reach Paradise, whereas God's signs manifested to Prophet Muhammad ﷺ are directly related to God and are not associated with this world.

The Prophet's Vision of His Lord

God revealed to His servant what He revealed. The Prophet's heart in no way falsified what it saw. Will you then dispute with him about what he saw? And he saw Him again another time at the Lote-tree of the utmost boundary, at the Garden of Abode. Behold the Lote-tree was shrouded with what shrouds. His sight did not swerve or waiver. Indeed he saw of the Signs of his Lord, the Greatest.[11]

Imam Nawawi and the late Imam Metwalli Sha'rawi concur with the majority of scholars in interpreting these verses to mean that the Prophet ﷺ saw his Lord another time, not that he saw Gabriel ﷺ another time, as other scholars assert. Imam Nawawi relates in his commentary on *Sahih Muslim*, "Most of the scholars say that the Prophet saw his Lord with the eyes of his head—*ra'a rabbahu bi 'aynay raasihi*. The Prophet came all the way to the Divine Throne (*'arsh*), reached *qaaba qawsayni* (the distance of two bow's length), and reached the Paradise of Jannat al-Maa'waa near the Furthermost Lote-Tree (*sidrat al-muntahaa*).

---

[10] Suratu 'l-Isra (The Night Journey), 17: 1.
[11] Suratu 'n-Najm (The Star), 53: 10-19.

After all this Imam Sha'rawi asks, "What would make the Prophet's sight swerve? Some say it was Gabriel 彅, but the Prophet 舙 had seen Gabriel 彅 many times and Gabriel was with him for the duration of the Night Journey and Ascension. It is irrelevant to say at this juncture that the Prophet's sight did not swerve or waiver, because if this was in reference to Gabriel the Prophet had many opportunities to see him already. God doesn't say anything irrelevant which is why I side with the majority of scholars (including Imam Nawawi) in saying that with his physical eyes the Prophet 舙 saw God, the Exalted."

Indeed he saw of the Signs of his Lord, the Greatest.[12]

What then could the Greatest Sign be for the Prophet 舙 other than the vision of his Lord? For the Prophet 舙 saw all seven levels of Paradise, then ascended further than any creation before or after, to *"two bows-length or nearer."* It is stated in hadith that the greatest reward for believers in the next life will not be the pleasures of Paradise, but the vision of their Lord every Friday. If the believers, the common and the special, are going to see their Lord in the afterlife, then clearly nothing less than that could be "the Greatest Sign" for His Beloved Prophet Muhammad 舙.

And We granted the vision which We showed you (O Muhammad) but as a trial for mankind.[[13]

Regarding this verse, Ibn 'Abbas said, "God's Messenger 舙 actually saw with his own eyes the vision (of all which was shown to him) on the night of his Night Journey to Jerusalem (and then to the heavens)..." That is the greatness of Prophet Muhammad. No one saw his Lord other than Muhammad 舙, making him 舙 the only true monotheist—*muwahhid*. No one except Muhammad 舙

---

[12] Suratu 'n-Najm, (The Star) 53:18.
[13] Suratu 'l-Isra (The Night Journey), 17:60.

achieved a perfect grasp of Divine Unity—*tawheed*. Everyone else's understanding of *tawheed* remains imitative (*taqleed*).

Prophet Abraham ﷺ was the father of the prophets and was granted spiritual vision to see the workings of the universe and Prophet Moses ﷺ was granted to speak with his Lord. But Allah moved Prophet Muhammad with his physical body in defiance of the physical laws of the universe to the Unseen, a place where there is nothing and no possibility of anything—*"laa khalaa wa la malaa."* Allah took Muhammad there and revealed to him Himself, in the manner He wished. How this was we do not know. It is unseen and unknown (*ghayb*). Thus, as Ibn 'Abbas ﷺ said, it is a matter to be believed with acceptance, not a matter to be questioned.

Explanation of the Idol Verses

> *His sight did not swerve or waiver. Indeed he saw the*
> *Greatest Signs of his Lord. Have you seen Laat and*
> *'Uzza (two pagan idols) and the third one Manaat*
> *(another idol)?*[14]

Why does Allah mention these three false deities, Laat, 'Uzza and Manaat, which the polytheistic idolaters of Mecca worshipped, immediately after mentioning the *"Greatest Signs of his Lord"* in 53:18? Scholars say that 53:18 shows that Muhammad ﷺ reached perfect grasp of Allah's Unity, while the verses 53:19-20 by contrast show these idols as nothing more than fabrications of their makers. If *"Greatest Signs"* referred to Gabriel then it would not follow to mention the false idols after it.

Prophet Abraham ﷺ mentioned a star, the moon and the sun— three entities of this worldly life—as objects falsely taken as gods besides God. And in the Chapter of the Star (an-Najm), Allah

---

[14] Suratu 'n-Najm (The Star), 53:17-20.

mentioned al-Laat, al-ʿUzza and Manaat, again three false gods, immediately describing Prophet Muhammad's seeing his Lord, as explained by most scholars. Both these revelations reject the false concept of idol-worship, and subtly stress the false notion of a trinity, which pervades most forms of idolatry. Oneness is for Allah the Exalted and Glorious, the One—al-Wahid, the Unique—al-Fard, the Eternal—as-Samad.

OF JEWELS AND SAINTS

*J*ust as from the dust of Earth emerge diamonds, emeralds, rubies and sapphires, so do some human souls get polished into precious gemstones capable of holding, reflecting and transmitting light. When a man or a woman becomes like a jewel, he or she is being perfected by a saint who oversees the spiritual energies for a given part of the globe. Every area has such a *wali*, an enlightened guide who is in charge of it. Such saints direct and modulate angelic light by which they transmute rough stones into glowing gems and transform souls into vessels of heavenly light. The Earth, in its fashion, swallows carbon and, over time, within its depths, under tremendous geological pressures and temperatures, may send the element back to its surface as a diamond. Just so, a *wali* can focus Divine light upon a human soul and forge an enlightened being, as rare and precious as any crown jewel.

God, the Exalted, sends certain people before these guides to be polished. While it may take millions of years at high compression to turn a lump of carbon into a diamond, one look from a *wali* can change a normal human being into a saintly soul.

Look at Professor Ahmed. Is he the same as when he came first to our master, Mawlana Shaykh Nazim ق? No. Before, he was proud of himself. Before, he was proud of his science, his many PhDs; proud of what he was doing. Now he looks at that and no pride comes to his heart, because he learned to be humble and to embrace that reality. He helped design the Hubble Telescope so that mankind could see into distant space and time.

Yet, when he sat at the feet of Mawlana Shaykh, he saw even further, and instantly found his knowledge to be nothing in the presence of a true knower. All his knowledge became like *epsilon* before infinity. That person, Nazeer Ahmad, is one of the rare followers of Mawlana Shaykh.

In the books of *seerah*, where the Prophet ﷺ reports a description of the heavens, one reads of entire palaces composed from a single huge pearl or diamond. On Earth, pearls can be made by seeding oysters with grains of sand, which the creature then coats with layers of lustrous stone. For pearls within humankind, the real manufacturing of such jewels is done by the angels, from the lights that come through the eyes of a *wali*. Different people are affected by this light in various ways, depending on the level of the presiding *wali*. If he is a powerful *wali*, the most precious gems will be produced. If he is less powerful, the result will be semi-precious stones, and so on.

Remote Sensing

Sometimes the *awliyaullah*[15] look at those who are very knowledgeable in their fields and polish them. This can double or triple the knowledge of such individuals, alter their patterns of thought and expand their horizons. Even though these scholars and specialists may be involved in, worldly (*dunya*), work, if they are under the guidance of Mawlana Shaykh he may clothe them with certain powers enabling them to carry the realities those attributes. In effect, as Mawlana dresses people, they become his eyes, each according to his own level. Through their eyes, Mawlana can see other people. Whenever the shaykh wants to look at the people around his followers, he will use the eyes of the disciple (*mureed*) to see who is there and attract them to the

---

[15] Plural of *wali*, saints.

disciple as though to himself. This is deep wisdom and is normally hidden.

This is why the Prophet ﷺ told the Sahaba, (his Companions,) to travel. Like ripples spreading in a pond, the Prophet's Companions fanned out across the Earth, attracting people to their faith. In so doing, these emissaries became healthy—not necessarily in the physical sense, but in their spiritual lives. This is because, as the Prophet ﷺ used them to attract people, he cleansed them.

When a shaykh uses someone as his eyes or his voice, they are purified and become suitable instruments for the special function of transmission. Clear minds, pure hearts, can accurately forward messages, like efficient parts of a well-designed telecommunications system. On the other hand, broken wires or dirty lines will garble or confuse the meaning: no one will hear or be attracted to the message. So the shaykh refines his disciples. They become subtle: sensitive to the appropriateness of their words and manner for given audiences. Not everyone can do this. The ability to speak effectively to a wide spectrum of human types is rare indeed. Through the inspiration and guidance of a spiritual master, such things become possible.

This is the, wisdom (*hikmah*), behind Mawlana Shaykh Nazim's global reach. He has disciples and students at various levels of ability around the world and through them he is able to catch anyone wherever he likes. By this means his wisdom is spread universally and he has knowledge of every place his disciples are present. While he may physically appear to be in one place at one time, he resides at the center of a sensory net, which sends and receives information on a moment-to-moment basis. But unlike the Internet, his net is made of human souls connected together in a special design, specifically suited to radiate angelic influences, a major lifeline for humanity in a time of increasing crisis.

Go West

Prophet Muhammad ﷺ said, "Seek wisdom, even in China."ⁱ One of the many meanings behind this is his encouraging the Companions to reach as far as China because he could use them (and later the *awliya*) as points of transmission who would, in turn, attract followers to the Way (*tariqah*). That is why you can say that Grandshaykh Nazim ق has 1,000 disciples, or 100,000 disciples. But in reality there are far more: not in the physical realm, but in the spiritual realm, where there are millions. That is why the Community of the Prophet ﷺ is divided between 124,000 *awliyaullah*. Every *wali* has his own group.

I was explaining the hadith, "Seek wisdom, even in China." When the Prophet ﷺ was in Mecca and they were abusing him and torturing the Companions, some of these early Muslims were not able to defend themselves or to endure the pain and suffering.

The Prophet ﷺ said, "Seek wisdom even in China."[16] When the Prophet was in Mecca, he began sending his followers to various parts of the planet. So where did he send them? He sent some of them to Abyssinia, to a kingdom ruled by a Christian king, no less! The Prophet ﷺ sent them from Mecca to Abyssinia. What direction is that? It is West of Mecca. So the Prophet ﷺ in this instance is saying, "When you are in difficulties seek asylum in the West." It is one of the subtle indications (*ishaaraat*) that the Community is going to find its peace and safety in the West. While he could have sent them south to Yemen, he did not. He did not send them to north to Russia. Instead, from Mecca he sent

---

[16] al-Bayhaqi in *Shu'ab al-Imaan* and *al-Madkhal*, Ibn 'Abd al-Barr in *Jami' Bayaan al-'Ilm*, and al-Khatib in *al-Rihla fi Talab al-Hadith*.

them West. That is the first indication that there were going to be Muslims inhabiting the West.

So what was he doing with these Companions? They served as bridges to the king of Abyssinia, whose title was Negus. What did the king do? The Negus accepted them, and accepted Islam. Did America accept Islam or not? Did Europe accept Islam or not? Did the Prophet ﷺ try to fight the Abyssinians? No. That is an indication that when you seek asylum in the West you do not seek to fight.

Then the Prophet ﷺ migrated to Madina where he established the Islamic state. At that time what did the he say? He said, "Seek wisdom, even in China." Where is China? It is to the East of Madina, slightly north. So here lies another subtle indication, "Find asylum in the East." That is another interpretation of this hadith. For that reason you find many Sahaba in China, for they understood the subtle meaning of this hadith of the Prophet ﷺ.

Today this hadith is commonly thought to mean that, if knowledge is far away or difficult to obtain, we should nevertheless, strive for it. But the meaning is also that the faithful could go to far places and find asylum. For example, emissaries were sent to Central Asia, far to the east and north of Madina—in the direction of China. Many links to Central Asia were established: Bukhara, Kyrgyzstan, Iran, Tajikistan Pakistan, India, East Asia, all these places are to the east.

And what happened? The Prophet ﷺ moved many Companions there. So it became like a bridge, spanning the gulf between East and West. He did not say, "Seek war, even in China," nor did he say "go to Abyssinia and fight." Rather he ﷺ said, "I am sending you to a merciful king." So the Prophet ﷺ sent his Companions because they were, in effect, all *awliyaullah* and through them he spread angelic power. Even today, the *awliyaullah* convey this angelic power everywhere, attracting people to the path.

In Istanbul, there is a door, called the gate of Bayazid, near the Grand Bazaar. One day Grandshaykh 'Abd Allah ad-Daghestani ق and Mawlana Shaykh Sharafuddin ad-Daghestani ق, went to this door. They stood on either side of the gate and held their hands together over the entrance. Mawlana Shaykh Sharafuddin ق said, "It has been ordered that anyone who passes under our hands will enter the *shafa'a*, intercession, of the Prophet."

With that simple action, the Prophet ﷺ used his power to allow people to enter Paradise. And so they stood there, holding their hands, in an arch over the heads of people from morning to evening, neither eating nor drinking, allowing people to pass between them. *Awliyaullah* are granted these special powers. People who don't understand their behavior or powers cannot accept such actions. We ask Allah to open our eyes.

There is yet an even subtler indication in these hadiths urging the Companions to travel to distant places for the sake of refuge or knowledge. In them is a push to the seeker—for traveler here may be interpreted as a seeker in the Way of God—to push himself or herself to ascend ever higher and farther, traveling to distant "lands" of spirituality. The meaning of "lands" is different levels of understanding—levels where the "language" is far different from the one we know, the tastes, smells, sights and sounds are all at a higher level of understanding. To do this, the seeker then must prepare himself well, taking with him supplies, and riding a sturdy mount or vehicle in order to cross the vast deserts or oceans in his path. The supplies are love of God, tempered by fear of God and yearning for the Divine Presence. The oceans are those of Divine Knowledge, which as the seeker traverses, will fill his heart and soul with knowledge, gnosis and the taste of realities. The deserts are the huge empty spaces in the heart and the obstacles are the temptations of ego. Brigands on the way are the rapacious whisperings of Satan and the weapons against them are the sword of ablution and the shields of remembrance and prayer.

Thus the man or woman of God, is always a traveler, meaning that the seeker never stops seeking. For after one "land" there is another, and after it yet another. For this the Prophet ﷺ said, "My connection with the world is like that of a traveler resting for a while underneath the shade of a tree and then moving on."[17] This can be taken as "whatever level of closeness to God I reach, I am never content with, but I must keep moving and never stopping except briefly, in acquisition of Godly wisdoms and realities."

The Humble Shepherd

Today, you cannot find anyone who does not think very highly of himself. Though someone might deny it, he is lying. There is a story about one of the disciples of Grandshaykh Jamaluddin al-Ghumuqi al-Husayni ق. This disciple was not good for anything. Everything he touched turned out poorly. Finally the shaykh got fed up and said to him, "Look, I have a flock of sheep that I want you to tend. You will take them up into the pastures in the morning and bring them back in the evening. That way you will be kept away from the other disciples and stop contaminating them." So that follower took on the duties of a shepherd going up into the mountains and back again each day.

Now whenever an occasion arose, he would take one or two of the lambs and sacrifice them, and distribute the meat to the poor. When Mawlid an-Nabi, the celebration of the Prophet's Birthday, ﷺ, came, one lamb would be gone, then later two lambs, and so on. The meat was distributed each time: for the tenth of

---

[17] Ahmad, Tirmidhi.

Muharram[18]; for the fifteenth of Shaban[19]; for Rajab[20]; for Ramadan[21]; for Eid al-Adha[22]—until, finally, the whole flock was finished. When the shaykh went to check on his flock, he asked, "What happened?" The disciple-cum-shepherd explained that he had slaughtered the sheep and had given away the meat to the poor for the love out of the Prophet ﷺ. "For Mawlid an-Nabi, for Rajab, for nisf-Sha'ban... I gave all to everyone."

The shaykh decided to teach him a lesson. He told the disciple, "You are the worst of my students!" The shaykh loudly berated him, shouting, "You are the worst of the worst; the lowest of the lowest! Don't come here again! You are a bad influence on everyone!" The shaykh told the others to throw him out and to avoid him on sight.

At this point the shaykh looked into the heart of his disciple and saw that his love for his shaykh had not changed. Today, where would you find this? If you correct a disciple with one word, he becomes upset and is rude to his shaykh. He says, "O who cares for *tariqah*? Give back my initiation, my *baya'*!"

So the other disciples threw the shepherd out. At that time, the Russians were in control of the area and very few mosques were open. The Sufis went to the mosques at night. The Russians didn't interfere because, for the most part, the people of *tariqat*, the Way, were not involved in politics. This was in the time of Sayyidina Jamaluddin al-Ghumuqi al-Husayni.[23]

---

[18] 'Ashura, an important holy day in spiritual Islam.

[19] Nisf Sha'ban, the spiritual New Year in Islam.

[20] Laylat al-Isra wa'l-Mi'raaj, the holy Night Journey and Ascension.

[21] Islamic month of fasting and special prayer.

[22] Holy day celebrating Abraham's submission to His Lord's Will.

[23] See Mawlana Shaykh Nazim's lecture "The Final Limit" in *Mercy Oceans' Lovestreams* p. 101-110.[23] 35th master in the Golden Chain of the Naqshbandi –Sufi Order, Sayyidina Jamaluddin al-Ghumuqi al-Husayni lived in Daghestan, in the

So the outcast disciple crept into the mosque and hid behind a pillar. He sat and talked to himself, "*Subhanallah*. The shaykh ordered you to do this, you failed. He ordered you to do this—you failed. At the end he ordered you to take care of his flocks—you failed. You are the worst of his students!"

Now at that moment, his shaykh was also in the mosque, hidden from sight, and he was listening to his disciple.

The disciple continued to talk to himself. It was as if he were talking to someone reflected in a mirror. He said, "You are the worst; you are worse even than Iblees—Satan."

Most people could not accept the idea that they are worse than Satan. But keep in mind that while Satan disobeyed, he still believed in God. He is *muwwahid*—a monotheist.

The disciple continued, "I swear that if it is not the truth that I am worse than Satan, then my wife, Fatima and I will be divorced." So sincere was he that if there had been in his heart any fraction, one hundredth, one thousandth, or an even smaller amount not accepting this, then he would have been divorced from his wife upon the spot. Who can do that? Who can say that? But this disciple was truly believing he was worse than Iblees.

When his shaykh heard all this he emerged from his hiding place and called his disciple to sit in front of him. The shaykh

---

Caucasus mountains of southern Russia. In the latter days of his time as leader of this Sufi Path, Shaykh Jamaluddin led his disciples in fierce battles against the Russians when they sought to prevent the free practice of the faith. Under his guidance the famous Imam Shamyl fought pitched battles against insurmountable odds against well-armed Russian troops. The outcome was a stalemate, which ended only after 35 years of intense struggle. Following this many disciples of the shaykh emigrated from Russia to Turkey in order to escape the ongoing persecution.

pointed to the heart of his disciple with his *shahada* finger[24] and poured forth into his heart the six latent powers that exist in every human being: *haqiqatu 'l-jadhbah, haqiqatu 'l-fayd, haqiqatu 't-tawajjuh, haqiqatu 't-tawassul, haqiqatu 'l-irshad, haqiqatu 't-tayy.*

In each human being there exist six latent powers:

- The Power of Attraction of either objects or people to the shaykh—*Haqiqatu 'l-jadhbah*;

- The Power of Emanation or outpouring of experience from the Prophet ﷺ through the chain of transmission to the heart of the disciple—*Haqiqatu 'l-fayd*;

- The Power of Alignment of the shaykh's heart towards the disciple's, and of the disciple's towards his spiritual goal—*Haqiqatu 't-tawajjuh*;

- The Power of Connection to Divine power and favors through the Golden Chain—*Haqiqatu 't-tawassul*;

- The Power of Guidance to the destination embarked upon through the spiritual connection—*Haqiqatu 'l-irshad*;

- The Power of Folding Time and Space—*Haqiqatu 't-tayy.*[25]

These six powers exist in the heart of every one of us. If Mawlana Shaykh Nazim ق were to open that light in everyone of us, that light would attract all America—and even more. But he is

---

[24] Index finger, named *shahada* finger or finger of testification to faith because it is raised when reciting the affirmation of God's Oneness and Prophetic dispensation: *"ashhadu an La ilaha ill-Allah wa ashhadu anna Muhammadan Rasulullah* – I bear witness that there is no god except the one God, Allah and I bear witness that Muhammad is the Prophet of God", whose sincere recitation is sole and sufficient condition to enter into the faith of Islam,

[25] See Mawlana Shaykh Nazim's lecture "The Final Limit" in *Mercy Oceans' Lovestreams* p. 101-110.

not opening that to us. Why? Because for them to be opened each one must first realize how bad he or she is.

Who thinks of himself as bad? No one: we think of ourselves as perfect. But in reality we are full of the *tifl al-madhmoumah*, the spoiled childish ego. How can our hearts be open to feel and see unless we clean ourselves? This is why Sayyidina Bayazid said, "I respect the young ones because they have less sin and I respect the older ones who have more worship, *'ibadah*." But what about us? We respect ourselves only. Can anyone say one word against us? No. We go crazy at even the slightest criticism. May Allah forgive us.

What did Iblees do wrong? Compared to us what he did was nothing. He disobeyed one time. How many times do we disobey? How did he disobey? He refused to make prostration, *sajdah*, to Adam ﷺ. Iblees thought he should only make *sajdah* to Allah. He did not realize that *sajdah* is a prostration of respect, *sajdat al-ihtiram*, to the light of the Prophet ﷺ. Allah gave the order but in reality He didn't want him to obey it. Why did Allah order him to make *sajdah*?

Think! If He wanted him to make prostration, *sajdah*, wouldn't He have been compelled to do so? With this disobedience, Allah knew that Iblees would go after His servants. He knew he would provide temptations to all mankind. This became the function of Iblees. Is that Allah's Mercy where He said:

> But My mercy extends to all things. That (mercy) I shall
> ordain for those who do right, and practise regular
> charity, and those who believe in Our signs.[26]

This teaching is not found in any other *tariqah*—no other shaykh can teach what Mawlana teaches. There is only one source

---

[26] Suratu 'l-'Araaf, (The Heights), 7:156.

left that has this kind of knowledge. Even the Jinn do not possess this kind of knowledge. It is only from Mawlana Shaykh Nazim ق. This kind of knowledge passes from the Prophet to Mahdi, from Mahdi ؏ to the Ghawth, the spiritual saint at the top of the saintly hierarchy whose assistance is sought by believers,ii Mawlana Shaykh Muhammad Nazim al-Haqqani ق. Go East! Go West! You will not find such knowledge anywhere else. When Mawlana Shaykh says something, he raises you to that level. As soon as you heard that story of Sayyidina Jamaluddin, Mawlana Shaykh raised you to that level. His teaching stories do not just go in one ear and out the other. He has the power to raise his disciples because, when you hear his stories they become part of you.

That is why on the day of your death, with your last seven breaths, the Prophet ﷺ is there, present. He ﷺ shows you what you have received of high levels and positions of status through your connection with *awliya*.

He Said, She Said

Today people do not understand this kind of teaching. They are only looking for *"qaala wa qeela wa qaaloo, wa ma qaaloo*—he said, she said, they said, they did not say." Today, most knowledge is dry and derivative. Scholars endlessly quote one another, serving up the same old dish warmed over and over again. When a professor writes a book it is filled with footnotes. If you don't have footnotes they say it is not academic. In reality, knowledge is not a dead, static thing, pressed between the pages of a fading book. With each moment, knowledge rises higher. As the Prophet ﷺ ascends, so knowledge grows and spreads from him. Knowledge multiples as the Prophet ﷺ is raised up: it doubles with each moment. From the time of creation until now the Prophet ﷺ is in continuous ascension. Knowledge, like a living thing, grows and transforms with that upward movement. For such knowledge, we don't need to refer to footnotes or indirect sources. The *awliyaullah* have direct access: they don't need footnotes. No one can question their authority.

In the past, no one would question a *wali*. In contrast, today in most places, people don't consider or believe in any *wali*. They believe in scientific theories and philosophies. In the modern world, who will listen to *awliya*? Who is there to teach among the educated classes, who believe they already know everything?

Natural Disasters

There are still some places where things are different. When I traveled to Indonesia, one *zawiya* we visited could hold perhaps 500 people. When we went to give a lecture outside, there were twenty or thirty thousand people waiting to listen. Sometimes the crowds are like that in Pakistan as well. One time I went to speak at the largest stadium in Jakarta. It can hold 250,000 people and the crowds overflowed even that. Another time 150,000 people came to the Istiqlal Mosque in Jakarta. All of them took *baya'*, initiation. They are pure. They move with their emotions. On another trip to Malaysia the crowds were overwhelming. The army had to clear a path before we could even reach the *zawiya*. I entered and prayed Maghrib, the sunset prayer, and Isha, the night prayer, and did *dhikrullah—remembrance of God*. When we went to leave, at least 20,000 people had gathered outside. Our way was blocked. The army had the people sit down in the road so that we could pass. Even then, they jumped up and grabbed at my *jubbah*, cloak, and beard. It is good that I took three *jubbahs*.

The people there think with their love, just as it was in times past. There are some remarkable examples of devotion and piety in that part of the world. At a special gathering for praising the Prophet ﷺ, *majlis salaat 'ala an-Nabi*, they read *Dala'il al-khayraat*; each day reading one chapter of *salawat*, invocations for blessings on the Prophet ﷺ. In one village near Jakarta this is the tradition and it has lasted for 250 years. From the time of 'Asr, the afternoon prayer, to Maghrib, the sunset prayer, all 40,000 of the inhabitants close the town and go to the mosque. They recite seven *hizb*, sections, which is one chapter, *juz*, every day. This has gone on for 250 years without interruption. Each and every day they continue this practice. As one shaykh dies, the next one comes; when that shaykh dies then the next one comes. To this day they are sitting in recitation. Where in the modern world would you see that?

By comparison, here in the West, we live on artificial fruit. Wherever modern civilization has reached, people must live on the thin diet of plastic fruit. There is still real fruit in the places I have described, because the trappings of modern civilization have not yet swept their culture aside. The new civilization is, in fact, not civilization at all, but rather the culture of Satan. The Civilization of Rahman still exists, preserved in out-of-the-way places in the world. As soon as the culture of MTV and "civilization" enters a place, it destroys everything. No one can think anymore. The lower instincts are glorified. They take over the whole mind. People become trapped in the rush to make money, to eat and to live for the next sensual pleasure. They are turned upside down: their baser natures rise above what should have been their ruling judgment and conscience.

The noise and clutter of the new culture are drowning out the old. Here in the San Francisco area, we are sitting in a region of nearly seven million inhabitants, and this evening only twenty or thirty people have come to listen to this talk.

THE OMNIPRESENT WITNESS

Authority and Submission

God, the Exalted, said:

> *Obey Allah, obey the Prophet and obey those who are in authority.*[27]

The phrase, "...*obey those who are in authority*," could have many meanings. Anyone can be in authority in a given situation. A policeman, a king, a senator: all might have authority; each according to his own situation. We also have authority over our minds and hearts. So what is God, the Exalted, saying when He tells us to obey those who are in authority? If I think that I have authority, then I have to consider what kind of authority that might be. We all tell ourselves that we have authority. Even Iblees,[28] though God, the Exalted, cursed him, thought and still thinks that he has authority over human beings.

In some ways, through trickery and deceit, Iblees has proven that he has that authority. How? He whispered in the ear of Adam 舔 and told him to eat of the forbidden tree. So what happened? Adam 舔 ate. This made Iblees happy that he had authority over even a prophet, such as Adam 舔. He was able to whisper in the ear of Eve and Adam 舔 and they ate from the tree. If that is the case with Adam 舔 how could we think that we have authority over ourselves: we, who are not prophets, but merely ordinary people? This is one of the chief illusions of our existence!

---

[27] Suratu 'n-Nisa, (Women), 4:59.
[28] Satan's proper name in Arabic.

We tell ourselves that we are in charge; we are clever; we are knowledgeable. Shouldn't everyone listen to us?

This illusion can only be broken with *wilayah*, sincerity and piety. Our first goal should be submission: to submit to everything, to accept Allah's Will. That means you must know that you have no authority.

Once, a disciple asked Grandshaykh, "If everything is written for us, then what difference does it make what we do?" Grandshaykh's reply turned on a subtle point and had to be explained to the disciple twice. "We don't know what is written for us. Therefore, we have the responsibility to choose our actions. Discussions of free will versus predestination are empty talk." This answer requires some thought. By not knowing what lies in wait for us just around the corner, our probable surprise, perhaps even displeasure as the next event unfolds, must not overcome our ability to accept the challenge of that event with grace and humility.

Ideally, with consistent acceptance over the course of a lifetime, one might ultimately reach complete submission to God, the Exalted. In the highest example of this type of acceptance, the Prophet ﷺ responded to a twist of fate that resulted in the Hijrah. When a plot was hatched to assassinate him in Mecca, he was apparently forced to escape to Madina. Imagine it! The Prophet ﷺ, who would later travel to Masjid al-Aqsa and back again in an instant riding on the back of Buraq, was outwardly reduced to somewhat ordinary maneuvers to escape his persecutors. By all appearances, he was running away, just as any ordinary person would do. Why didn't he ﷺ simply ask his Lord to order His angels to escort him beyond the reach of his enemies? Why did the Prophet ﷺ go through such agony, and suffer such a painful journey through the desert to reach the cave with Sayyidina Abu Bakr as-Siddiq ؓ? Perhaps God, the Exalted, wanted events to unfold in just a certain way to touch as many people as they did and advance the Prophet's ﷺ mission along specific lines. There are several secrets behind the Prophet's ﷺ restraint, the highest of which is, he did not want to presume that he had any authority over Allah's ﷻ Will. He was in perfect submission and apparently decided to deal with the situation without requesting an army of angels to come to his defense.

Certainly such a direct, Divine intervention would have amounted to a spectacular rescue, (and would have given the Quraysh pause), but would it have been appropriate? The Prophet ﷺ is the perfect *muwwahid*—monotheist. The meaning of *tawheed* is to see that everything is coming from God, the Exalted. That means every action that the Prophet did is in accordance with Allah's ﷻ Will. He was obeying that authority. He was able to say *Bismillahi 'r-Rahmani 'r-Raheem*, and be instantly transported to Madina. He is present and seeing, *Haadir* and *Naazhir*. And the one who is present and seeing, can he not move in one moment from Mecca to Madina?

The Prophet's Omnipresence

What is the meaning of *Haadir* and *Naazhir*? What are the two aspects of omnipresence? *Haadir* means to be present with the body and *Naazhir* means he is looking at us. That is the common meaning that we can understand. But is that what it means for the Prophet ﷺ? *Haadir* means he is in the Divine Presence and he has never been away from that Holy Presence. When he went to the Station of "*qaaba qawsayni—two bow's length*," he is there. His *ruhaaniyya*, his spirituality, is always there; he is Present there and Looking to his Lord. Never do his eyes move or shift away from his Creator.

That is why Imam al-Nawawi in his book *al-Adhkaar* interprets this verse:

*His sight did not swerve or waiver. Indeed he saw of the
Signs of his Lord, the Greatest.*[29]

as meaning, "He saw his Lord with the eyes of his head."[30] Do you
think that the one who could look at God, the Exalted, with his
eyes would look anywhere else? Although the Prophet ﷺ went
back to earth, to fulfill his mission—he listened and obeyed—yet
he is simultaneously always Present in the Divine Presence,
gazing without cease. When he was at *"two bow's length or nearer,"*
and God, the Exalted, manifested His Reality to the Prophet ﷺ
with His Beautiful Names and Attributes do you think the
Prophet ﷺ would look anywhere else?

His presence is there; his eyes are there, even though he is in
the *dunya*, this world. When he is there, that means that he is
receiving. What is he receiving? "What no ears have heard, what
eyes cannot see and what no human heart has ever conceived."
The Prophet ﷺ is observing creation as it emerges from non-
existence into existence. He is Present and witnessing all these
things.

When you go to a lecture you have to be present to listen, do
you not? When you go to the auditorium, you sit and listen and
watch the speaker. You do not go there to sleep, nor do you go
when the auditorium is empty. What do you do there?

Al-mahboob ma' man ahab—The beloved is with the one who
loves him or her. Or: *al-muhib ma' man ahab*—The lover is with the
beloved. So, the lover is going to be there and is going to know
that this is the auditorium that the beloved owns. He is drawn
there to sit, but not when it is empty. The one who loves must be
with the one who is loved. He ﷺ is in the Station of *"two bow's-
length or less."*

---

[29] Suratu 'n-Najm, (The Star), 53: 10-19.
[30] Arabic: *ra'a rabbahu bi 'aynay raasihi.*

What is the Prophet ﷺ doing in that station? He is not sitting alone, by himself and waiting, nor is he sitting there to watch colorful lights shining from the Creator. No, he is not interested in that, nor in any sort of heavenly pleasure. We are speaking of the Prophet ﷺ. We might be interested in heavenly pleasure, if God, the Exalted, gave it to us. We might request and beg for it. But is the Prophet ﷺ merely interested in heavenly pleasure? No he is not. He is interested in the One Who created heavenly pleasure. He is interested in the One Who has been described by the Beautiful Names and Attributes as Allah and Who manifested himself with all His Beautiful Names and Attributes to His Prophet ﷺ? Clearly, the Prophet ﷺ holds a special place in Allah's ﷻ creation.

Unlimited Greatness

When we say *Allahu Akbar*, we recognize that there is no limit to God's Greatness. There is no limit to His creativity; no limit to His power; no limit to His Beautiful Names and Attributes. The Divine Names and Attributes are endless, because they expand and multiply at every moment. As creation expands, it rises and at each point in this ascension everything transforms. And as the Prophet's ﷺ ascension continues, it is always in the Station of *"two bow's-length or less."* The greatest things mankind has conceived of are nothing in the face of this vast and continuing expansion. Parallel universes, higher dimensions, the macrocosm, Plato's archetypes: all of these conceptions amount to only a fraction of an atom when compared to what issues forth in an instant from the Divine Fountain of creation. This is connected with the manifestation of His Description: *Allahu Akbar.* That word indicates something huge: beyond description. So think! The Prophet ﷺ is there, witnessing each moment as creation emerges and is stretched into an infinity of worlds and times. And what is he doing there? Is he sitting passively? Or he is receiving from

God, the Exalted, at each and every moment, the Essence of these Beautiful Names?

Because God, the Exalted, is the Creator, al-Khaliq. He did not create for a moment and then stop. As the Creator, He is creating at every moment. Even within the part of creation that we can see, there are billions of galaxies expanding in all directions. There is no way to describe what God, the Exalted, is creating because He is the Creator. That is the meaning of *Haadir*. The Prophet ﷺ is at that point and sees creation being created. Not only does he observe this process, but he is dressed with the manifestation of all that is being created. He is the Chosen One, al-Mustafa. He is Master of all servants that God, the Exalted, has created: Sayyid al-Akwaan. The stars are his servants, as are the galaxies.

And we have subjected to you whatsoever is in heavens
and whatsoever is on earth.[31]

All that is inside and outside are servants to God, the Exalted. All the elements in the periodic table are making *tasbeeh*, glorification and praise of God. So God, the Exalted, is creating, and the Prophet ﷺ is Present, *Haadir*, and *Naazhir*, observing the secrets of creation as they are made manifest.

What we normally explain of *Haadir* and *Naazhir* is limited; it conveys nothing of its true import. We care not what ruling other scholars make on such matters and certainly we have no concern for what the Wahabis say about it. You must understand that *awliya* don't address the mind. They speak from East to West and North to South. Today, such depths of knowledge only comes through Mawlana Shaykh Nazim ق. No one can bring this sort of knowledge except from that tap. That source is really one drop from a special ocean. He is taking from the ocean of knowledge in the heart of the Mahdi ﷺ and relaying it to humanity. In effect, we

---

[31] Suratu 'l-Jathiya (The Kneeling), 45:13.

are like a radio station. We receive and transmit the voice of Mawlana.

So the Prophet ﷺ is *Haadirun wa Naazhirun*: Present and Seeing. In turn, the saints and *awliya* walk on the path of the Prophet ﷺ and are able to relay certain aspects of his unique witnessing. When a scientist is in a laboratory and doing an experiment, he has to be very precise to make the experiment a success. He must pay careful attention to the smallest of details. In the laboratory classroom, the students will watch their professor closely to see what he is doing. They are being trained to understand his methods and to take notes. But the Creator does not proceed in this fashion. He creates from His *qudrah*, His infinite Power, and His *Irada*, His Will. When the Essence wants something, the Divine Will is asserted and knowledge of it comes through the Attribute al-ʿAlim. This, in turn, immediately produces the Plans and when the Plans are produced, the Attribute al-Qaadir, the All-Powerful, will create what has been willed.

The Prophet ﷺ has reached the level of the highest servanthood, and watches this process of creation. This was granted to him ﷺ because he reached the Station of *"two bow's-length or less"* and made prostration there, in that Presence. Not even the archangels: not Gabriel ؏, Mika'eel ؏, Israfeel ؏, nor Azraeel ؏, reached this level—only the Prophet ﷺ. This happened because he ﷺ was accepted and invited. So when he ﷺ is in that place of witnessing, he ﷺ is seeing. He is *Haadir*. When he sees something it means he sees every smallest detail.

There have been *fatwas* saying that because the Prophet ﷺ is *Haadirun wa Naazhirun* he can see you and me. However, this is only a small part of the meaning. He is seeing whatever creation is being created in different parts of this universe: this planet is only like the head of a pin when compared to the vastness of the universe. If we suppose that the Prophet ﷺ only sees us we are diminishing his level. And while he does, indeed, see us individually and hears the leaves of the trees and stones of the earth praising the Lord, he is also hearing this chorus of praise as it rises across all of creation. It would be a mistake to imagine his witnessing is limited to the Earth. On the contrary, his servanthood extends to every star and every planet.

Paradises Pleasures

Yet that is not all. The Prophet's ﷺ omnipresence extends beyond the Universe we see through telescopes. In the observable world there is a void between things. Look across this room, you only see heads of people. Between them you see clear space. However, in Paradise there is no empty space. Here there are empty spaces between things. Yet in Paradise, even the smallest fraction of an atom yields pleasure. Unlike our earthly pleasures, the pleasures of Paradise are lasting. Here we eat ice cream, get married, go on a honeymoon—but these pleasures are fleeting. People take great pleasure in sex and devote much of their lives to its pursuit. Yet how long does it last? A few moments in time: then it is finished.

Our earthly, *dunya* pleasures are like the spit in your mouth when compared to the pleasures God, the Exalted, bestows in Paradise. From every void that you think is a void here, in Paradise there is no comparable void. There, every space is full. And from every particle of space in Paradise you take a pleasure that is incommensurable with any sexual or animal pleasure. Experiences in Paradise have different properties than those we encounter here on earth. Aside from being richer and stronger, in Paradise the succession of pleasures never stops. And yet, with each new pleasure, the savor of the former experience is retained. As these ecstasies arrive, they do not cancel one another out, nor do they mingle. The multi-dimensional nature of paradisiacal pleasures allows them to persist over time, while remaining distinct events. Even as a normal person enters Paradise and ascends through its levels, the successive pleasures do not override one another nor conflict. They rise with you on your journey as discrete, yet apparently continuous encounters, each resonating simultaneously and yet distinct from all the others.

The Prophet ﷺ is always there at the point of emerging creation. First, he is dressed by the Beautiful Divine Names as they manifest—then they pass through him to the rest of creation. Because he is the unique perfect servant of God; he is the only one in continuous *sajda*, prostration and adoration of His Lord; he never raises his head. That is Maqaam al-'Abdiyya—the Station of Perfect Servanthood. That is why God, the Exalted, said to Adam ﷺ:

If Muhammad was not in existence, I would not have created you.[32]

The meaning of "you" here is not just the creation of human beings. It means everything. Every moment there is a creation. Every moment creations are created and manifest to the Prophet ﷺ and from Prophet ﷺ on to us.

This is the meaning of *Haadirun wa Naazhirun*. Why does it come through the Prophet ﷺ? Because, he is obeying the authority of Allah, Glorious and Exalted. If you obey that authority, you will be inheriting aspects of these secrets. You will not be like the Prophet ﷺ, for no one can be like Him, but you will be inheriting certain aspects of these secrets through that chain of sainthood. From one saint to another, you will be dressed with these qualities that can neither be described nor understood. This is the meaning of the verses:

---

[32] Hakim in *al-Mustadrak*.

Obey Allah, obey the Prophet and those in authority
among you,[33]

and

Whoever is obeying the Prophet is obeying God.[34]

Who is obeying the Prophet ﷺ? Does *"those in authority..."* mean you? Who are the true authorities? They are the *awliya*.

In the final sense, you cannot reach the level of *"Obey God."* To obey God one must know what God wants from us—not only at the level of Divine Law, but at the level of reality. One must know what we promised to fulfill and obey on the Day of Promises. So in reality, only Sayyidina Muhammad ﷺ is practicing true obedience.

Then what must one do? *"Obey the Prophet."* But who can obey the Prophet ﷺ? We ordinary people cannot. We are not obeying anyone. The ones who can obey the Prophet ﷺ are those whose hearts are sincere. Then humble yourself and go to the lowest level. *"Obey those who are in authority."* Who are they? They are *awliyaullah*, the saints. So that is why God, the Exalted, placed them all over the world. As long as men are living they are living among them. For this reason when a shaykh dies his followers must take the hand of a living one.

There is a clear chain of command. If you have a true guide, then you listen and obey. When you obey, the guide takes you to presence of the Prophet ﷺ. The Prophet ﷺ then takes you to Presence of the Lord ﷻ. This is the meaning of:

If they had only, when they were oppressors to
themselves, come unto thee and asked Allah's
forgiveness, and the Messenger had asked forgiveness for

---

[33] Suratu 'n-Nisa, (Women), 4:59.
[34] Suratu 'n-Nisa, (Women), 4:80.

them, they would have found Allah indeed Oft-
returning, Most Merciful.[35]

This verse means one must come to *awliya*, and the *awliya* take
you to presence of the Prophet ﷺ and then the Prophet ﷺ will
make *istighfaar*, asking forgiveness on your behalf. Would God,
the Exalted, refuse such a request? Undoubtedly not. He is the
All-Forgiving, the Merciful. May God, the Exalted, forgive and
bless us all!

Abu Jahl and the Pit

There was a man who lived at the time of the Prophet, who
refused his message called Abu Jahl.[iii] One day he prepared a trap
to harm the Prophet ﷺ. He invited him to his house to eat.
Sayyidina Muhammad ﷺ was happy, thinking that Abu Jahl
finally wished to accept Islam. Abu Jahl dug and concealed a pit
in the path to his home, in order to capture the Prophet ﷺ. At least
this is how the story is related in the *seerah*: that the Prophet ﷺ was
fooled by this trick and did not detect Abu Jahl's true intentions.

In the larger sense, God, the Exalted, is showing us our
ignorance: we fall into the pit of ignorance at every turn.
Although it is the *seerah* that says the Prophet ﷺ was taken in by
this trick, it must be understood that the Prophet ﷺ was above
this. Only an ignorant person would say that the Prophet ﷺ did
not know what Abu Jahl intended.

In the common recounting of the event, when the Prophet ﷺ
approached the hole that Abu Jahl had placed in his path, God,
the Exalted, saved him and caused Abu Jahl to forget about the
hole and subsequently fall in it himself. However, if we accept this
version, we are blind. In reality the Prophet ﷺ knew Abu Jahl had
dug a hole just outside his house. How could it be otherwise? The

---

[35] Suratu 'n-Nisa, (Women),4:64

Prophet ﷺ was looking at the Preserved Tablet[36] and therefore knew all along that he was walking into a trap. He answered Abu Jahl's invitation following *Iraadatullah*, the Will of God. It would never have occurred to him to do otherwise. As he walked towards the house he said to his Lord, "I am Your servant, and I do what You want. I will fall into the pit the just as Sayyidina Ibrahim ﷺ, willingly walked into the fire." Prophets do not follow their own will: they follow God's Will. "If I fall, I fall. I am showing submission."

> *Say (O Muhammad)!: "I am but a man like yourselves,*
> *(but) the inspiration has come to me..."*[37]

Only block-headed people would say that the Prophet ﷺ is a person like you and me. Does revelation come to a common person? He is a perfect servant to God, the Exalted, submitting to His Will and not to his own. For the Prophet ﷺ, to demonstrate any will of his own would be *shirk*, idolatry. In this instance, the meaning of *shirk* is to be self-willed. Absolute Will is reserved for God alone. The Prophet ﷺ knew that reality.

So the Prophet ﷺ went to Abu Jahl's house only to find that his host had fallen into his own trap. The Prophet ﷺ did not take advantage of the situation, even though Abu Jahl was his enemy. He didn't tell him, "Take *shahada*[38] if you want me to take you out of the pit." He didn't tell him, "Believe in me and I'll pull you up out."

---

[36] Preserved Tablet, Arabic: *al-Lawh al-Mahfoudh*. A heavenly record in which God has written the destinies of all created beings, prior to their creation in this world.

[37] Suratu 'l-Kahf, (The Cave), 18:110.

[38] Shahada: the testification of faith by which one becomes Muslim. "*ashhadu an La ilaha ill-Allah wa ashhadu anna Muhammadan Rasulullah* – I bear witness that there is no god except the one God, Allah and I bear witness that Muhammad is the Prophet of God."

Instead, the mercy of God filled the Prophet ﷺ. He looked at Abu Jahl down in the hole and said, "I am taking you out of hellfire, because you are my relative. You are my cousin, my blood:

> Say: "No reward do I ask of you for this except the love
> of those near of kin."[39]

And

> with the believers kind and merciful.[40]

God, the Exalted, is showing us here that through His messenger, He cares for all of us; He is watchful over us, and is merciful. *Ra'ufun raheem* are *Siffaatullah,* God's own Beautiful Attributes with which He, the Exalted adorned the Prophet ﷺ. Because he was dressed with heavenly kindness and mercy he gave his hand to Abu Jahl saying, "Come out. I don't need anything from you. Believe in me or no, I am the mercy to all creation—*rahmatan lil-'alameen.*" From the mercy that Allah sent him, he pulled him out without conditions.

Oceans and Drops

Whatever we say about *'azhamat an-Nabi*—the immense greatness of the Prophet ﷺ, is but a drop from the oceans of our master Mawlana Shaykh Nazim ق, and whatever he possesses is but a drop from Sayyidina Mahdi's ocean; and whatever al-Mahdi ﷺ possesses is but a drop from Sayyidina Muhammad's ﷺ ocean.

When Sayyidina Mahdi ﷺ appears, the secret of the Qur'an appears—Khaamis al-Qur'an. As it stands now, people are extracting only the literal meanings from the Qur'an. Based on these limited commentaries, *tafseers*, millions of books have been

---

[39] Suratu 'sh-Shura, (The Consultation), 42:36.
[40] Suratu 't-Tawbah, (The Repentance), 9:12.

published over 15 centuries. When the Mahdi 舎 comes, such *tafseers* will be put back on the shelf, they will no longer be relevant. New commentaries and new interpretations will appear. That will be the time of *waqt al-barzakhi*: the time of connection between earth and heavens. When the cycle of the Mahdi 舎 comes, everything will begin to open from the afterlife. *Awliyaullah*'s hearts are boiling because of what they see of these realities already, but God has not given them permission to reveal it yet. So people are waiting, according to the principle, "Waiting for relief is a form of worship." They are waiting for release.

Expectations are running high as humanity waits for the coming events. That is why it is very important to keep waiting and worshipping. Look how the Jews are waiting and preparing for the Messiah. Look how the Christians are preparing for the coming of Prophet Jesus—Jesus Christ 舎. Why are we not preparing? Look at all the mosques. Does anyone mention Sayyidina Mahdi 舎 and Prophet Jesus 舎? If you go to synagogues you will hear how much they speak about the Messiah. If you go to churches you will hear how much they speak of the coming of Jesus 舎. The Jews and Christians are actively awaiting the Messiah: perhaps he will turn out to be al-Mahdi 舎.

Seeing the Prophet

In reality, we are waiting for Sayyidina Muhammad 舎. When *Iraadatullah*—Allah's Will, manifests, don't think it is only Sayyidina Mahdi 舎 and Jesus Christ 舎 who will arrive. When they come great miracles will also come. In *barzakh*, the intermediate life between the worldly life and the hereafter, *awliya* move freely. What about the Seal of the Prophets Sayyidina Muhammad 舎? Do you not think he can appear to *awliyaullah* in reality? And if he chose, could he not appear to any one of us in reality? Would this be so difficult for him?

41

The Prophet ﷺ said:

Who saw me in the dream he will see me in reality (*fee al-yaqaza*) for Satan never can take my form.[41]

So many people have come to me and said that they have seen the Prophet ﷺ in a dream. Others have said that they felt his presence when they closed their eyes while in a waking state. Still others have said that they had seen him as a shadow moving. One nine-year-old girl called me to say she had seen the Prophet ﷺ actually standing in front of her. If that can happen to this child, why can't it happen to any of us? Perhaps it is because children at that age are pure and innocent and their special status allows them to see such things.

Every night there are 124,000 *awliya* meeting with the Prophet ﷺ. Do not think that there were no more *awliya* left to take direct orders from the Prophet ﷺ. Each moment there are orders from the Prophet ﷺ for each one of us to obey. In many books it is written that everything is coming from the Prophet ﷺ through the Sahaba: "*Qeela, wa qaala, wa lam yuqaal*—she said, he said, and that was not said."

It is our responsibility to obey orders, and always has been from the beginning of our pledges to follow Islam: "*Aamanaa wa sadaqnaa*—we accepted and we confirmed what was said." The Prophet ﷺ is ascending with each moment. With each level in that ascent, new and higher knowledge is unfolding. In every moment there is *it'at ar-rasool*—obedience to the Prophet ﷺ. And with it come new orders, new levels of responsibility and higher standards of behavior. Word of these developments comes to us through the *awliyah*.

---

[41] Bukhari.

42

Why was 'Abdul Qadir al-Jilani was called Ghawth al-'Azham, the Greatest Helper Saint? He was called this because he brought fresh knowledge. It is the role of certain other *awliya* to keep quiet while others, such as Sayyidina Muhyiddeen ibn 'Arabi, were allowed to speak. He brought new knowledge in his time. Where do you think he brought this knowledge from? No, he brought such wisdom from the Prophet ﷺ. If the *awliya* wanted to write what 'Abdul-Qadir Jilani and Muhyideen ibn 'Arabi brought it would fill this entire earth with mountains of words.

THE BRIDGE OF TIME

The Eternal Now

The Prophet's possesses the qualities of omnipresence, *al-Haadir*—
is the one who is present, and *an-Naazhir*—the one who is
monitoring, looking and observing.

If he is present as creation emerges into existence, then he is
always in a "present" zone—a place which transcends our
ordinary notions of time. There is no past for him. Because, if that
moment is now, if we imagine my hands are the hands on a clock,
when it makes a tick, then that is the present. Then when the
second hand moves one tick, that become past and the second it
moves to the next position it becomes present, which a moment
before was waiting in the future. Look at my hand! This is an
important point. It is still there, it is still present, which means that
everything is still present: my fingers, the palm of my hand, its
front, its back—all are still there.

If I pass this rosary, *tasbeeh*, through my fingers, moving each
bead, one by one as I count them, does it mean a bead ceases to
exist just because I have passed it and moved on to the next? The
beads are still there, in exactly the same order in which they were
originally strung. The sense of touch in my fingers might think
that the previously counted beads have died, but the higher sense
of my sight tells me they are still hanging below my hand, waiting
for the next cycle. The moments of our lives are like these beads.
Our senses convince us that, because the passage of time has
moved certain experiences out of our immediate line of sight, they
have died a qualified death in a strange domain called the past.

But those moments are still there, intact and living somewhere in a higher dimension, just beyond the reach of our ordinary senses.

There is no such thing as past and future in the heavenly time of God, the Exalted. For Him, both above and outside of time, all events unfold simultaneously. For us, time must unfold in a linear fashion, one event after another. We watch the clock. It moves forward, one second, then that second becomes the past, while the next second sits waiting in the future. But outside the limitations of our senses, all of these moments exist at once. That is why we say *"Huwa 'l-aawwalu wa 'l-aakhiru—He is the First and He is the Last,"*[42] because there is no beginning and no end. To Allah there is only the present. There is no counting of years. For us to understand the quality of Allah's swt Time:

> *Yet they ask you (O Muhammad) to hasten on the*
> *Punishment! But Allah will not fail in His Promise.*
> *Verily a Day in the sight of your Lord, O Muhammad, is*
> *like a thousand years of your reckoning.*[43]

One day to God, the Exalted, is like one thousand years of what we count. And in another place Allah says:

> *The angels and the spirit ascend unto Him in a Day the*
> *measure whereof is fifty thousand years: Therefore, [O*
> *believer,] endure all adversity with goodly patience.*[44]

When the angels and the Ruh, the Holy Spirit, make an ascension to the Divine Presence of one day, that day equals 50,000 of our worldly years. This means that there is a flexible connection between the earthly and heavenly units of time. As it spans between the heavens the earth, time twists and stretches. Where time relationships can be compressed in such extreme

---

[42] Suratu 'l-Hadid, (Iron), 57:3.
[43] Suratu 'l-Hajj, (The Pilgrimage), 22:47.
[44] Suratu 'l-Ma'arij, (The Ascensions), 70:4.

ways, the relative positions of past-present-future can also be transposed, amounting to a chain of causation we cannot even imagine. Days, hours, minutes, seconds, ages, eternities, eons—all these units flow and merge, intermingle and swirl against the backdrop of creation. In the highest sense, for God, the Exalted, there is no time. His Greatness transcends all aspects of time, space and matter. When angels ascend to the Divine Presence, they need one day: one day that for us would last 50,000 years; a ratio of 18,250,000 to 1 between heavenly and earthly time.

We can gain insight into one aspect of Allah's Greatness by examining these relative aspects of time. One heavenly hour would translate to 2,083 years on Earth. One heavenly minute would equal 35 earthly years, and a heavenly second would correspond to 211 days. An average human life of seventy years would amount to only two heavenly minutes. Where is our ordinary experience of time in this scale? From one heavenly minute to another there are massive changes. If that single minute to us is 35 years—imagine how much happens on earth in 35 years! In one 35-year "minute" to another, how many people will die, how many people will come to this world and how much will God, the Exalted, add to the creation that He is manifesting to the Prophet ﷺ. He said in a Holy Prophetic narration:

> I was a hidden treasure, I wanted to be known; so I created creation.[45]

He weaves the fabric of creation from His Beautiful Names which emerge from the Divine Essence: Huwa. Of which creation do we speak? This universe? This cosmos, even in all its vastness, is nothing more than the head of a pin when compared to what God, the Exalted, brings forth in the act of creation.

---

[45] Razi, Suyuti, Jarrahi. This is a *hadith qudsee*, meaning God's Words relayed on the tongue of the Prophet ﷺ, which are not part of the Qur'an.

The Lord's Continuous Creation

Just as the background radiation from the Big Bang is all around us, so creation is there. That is:

From Him seeks (its need) every creature in the heavens and on earth: every day in (new) Splendour does He (shine)![46]

Nothing can be given as Allah's ﷻ Likeness for *"there is nothing whatever like unto Him."*[47] Such descriptions are put forth, but only in order to convey to us a slight glimpse of His Greatness. Like a vast cosmic fountain, torrents burst forth from His Divine Wellsprings, and each of the deluges that emerge in turn split into streams and multiply yet again. Divine Greatness rushes forth creating primary, secondary and tertiary manifestations spreading throughout all of creation. We cannot imagine what this means. String theory physicists have begun to propose models of a space whose fabric stretches at all points, not unlike a giant sponge swelling with water. In a sense, modern science is approaching the notion of a universe in a state of continuous creation.

A majestic and sweeping description of the universe occurs in *Nuzhat al-Majalis* in a tradition in which a believer asks God, the Exalted, to set forth a vision of Paradise. Instead of indicating the scale of creation in terms of mathematical formulae, this version paints a vivid picture of the flight of an angel. It is related that God, the Exalted, ordered the archangel Gabriel to fly with all six hundred of his wings across the span of the universe in search of its limits. Years before, when he had carried the revelation to the Prophet ﷺ, this same angel had flown on only two wings. Now he flew for 70,000 years, grew weary, then stopped and cried, "O my

---

[46] Suratu 'r-Rahman, (The Merciful), 55:29.
[47] Suratu 'sh-Shura, (Consultation), 42:11.

Lord! It is not finished." God, the Exalted, answered, "O Gabriel, the distance you have traveled is only one corner of Paradise."

Everything about the Divine realm has a growing, living quality about it. Consider the compounding effect of our recitation of the Divine Names like al-Kareem, ar-Raheem, al-Hakeem, al-Wadud. For example, when we say "Ya Haleem, Ya Haleem," the first time we say it, God, the Exalted, manifests this Beautiful Name and dresses us with its manifestation. When we recite it a second time, that "Ya Haleem" is a completely different manifestation from the first one, and it is so much higher that the first one cannot understand the second. The difference between the two is like the difference between the universe and the heavens.

Don't think that the Divine Attributes are merely different names for God, the Exalted. They are full of knowledge and they carry that knowledge by Allah's *Qudrah*—His Divine Power. When we say ar-Raheem, that Divine Attribute the Compassionate understands every particle of knowledge inside it. When you repeat the name, the effect multiplies both in terms of quality and quantity.

That is how we describe that verse *"every day in (new) Splendour does He (shine)"*[48] every moment every Divine Attribute is in a new *shaan*, a new manifestation that God, the Exalted, opens to that attribute from His Essence. The mind cannot understand that.

Then which of the favors of your Lord will you deny?[49]

You cannot apprehend Allah's ﷻ Greatness. Each time you say *Allahu Akbar*, God, the Exalted, opens more of His Greatness, and

---

[48] Suratu 'r-Rahman, (The Merciful), 55:29.
[49] Suratu' r-Rahman, (The Merciful), 55:13.

each repetition of the phrase is at an incommensurably higher level that the last.

In the Divine Presence

As we described previously, when the Prophet ﷺ was in the Divine Presence, *Haadir wa Naazhir,* Present and Observing, wherever he looked there was no empty space. Emptiness would suggest a weakness in the fabric of Paradise. It must be full, like this bottle of water. Each and every drop of Paradise gives pleasure. In the heavens everything is full. It is not like here, where you see empty places and areas of vacuum. Each point of space there contains its own pleasures. So the Prophet ﷺ is in that presence, absorbing the ecstasy of this immeasurable knowledge. God, the Exalted, is dressing him with the manifestations of His Names and Attributes. All the while the Prophet is *Naazhirun*: "looking," as Imam Nawawi said, "with the eyes of his head." So, would someone in this position, observing all these wonders, be willing to come back? No. However, God, the Exalted, ordered him to come back. For that reason alone, he came back.

Grandshaykh said that among the *awliyaullah* it is understood that the Prophet ﷺ did not come back in the same manner as he went. He went with his full capacity when he reached the Divine Presence. He was *Haadirun wa Naazhirun,* so part of him will never leave. This condition explains why the *awliyaullah*, who manifest some aspects of the Prophet's character, can appear to be in different places and personalities at various times. Imagine then the power of the Prophet ﷺ, whose body came back, but whose spirit remained above, with the Divine Presence. So while he was on Earth, in Mecca, yet he also remained observing the Will of God, the Exalted, on every aspect of human life. He, therefore, is the Master of creation, *La ilaha illa-Llah Muhammadun Rasulullah.*

It is important to note that Allah did not say, *"Jibreel Rasulullah,"* nor did He say *"Jannat Rasulullah."* He said, *"Muhammadun Rasulullah."* And the Prophet ﷺ said:

I am the master of the sons of Adam and I say it without pride.[50]

Allah named him the King of creation. His responsibilities cover the universe. That is why Allah gave the Prophet ﷺ *shafa'*, intercession, on Judgment Day. He says to him "do what you want." For those who say *La ilaha ill-Llah Muhammadun Rasulullah*, God, the Exalted, will say "Take them to Paradise." This will be the case even if they have pronounced only one *salawaat*.

So the Prophet ﷺ saw the realities of the conditions around him and knew he had to carry the abuse and torture of people. The oppression of the Quraysh led to the migration of Muslims both West and East. These early Muslims acted as bridges across the world. The Prophet ﷺ ordered these migrations. There is a subtle wisdom in each of his actions. This wisdom is contained in the verse, *"every day in (new) Splendour does He (shine)."* Every instant, God, the Exalted, is in *shaan*. *Shaan* means that in every moment He makes His creation appear. The Prophet ﷺ sees this ongoing wonder, and yet he returned to earth. He traveled from place to place on this planet and carried out his mission. He went into the desert, to the Cave of Thawr, and traveled to Madina from Mecca. Just as the early migrations created a bridge to the rest of the world, so the Prophet's ﷺ dual locations in space and time create a bridge from the Divine Presence to the Earth. He became, in effect, a channel between the upper and lower dimensions of creation.

---

[50] *Musnad Ahmad.*

THE ADVOCATE OF MERCY

Heavenly Records

> *Obey Allah, obey the Prophet and obey those in*
> *authority among you.*[51]

This important admonition is based on the fact that we are under constant observation. The kind of observation meant here is above and beyond the ordinary type of security surveillance practiced by governments and corporations: it is of a higher sort that can neither be contested nor denied. Indeed, God, the Exalted, is observing us and He has assigned certain angels to write what we do of good and evil. They create a complete record of all our actions, something rather like a movie of our lives.

This special record that the angels keep cannot be altered or falsified. Just as a good, clear film can capture all the details of a complex sequence of events, the angels note our actions in all their detail. It is said in the Holy Qur'an, that the angels have been entrusted to write these special records. Consider then, what this writing might be like. Even a videotape can be tampered with, but not so the angels' writing. In a trial proceeding, the defense might argue that a tape presented as evidence was forged or filmed with an impersonator. However, this could not be the case with the writing of the angels. Their writing is infallible, beyond language, beyond multiple interpretations.

Imagine what sort of technology might be involved here. Just as modern recording methods capture photons and sound waves

---

[51] Suratu 'n-Nisa, (Women), 4:59.

in various media, the angels must also employ energy wavelengths in their work. Whatever the method of this writing is, it was given to the angels by God, the Exalted. That technology cannot be described, but it is something like a record that can bring back any moment of your life and, in some inexplicable way, cause it to be re-enacted. It goes beyond a mere copy of your life's events, it is almost as though it were the events themselves, held somewhere else in another dimension waiting to be brought back to life.

Sometimes, during brain surgery, patients tell of "re-living" events in their lives when electrodes are touched to certain parts of the cerebral cortex. They say that the experience is definitely not a memory. They actually go back in time to the point of the original events and retrace their steps—even for things that they had entirely forgotten or had faded beyond voluntary recall. They are not just looking at images or actors on a stage—they are there! Perhaps the angels' records are something like this, something kept somewhere just outside of our normal experience of sequential time—an entirely parallel existence, that persists beyond of our normal consciousness.

With this sort of record hidden in the wings of the human stage, everyone might ponder the consequences of their actions more carefully. Indeed, Judgment Day may consist of a detailed review of these digital, Technicolor, Dolby soundtrack films of our various careers. Had we thought about being in the eye of such a celestial camera at every moment, our behavior might have been of a higher order. After all, it's only human nature to behave better when you know someone else is watching.

And so, the Recording Angels create an irrefutable record of a particularly vivid sort. The good actions are recorded by the angel to the right, and the bad to the left. They witness our actions, verify the record, and stamp them as notarized. God, the Exalted, has authorized them to do this, and their observations are total.

However, the angels do not necessarily have the last word. In his mission of transcendent mercy, Prophet Muhammad ﷺ may intervene at the point of judgment. He said:

I observe and see what all the members of my Community are doing and I record it. If I find good, I praise God, the Exalted, and if I find other than that I ask forgiveness for them.[52]

Consider then the greatness of the Prophet ﷺ. That means he has the ability to erase whatever the angels have recorded. In effect, he is saying that the heavenly technology that God, the Exalted, gave him is higher than what was granted to the angels. The Prophet ﷺ is the Arch-Intercessor and, as such, he can write over any part of the angelic records he chooses. Even though the angels maintain an undeniable record of our actions, the Prophet ﷺ has special authority over the evidence presented in the courtroom at our judgment.

That is why Prophet ﷺ said: "I am master of the Children of Adam."[53]

Prophet ﷺ will not leave the Community exposed to the angel on the left. The angel who records our bad actions would be ashamed to expose the Community of the Prophet ﷺ. There is a hadith of the Prophet ﷺ concerning the Day of Judgment. Even if someone has been a sinner his whole life, if he believes in God, the Exalted, and the Prophet ﷺ, he can receive mercy on Judgment Day. There are many people who are Muslim in name only: they believe but don't perform the obligations of Islam. On the Day of

---

[52] al-Bazzar and Qadi Iyad in his *Shifa*.
[53] *Musnad Ahmad.*

Judgment when that person comes in front of the *Meezaan*, the Scale, God, the Exalted, will question him and order the Scale to weigh his actions.

A Single Divine Manifestation

(Allah) Most Gracious! It is He Who taught the Qur'an.
He has created man.[54]

Such is the greatness of God, the Exalted! His manifestations of the Divine Name ar-Rahman are like a fountain where every drop of water multiplies as it flows forth. The reality of that Attribute emerges from the Essence in ever expanding circles. Mercy showers down on us from a concealed place. No one sees each new drop before it materializes from the reality of the Divine Name Huwa, where Allah said:

I was a hidden treasure and I wanted to be known so I created creation.[55]

It would not be correct to say that these Attributes are created as they come into view. They are not *makhluq*—created. They are ancient and have always existed in the Essence. They are *azaliyya*, pre-eternal, pristine, *abadi*, eternal, not created. We are created. But the Qur'an, Allah's ﷻ Ancient Words, Kalaamullah al-Qadeem, is not created. The Qur'an originates from the Beautiful Manifestation of the Divine Name ar-Rahman. It is a mercy for everyone. It is clear that the Qur'an stems from this one attribute—remember that all save one surah of the Holy Qur'an begin: *"Bismillahi 'r-Rahmani 'r-Raheem*—In the name of Allah, the Most Gracious, the Merciful."* Mercy bursts forth from the Qur'an generating an infinite number of meanings. Its words are living things and no one but God, the Exalted, and the Prophet ﷺ can see

---

[54] Suratu 'r-Rahman, (The Merciful), 55:1-3.
[55] *Hadith qudsi* cited by Razi, Suyuti, Jarrahi.

how the continuous ascension and movement within this creation weaves these meanings into new patterns.

From the mercy of *"It is He Who taught the Qur'an,"* that first understanding of the first Attribute that was explained to the Prophet ﷺ, the whole of creation came, *"He has created man."* All of this came with the first manifestation at the first moment. What about the second manifestation, the third or the fourth? What more is coming? What can we say about it?

With one manifestation of ar-Rahman the entire universe was made manifest. The power of this Divine Mercy rings throughout the first surah of the Qur'an. How many emanations of this Divine Attribute have become reality in our era—in the future, past and present of Allah's Name *ar-Rahman*? Can you imagine? And what will emerge from them as time moves forward? This was just one emanation—think how much of creation has originated from this one instance of one Divine Attribute.

The Cosmic Balance

It is He Who taught the Qur'an.[56]

Through the Qur'an, human beings have been taught many things. The holy book covers vast areas of science and deep knowledge. Whether describing the precise motions of the Sun and the Moon, the kingdoms of animals and trees, the different levels of creation: all these topics revolve about a central vision of the cosmic order. This vision implies a certain balance in creation; a balance maintained and organized in the reciprocal love demonstrated by the Creator for His creation and His creatures returning that love and respect in the act of prostration. In this regard, the Qur'an is a discourse on the science of love and mercy,

---

[56] Suratu 'r-Rahman, (The Merciful), 55:1-3.

both given and returned. Everyone living is in prostration. As He raises the heavens, He maintains the structure in balance.

In order that ye may not transgress (due) balance.[57]

This balance should not be subjected to misuse or interference, either by humans or any other agents in the universe. The universe was not meant to shake. Its stability somehow rests on the free flow of love and mercy, a flow which connects the upper and lower levels of the structure. Any blockage of this flow constitutes a pocket of darkness and stagnation.

So the Holy Qur'an issues forth from that one Attribute: ar-Rahman, The Most Merciful. This is why the Prophet ﷺ said, "When I am observing you, if I see good I praise God, the Exalted, and if I see other than that, I seek forgiveness for you." This means, "I erase everything. Don't worry about what the angels write. Allah gave me *shafa'a*—the power of intercession."

Value of Praising the Prophet

There was once a sinner who arrived at Judgment Day. On one occasion in his life he attended and heard someone say, "*Allahuma salli 'ala Sayyidina Muhammad*—O Allah bless our master Muhammad ﷺ," and upon hearing it he repeated it. So, in his entire life, he recited praise on the Prophet ﷺ one time; one *salawaat*. On this account, he received mercy. Do you doubt that any Muslim or believer who recited one *salawaat* on the Prophet ﷺ, even just one time, would not receive mercy?

Even a non-believer, taking it even further, might receive such a mercy. For example, someone might read a book where the *salawaat* is written after the Prophet's ﷺ name. Seeing the simple words wishing peace upon the Prophet ﷺ, could bring light into

---

[57] Suratu 'r-Rahman, (The Merciful), 55:8.

his heart and guide events in his future, leading him, one day, to take *shahada*.

So on Judgment Day, according to Grandshaykh, there is hadith of the Prophet ﷺ about this sinner that says he will be standing at the *Meezaan*, the Scale, and he will put his bad *'amal*, actions, in the left side of the Scale. He has no good deeds, so the Angel on the right says he has nothing to give. And he only has one *salawaat 'ala an-Nabi*. The bad side is heavier and the Scale tips. Then they put that one *salawaat* on the Scale. What happens when your bad actions are heavier? "Take him to hellfire." "But wait, he did one *salawaat*." What did the Prophet ﷺ say? "Whoever prays on the Prophet ﷺ, Allah will pray on him ten times."[58]

Can you imagine anything more powerful than the Divine *salawaat*, God's praise of His Prophet ﷺ? Can any darkness be cast upon that *salawaat*? He gives a heavenly *salawaat*. Those ten *salawaat*s come from the heavens with a force beyond our imagination. This is real power. If you were to measure the weight of all human *salawaat* from Adam ﷺ on up to Judgment Day and place them on the Scale against that tenfold *salawaat* of God, the Exalted, and His angels, do you not think that this will outweigh those sins? Immediately that Scale will fly off its stand. The Prophet will say, "Do you not feel shy?" Immediately the Scale will tremble and the bad actions of that servant whose actions it is weighing will be tossed out of the left side of the balance.

Do not worry! With this special *salawaat* you will go to Paradise. Finished! This everlasting mercy for all mankind came from one manifestation of one Divine Attribute. Imagine then, the blessings that must issue from all the other 99 Divine Names and Attributes as they become manifest, each with its own special characteristic.

---

[58] Bukhari and Muslim.

So God, the Exalted, has given authority to the Prophet ﷺ to look for our best actions. He has not been asked to look for ways to punish us. God, the Exalted, knows we are weak servants: *"man was created weak."*[59] We cannot do what we are obliged to do. God, the Exalted, has said that while we are running away from Him, He is running towards us.

Grandshaykh said that when the Prophet ﷺ simply moves his finger, there are 12,000 oceans of meaning and worlds of wisdom behind the gesture. In whatever he does in this life and in the life of the intermediary life, *barzakh*, there are fountains of knowledge that come forth, more than we can ever know.

Caricaturing the Prophetic Conduct

Today, people are in the streets protesting the Danish cartoons of the Prophet ﷺ. What? They object only to the cartoons? Look rather to the conditions in the Community: are we holding to the *Sunnah* of the Prophet ﷺ? What could foolish drawings do to touch or harm the Prophet ﷺ in any way? Perhaps of more concern is the fact that most of the Community is not currently following his practices, his *Sunnah*. Things like such cartoons are merely a distraction. Satan is playing with us.

As people who do not believe in Prophet Muhammad ﷺ, the thoughtless cartoonists have predictably shown their disrespect, but our disrespect from within the faith is a far deeper problem. Would the public have associated the Prophet ﷺ with bombs and destruction unless Muslim extremists had carried out their acts in the guise of Islam? People march in the streets to protest the cartoons and jump up and down yelling. What about all our other failings? As the Prophet ﷺ said, "Whoever revives my *Sunnah* in a

---

[59] Suratu 'n-Nisa, (Women), 4:28.

time of corruption will take the reward of seventy martyrs."[60] What are we doing? The Prophet says, *"If ye do love Allah, Follow me, Allah will love you."*[61] Who is doing that today? No one.

The significance of the Prophet's actions and practices reverberates even today. His special qualities, by virtue of his power of being Present and Observing, touch us even at this moment. We must transcend time and embrace timelessness in order to comprehend the meaning of *Haadir* and *Naazhir*. Leave behind days, hours, weeks, months, years: the Prophet ﷺ sees all that is and all that will be. He is the light of God, the Exalted, and everything emanates from the Light of Muhammad ﷺ—an-Nur al-Muhammadiyya. Everything emanates from *ism* ar-Rahman, the Divine Name the Most Gracious.

Once we understand that light is timeless, everything becomes clear. Imagine a presence that touches every point of the universe in all of its time dimensions forever. The closest thing in science to this would be the behavior of physical light. It propagates across space at such a high speed that it is considered the upper limit of velocity in modern physics. Because of these properties, visible light has always worked as a metaphor for Divine Light and the light of the Prophet ﷺ:

God is the light of the heavens and earth.[62]

Mawlana Shaykh Nazim ق and Grandshaykh ق are saying that the worlds of science and spirituality are coming together like puzzle pieces. It is remarkable how our physical understanding and our spiritual understanding are merging in this age. Today, physicists discussing variations of the Unified Field Theory are beginning to sound more like Zen Bhuddists describing the

---

[60] Tirmidhi.
[61] Surat Aali-'Imraan, (The Family of 'Imraan), 3:31.
[62] Suratu 'n-Nur, (The Light), 24:35.

"Eternal Now" than modern scientists. Similarly, the Prophet ﷺ is the very source of light, so for him there is no before and no after.

To illustrate what Mawlana Shaykh is saying, it can be said that we live in world that is connected together by electromagnetic energy. From computers to satellites, from sunlight to the aurora—it is all composed of electromagnetic fields based on waves. Many quantum physicists studying the difference between waves and particles have come to the conclusion that everything is in a wave form until it is "witnessed." When we witness a wave pattern it changes character and becomes a particle running at the speed of light and that becomes permanent, timeless.

When we make an intention, *niyyah*, the intention of the heart is a wave that changes the pattern of electromagnetic energy that connects with the heart. That is an interpretation compatible with basic physics. So when we witness something, it is "recorded" in the very fabric of space and time. When we wish for something, it also is "recorded." When we plan something it is "recorded."

One day someone brought a picture to Mawlana Shaykh Nazim ق of the electromagnetic field surrounding a heart. He looked at it and said, "This is what we have been talking about for such a long time. When the heart changes with an intention it generates electromagnetic patterns. There is a point where time and energy collapse into one another."

Time is measured in different ways: there are limits to its measurement. Scientists say that the utmost accuracy of the best atomic clocks is somewhere between 10 to the minus 22 seconds and 10 to the minus 32 seconds (between 10^{-22} and 10^{-32}). Beyond that it does not make sense to talk about time. It only makes sense to talk about energy. When time is sliced into small enough increments, only the energy portion of the increment can be measured.

God, the Exalted, who has created the spirit, has placed it beyond time—it is pure energy. It transcends time and is uniquely a Divine creation. Modern physicists tell us that electromagnetic waves are of different lengths. Some have high energy and high frequency and are hot. Others have longer wavelengths and are cool. The universe is like an ocean swirling with energy. God, the Exalted, created the Muhammadan Light, an-Nur al-Muhammadiyya, so that this light could be witnessed; from creation, to creation.

Perhaps the Divine records that appear on our Day of Judgment are these same wavelengths, captured as particles, removed from time, and summoned to that point as the signature of our existence. Our lives are, in effect, captured as observed events, recorded, and judged. As such, this exact image of our history amounts to infallible evidence in the court of our final judgment.

However, even at this judgment we have an advocate for clemency. The Prophet ﷺ sees all and can intervene at any point. For the created universe we live in, the Prophet has been *Haadir* and *Naazhir* from time immemorial. He travels at the speed of light. One moment he is sleeping and Hazrat Khadija thinks he is still in his bed, yet in that time he travels to the heavens and returns and the bed is still warm. We, as disciples, must cultivate our thinking beyond the normal experience of sequential time. We are prisoners of time; yesterday, today and tomorrow. The Prophet ﷺ does not belong to time as we know it: he is timeless. The Prophet ﷺ said, in a holy hadith that Allah said, "Do not curse the Time, for I am the Time."[63]

---

[63] Bukhari.

TIME AND MEASURE

Difference Between the Qadiriyya and Naqshbandiyya

I would like to offer a few brief comments concerning the difference between the Naqshbandi and Qadiri Sufi Orders. Think of this as the first course of a spiritual repast—a short introduction to my talk today.

Qadiri comes from *qaadir*, power, so this Sufi Order take from the Divine Ocean of Power, *bahru 'l-qudrah*. Sayyidina 'Abdul Qadir al-Jilani was Servant of the Qadir, the Owner of Absolute Power. So they derive many of their practices from that Attribute. They emphasize *qudrah*, or power. That is why, throughout their history, there have been many miracles performed within the Qadiri Sufi Order. But not today. Today that ability is closed.

The Naqshbandi, on the other hand, inherit from the secret of the name Allah, the Name that encompasses all other Divine Names and Attributes. As a result, they focus on the *naqsh*—the engraving. They work to engrave on their heart the name Allah. So their focus is: "My God, You are my aim, and Your good pleasure is what I seek."[64] They focus on the true Reality of the Divine Essence. They don't focus on miracles, rather they hide their miracles. For them miracles are unnecessary. The source is the same, but they take from different Divine Attributes. One takes from *qudrah*, power, and the other takes from *naqsh*, engraving. This is a matter of *naqsh wa manqoosh*—the engraving

---

[64] Arabic: *ilahee anta maqsoodee wa ridaaka matloobee.*

62

and the engraved. Ultimately, all are taking from the Prophet of Allah ﷺ.

Timelessness

We are all familiar with time zones, especially when you fly from one part of the globe to another. Your position, East to West on the surface of the planet, determines what time of day it is. When it is darkest midnight on one side of the globe, in the same instant it is a sunlit high noon on the opposite side.

In effect, we live inside a huge celestial clock with many moving parts. Just as the hands of a watch sweep across its face measuring out seconds, minutes and hours, so the movements of the planets mark times within the solar clock whose face is the orbital plane girdling the Sun. Imagine rising up out of the solar system and looking back down from above. From this angle, would it not present the face of a strange clock with planets for hands and orbits for movements? The shorter hands would move more quickly: the Earth, Mars and Venus "hands." The longer ones would turn more slowly: the Jupiter, Saturn, Pluto and Uranus "hands."

Closer to home, as the earth turns on its axis, we experience the alternation of day and night, even though the Sun remains fixed and shining at all times. The two major motions of the Earth, its annual circuit about the Sun and its daily rotation around its own axis, combine to govern our days and seasons. The third element in this planetary dance, the orbit of the Moon about the Earth, contributes yet another measurement of time, the lunar month. This vast mechanism that divides the passage of our lives into days, months and years shows Allah's Greatness. Allah says:

It is He Who made the sun to be a shining glory and the
moon to be a light (of beauty), and measured out stages
for her; that you might know the number of years and

*the count (of time). Allah did not create this but in truth
and righteousness. (Thus) does He explain His Signs in
detail, for those who understand.*[65]

Who could have set these circles within circles, clocks within
clocks in motion? If you were to make a model of the Solar
system for your children you would need years and years to work
out the intricate relationships of distance and motion. No one can
do that. And yet, on a far larger scale, God, the Exalted, made this
Earth, which holds its place in the grand setting of the universe,
turning around itself and flying about the sun. That is one
meaning of *Allahu Akbar*.

The fountain of creation spouts forth the Divine Attributes in
the form of knowledge as well as the physical aspects of the
cosmos. The concepts embedded in the Beautiful Names of ar-
Rahman, The Most Gracious, and the phrase *"Allahu Akbar*, God is
Greater,"* generate understanding just as the Sun radiates light
and heat.

The sun, in its own right, is the master of a dance which
governs the movements of the Earth and her sister planets. The
kind of time represented by the level of the Sun in creation is
profoundly different from the experience we know as the
succession of day and night, light and dark on Earth, because the
Sun occupies a relatively stable position in the scheme. It is the
heart of the system, pumping out life-giving light, heat and
gravity that hold the local solar structure together. What could
comprise a night and a day for the Sun? The Sun is of a
completely different order than a planet. That is why Allah said:

By the Sun and his (glorious) splendour.[66]

---

[65] Surah Yunus, Jonah, (The Prophets), 10:5.
[66] Suratu 'sh-Shams, (The Sun), 91:1.

The idea that time might be different in different places in creation is an important one. Similarly startling is the notion that time might be experienced in drastically different modes, depending on the level of being of the entity perceiving it. We sense time mainly as a progression of instants, tiny slices of experience, more or less forming a whole that we typically think of as our history. It is as though we were locked in a tractor beam, inevitably pulling us forward through the years to our graves, all neatly broken up into little ticks of the clock. For God, the Exalted, without drawing comparisons, we can say by way of example that there is something utterly different—a Super-present—a possession of creation in its entirety from beginning to end, from eon to eon, all at once. Imagine, He can behold billions of years as a simultaneous event!

That means the Divine Focus is always on the present. It is not on something past nor something coming in the future. For God, the Exalted, everything is there, there is no before and no after, there is no knowledge that God, the Exalted, knew before and then later He knows something different. His knowledge transcends all events for all time. He knows everything, He is al-'Alim, The Absolute Knower. We say something has a beginning and an end, but for God, the Exalted, there is no beginning and no end.

Each one of us can time travel, in a sense, by reaching into our memories to retrieve some bit from the past or project our thoughts into the future by making reasoned predictions. Farmers plant their crops based on the seasons with the expectation of coming rain and harvest cycles. Economists predict market fluctuations based on mathematical probabilities. In either case, looking backwards or forwards in time requires a temporary escape from the overwhelming distraction of our five senses which sweep us along through each minute with the sensation of passing time.

Left unchecked and unexamined, this purely temporal experience of sights and sounds can leave us permanently Earth-bound. To look beyond the senses, to ponder the mysterious notion that time can stretch, bend, twist and even reverse itself can amount to a quest for a larger reality than that afforded by the fleeting experience we normally hold to be the present.

Medieval theologians characterized Heaven as the eternal realm and Earth as the temporal plane. Think of what the word temporal means: transitory, temporary, worldly, passing time. Our awareness of what we sense as the ordinary passage of time, the tempo of our experiences, is measured in the sensory world of sight, sound, visceral and somatic sensations. Therefore, our Earth-bound natures are very much linked to the moving point of sensation.

Consider the miraculous faculties of the saints and prophets: their ability to co-locate; send messages through telekinesis; fold space and exercise the power of attraction from great distances. These abilities would suggest that, given a certain level of spiritual development, some beings can step outside the normal space-time continuum, move away from the Earthly theatre and closer to the Heavens and, as a result, enjoy a greater freedom of movement and influence. For example, the notion that human consciousness could ride on a beam of light might seem perplexing to ordinary people such as ourselves, but perfectly natural to the Prophet ﷺ and the saints.

If the temporal experience is our lot in life, then what is timelessness for us? What is the opposite of a transient, fleeting ride on a sensory roller coaster? It is very hard for us to believe that the past is still there, and that the future is also now present. What would our timelessness look like?

Extended Geometry

Sometimes geometry can help to visualize difficult concepts. For example, our bodies, viewed over time, begin as single cells, grow, and then wither in the grave. In time-lapse photography, things like the lights on cars and people moving through the field of vision look like ghostly streaks in the picture. If the photographer's camera could back up far enough to get a time-lapse photograph of one person's entire 80-year life, it would reveal a very peculiar image of a long tube. This shape, expanding along its length from a single cell to the trillion-cell body of say, an 80-year old man would, over time, reveal a complex spiral of 80 turns, each turn as large as the orbit of the Earth around the Sun, a circle with a diameter of 186 million miles. If this man lived on the equator, he would be riding around the planet for 24,000 miles each day at 1,000 miles per hour, and around the Sun at 67,000 miles per hour.

The man's own senses would tell him that he was no bigger than his coat of skin, say 6 feet tall and, due to the moment of inertia, he would have no sensation of either terrestrial or solar speeds. But the angelic photographer could see a much larger form. It is as though each one of us were an electrical wire, where the consciousness of the present is one tiny charge of electrons coursing through the long, tube-shaped wire of our time-bodies over the course of its many coils, or years. The wire is there, before and after the pulse passes by any given point, or moment, in the line. If someone had enough spiritual energy to flood the entire line of his life as it extends in time with a "charge" of consciousness, all at once, he would possess all the seconds of his life simultaneously. He would be a very large being indeed, with a huge awareness of his life, nature, and perhaps even the rest of humanity.

Timelessness is extremely difficult to grasp, but to continue in geometrical terms, consider a sphere: it has a beginning and an end. It is round, so wherever you draw a line it comes back to the same point on its surface. On the other hand, picture a straight line extending out into space forever in both directions. In this example there is no beginning and no end. The line would suggest that space could continuously expand and stretch to infinity. Modern physicists propose just such a model: the observable universe is not only expanding and stretching, but much to their surprise, its rate of expansion is also accelerating. If we go along with the theory of the Big Bang, we assert that there must have been something that triggered the Big Bang, just as an explosion must be triggered. That means that what triggered it preceded the Big Bang. And what came before the trigger? Time must stretch out forever, forward and backward, just like our line.

Beyond and above physics, we know that the Light of Muhammad ﷺ was what triggered the Big Bang. And what could have ignited the Light of Muhammad ﷺ? Here we approach the very edge of existence itself. Allah created the Light of Muhammad ﷺ when there was no "before." God, the Exalted, precedes the before and has no end. In this realm, our ordinary conceptions of time dissolve into nothing:

> *Verily a Day in the sight of thy Lord is like a thousand years of your reckoning.*[67]

Divine Time Accounting

As we discussed earlier, the differences in time scales between the earthly world and the Divine Kingdom are vast. Similarly, cause

---

[67] Suratu 'l-Hajj, (The Pilgrimage), 22:47

and effect are magnified between these two realms. When you do one *salawat*, God, the Exalted, replies to you with ten *salawaat*. That means that when you do one minute of *'ibadah*, worship, you receive a reward of thirty years of worship. In one minute how "far" does God, the Exalted, "move" where He says, "If My servant comes to Me walking I will come to him running"?[68] When you recite the Opening, the first chapter of the Holy Qur'an, God, the Exalted, gives you the reward of thirty heavenly years.

Soulspeed

There are *awliyaullah* who can move faster than the speed of light. The speed of light is limited. When something is related to *akhira*, the afterlife, it is unlimited. The speed of light is 186,000 miles/second. While no one can imagine such a speed, still it remains in earthly limits. *Awliyaullah* move without limits. They move with the speed of the mind and even faster, with the speed of the heart. They can travel to the Sun or to an outer planet like Pluto with the swiftness of a thought. If they speak of Paradise they are there.

Imagine the mobility of people in even higher stations. The Sahaba and the Prophets must have powers of even greater dimensions. Consider the power of Prophet Muhammad ﷺ. He ascended to "*two bow's length*" and then returned to Mecca from the Ultimate Reality, and when he returned the mattress upon which he had been resting was yet warm. How far did he travel? It is not counted in light years, nor in *awliya* years, not even in prophetic years, nor in any measure we know of.

So when God, the Exalted, says, "I come to you running," how fast is He coming to you when you seek Him with a sincere heart? These are not theories; to *awliyaullah* these are facts. They speak

---

[68] Bukhari.

based on their direct experience of reality, no matter how much their statements run counter to our ordinary experience of space and time.

Everything in Measure

We are taught *"Every single thing is before His sight, in (due) measure."*[69] Everything in Allah's ﷻ Presence is in measure. That means even the cosmic distances we have been discussing are measured. Who is measuring them? Does God, the Exalted, need to measure? He does not, but to teach mankind He is giving us examples through the angels and the prophets.

> *He does take an account of them (all), and hath*
> *numbered them (all) exactly.*[70]

Ahsaahum—take an account of them—refers to the idea of sets or collections of things that contain subsets. In statistical exercises, you may gather things together and count them. You may count them one-by-one: *'addahum 'adda.*

> *He has full cognizance of them, and has numbered them*
> *with [unfailing] numbering.*[71]

God, the Exalted, created all human beings, but does He need to count them? If you have ten children, you know them. If you have one hundred you know all one hundred of them. If you have many relatives you know all of them. Think of Allah's ﷻ servants: would He not know all of them? And yet He is teaching us that He counted them in numbers. That means that He has given each one a specialty and that a particular angel has been assigned for each aspect of that specialty. As time passes, the angels succeed one another in tending the servants of God, the Exalted. Every

---

[69] Suratu 'r-R'ad, (Thunder), 13:8
[70] Surah Maryam, (Virgin Mary), 19:94.
[71] Surah Maryam, (Virgin Mary), 19:94.

breath you breathe is accompanied by an angel emerging and an angel entering. There are angels responsible for eyes, ears and noses. Grandshaykh said that with every single bite of food we take there are 300 angels extracting the minerals and vitamins and distributing them throughout the body. This is the case for a child's digestion as well as an adult's. And at each moment new angels come while others go.

Consider the technology used for kidney dialysis treatment. The machine filters and purifies blood just as a properly-functioning kidney does. Compare the sizes of the mechanical device versus that of the organ. The dialysis machine is huge and the kidney is tiny—yet it contains 100 million pores that can identify what is good for the body and what is harmful. Who made that kidney with 100 million pores which is able to identify and remove any poison, while isolating and absorbing a beneficial substance such as iron? This is beyond the realm of thought and even beyond the limits of imagination. For the one who was the Source of this we say *Haadirun* wa *Naazhirun*—Present and Observing. He is in that presence and looking at the Station of *"two bow's-length or nearer"*[72] At each moment the Prophet ﷺ is looking on as God, the Exalted, generates creation. As creation unfolds, the Prophet ﷺ observes and understands.

Given this pivotal point occupied by the Prophet ﷺ, do you think that he would run from Mecca to Madina in fear of the Quraysh? In reality, he remains at the Station of *"two bow's-length or nearer,"* the upper point of his ascension, and there he is still meeting with *awliyaullah*, may Allah sanctify their souls and bless them.

---

[72] Suratu 'n-Najm, (The Star), 53:9

71

From Muhammad to Muhammad

It is said that when Gabriel came to him with *wahiy*, (revelation), the Prophet ﷺ asked him, "O Gabriel who is giving you revelation?" Gabriel replied, "I receive the revelation from behind a heavenly veil." But Gabriel could not see his Lord. Only One can see his Lord. Gabriel said, "I receive revelation from behind a veil; a white hand extends forth and gives me revelations." (This is the explanation of *yad al-qudrah*—the Hand of Power). The Prophet ﷺ told him, "Next time, look to see who is behind that veil!" Grandshaykh mentioned, (and I have read it in many hadith books), that the next time Gabriel went before his Lord, he opened that veil and who did he see? He saw Muhammad ﷺ, and he said, "*min Muhammad ila Muhammad* ﷺ—from Muhammad ﷺ to Muhammad ﷺ." Does the one who is giving revelation to Gabriel and sending it to himself, need to run from Mecca to Madina? Then why did the Prophet ﷺ make that trip?

PATIENCE AND PURIFICATION

[A Friday Sermon]

The Art of Patience

O believers, O Muslims! *Alhamdulillah*, praise God, we are meeting again in an important holy month of the Arabic *Hijrah* new year, 1427, the month of Muharram. And today it might be the twelfth or 11th of Muharram, just after Ashura, a day which has seen many events from the time of Adam ﷺ throughout history. It is a day when the Prophet ﷺ entered Madina and saw the Jews fasting. He asked them why they were fasting. They explained that they were fasting and worshipping their Lord, because he saved Moses ﷺ on that day. He said, "We are also believing in Moses ﷺ, we are *ahaqq*, we have more obligation to Moses ﷺ to fast."[73] As-Saadiq al-Amin, the Truthful and Trustworthy Prophet Muhammad ﷺ said, "anyone who fasts that day, will be forgiven the sins of the past year."[74] Everything is by intention, *niyyah*, so if someone fasted for Ashura on Wednesday or Thursday, it will be as though you were newly born on that day

Islam came with mercy, *rahmat*. Islam's essential characteristic is mercy. That is what we, as Muslims, have to show to the rest of the world.

There are many problems and afflictions that Muslims are going to see in the coming years. Sayyidina Mu'awiyah ﷺ, related that the Prophet ﷺ said, referring to that time, "There would be

---

[73] Bukhari and Muslim.
[74] Muslim.

73

nothing left from the worldly life but affliction and confusion—*fitna*." There was *fitna*, trouble, that took place between Mu'awiyah ❀ and Sayyidina 'Ali ❀ at that early time in the Ummah. The Companions were fighting each other, just as again today Muslims are fighting each other. The Prophet ❀ predicted that in time there would be nothing left of this life except dissension and confusion. He warned, "Prepare for such testing patience."

If that could happen then, it can happen now. O Muslims, prepare for affliction and learn patience! In the face of difficulties, what do we have to do today? We must follow what the Prophet ❀ recommended, not what our ego is recommending. We are not following the *Sunnah* practices properly and therefore we are not achieving the state of *Ihsan*, the level of perfection of the soul, aimed for by the Sufis. Throughout history the Sufis have worked to purify the souls of their followers and students. They were teaching people to purify themselves in order to have patience. In effect, a large part of what the Prophet ❀ taught was patience.

Among Allah's 99 Beautiful Divine Names, the last is as-Saboor, The Ultimately Patient. All these Names and Attributes give, as much as we can comprehend them, qualified explanations of God, the Exalted. While His Nature can be indicated, it cannot be defined. God, the Exalted, is the Divine Name which encompasses all the Holy Divine Names and Attributes.

One of the Beautiful Names of God, the Exalted, relates to the Divine Essence. That Name is *Huwa*. In Suratu 'l-Ikhlas Allah says: *Qul Huwa*.[75] God, the Exalted, described the Essence to the Prophet ❀ by saying *"Qul Huwa—Say (O Muhammad) 'He!'"* And He is what? *"Huwa Ahad—He is Unique."* He did not say *"Qul huwa Allahu wahid—*Say (O Muhammad) He is One." *Wahid* is one

---

[75] Suratu 'l-Ikhlas, (Sincerity), 112:1.

74

level, and while we cannot say that one Divine Name is higher or lower than another, the distinction here is that the Oneness of Allah, *Ahad* is the Name that describes Allah's Absolute Uniqueness. No one can describe *Ahad*. If there is no way to describe *Ahad*, then there is no way to describe God, the Exalted. *Ahad* and *Samad* come one after the other. You go back from *Ahad* to *Samad* and from Allah to *Ahad*.

The Beautiful Names and Attributes appear like a fountain, a waterfall describing the Essence. And yet the Beautiful Names and Attributes are not enough to describe the Essence. Do you think that 99 Names are the only the names of God, the Exalted? We will not go into that discussion now.

So the last Divine Name of the 99 is as-Saboor, the Ultimately Patient. The Prophet ﷺ said, "Prepare patience." We are a nation told to have patience and God, the Exalted, will send His mercy.

Grandshaykh 'Abd Allah al-Faizi ad-Daghestani ق once said:

Patience is fighting all that the selfish ego, *nafs*, likes. There are three types of patience:

The first type of patience is patience with physical discomforts, such as getting up on cold mornings for prayer, having cold water for washing, waiting in line, being uncomfortable during illness, completing difficult tasks, and so forth. To remain patient and to be steadfast in your worship in spite of these difficulties is very valuable in the sight of God, the Exalted.

The second type of patience is even more valuable, and that is the patience to refrain from forbidden things. When you look at a woman, for example, say, "O my lower self! This is my sister! How can I look at her with bad eyes?" About this kind of patience there is a hadith: "To live as a servant and to keep away from forbidden things is more valuable than all the worship of all the angels, men, and jinn throughout all the ages!"

The third type of patience is the best of all. It is to be patient with the people who trouble you. Qur'an relates:

> You must carry some of you with others of you. We are
> trying some of you with others of you.[76]

Patience is a most necessary thing in the life of a man. If a man has hold of patience, all goodness is with him. Allah's eyes are on you…will you be patient?"

Bismillahi 'r-Rahmani 'r-Raheem, in the name of Allah, the Most Gracious, the Merciful is a phrase which describes the Attributes of God, the Exalted, from ar-Rahman, the Merciful, on through to as-Saboor, the Ultimately Patient. While we recite these Names and memorize them, what do we understand of them? The final understanding rests with Him, because He is al-'Alim, the Absolute Knower. He knows everything, because He created everything.

Grandshaykh 'Abd Allah al-Faizi ad-Daghestani ق related that the Mahdi ﷺ, the keeper of this time, told him:

> O my Brother, Shaykh 'Abd Allah! In our time, the sign of a good character, and the highest degree of *Jihad al'Akba*r (fighting with your ego), is to carry other people's bad characters, to bear with them, and to tolerate them. As much as we have patience with people, forbearance, we have good character. It is the sign of good character in our time.

So prepare patience. Don't make *fitna*; dissension. *Fitna* is everywhere. God, the Exalted, will defend the believers. You don't

---

[76] Surah Muhammad, 47:4

need to defend yourselves. Why should we have to run and defend ourselves and criticize this one and that one? If we submit to God, the Exalted, and be true to him, do you think Allah will leave us and not defend us? If Muslims submit to God, the Exalted, and the *Sunnah* of the Prophet ﷺ, God, the Exalted, will defend us. Why is Allah not defending us now? It must be because we are not obeying the Prophet ﷺ. *Ita'at* is submission. The ego does not accept to submit except to itself. That is the crux of the problem.

The Prophet ﷺ made the Sahaba submit to him. They said "yes" to whatever he told them; there was no question. When they entered Mecca, what happened? The Sahaba were preparing to kill everyone. In the year of the Opening, when the Prophet ﷺ returned to Mecca from Madina victorious over the tribesmen who had afflicted and tortured him and his Companions, the Companions were wielding swords seeking to fight the people who had harmed them. Instead, the Prophet ﷺ told his vanquished foes, "*Antum at-tulaqa*—you are the free ones. No one has the right to raise a sword." What can you change if you only bring suffering and problems to everyone?

Ahl as-Suffah: The People of the Bench

Today there is a big issue before us and no one knows how to solve it. How many times was the Prophet ﷺ tortured and abused? What did he do in the face of these trials? He forgave his tormentors. "*Antum at-tulaqa*: you are the free ones!" What can we do? We should follow the *Sunnah*. "Who follows my *Sunnah* loves me." What is the *Sunnah* of the Prophet ﷺ? It has so many facets.

Can we honestly say we are keeping the *Sunnah* of the Prophet ﷺ? God, the Exalted, said, on the tongue of His Prophet ﷺ:

If you love God, then follow me, He will love you. [77]

If there is someone we love and respect we will try to be like him and follow his example. Such practices can purify our characters. Do I lie? Do I cheat? Do I harm anyone? We must try, even if we do not succeed at every moment. Always question yourself. Should I do this? Should I do that? What can we do? One way to remember is to repent, *istighfaar*. Are we remembering to ask Allah's ﷻ forgiveness when we take account of our daily actions each night before sleeping?

The Sahaba were continuously purifying themselves. God, the Exalted, described them in Surat al-Kahf:

And keep your soul (O Muhammad) content with those who call on their Lord morning and evening, seeking His Face; and let not your eyes pass beyond them, seeking the pomp and glitter of this Life; nor obey any whose heart We have permitted to neglect the remembrance of Us, one who follows his own desires, whose case has gone beyond all bounds. [78]

God, the Exalted, told the Prophet ﷺ to be patient with the Sahaba. When he called for them, they stopped what they were doing and came to him immediately. They would sit behind the house of the Prophet ﷺ waiting. Today, the bench they sat on is called as-Suffah. The Sahaba used to sit there and remember God, the Exalted, in that very spot. If you visit there, you may find it near the Door of Fatima, but you must go around the place the authorities have closed. The bench is still there, just as the Ottomans preserved it. So what is the meaning of that bench? It means we must learn to cultivate patience. When we are patient, God, the Exalted, will support us:

---

[77] Surat Aali-'Imraan, (The Family of 'Imraan), 3:31.
[78] Suratu 'l-Kahf, (The Cave), 18:28

Whoever forgives and makes peace among his fellows,
God, the Exalted, will give him his reward.[79]

Why Are Muslims in such a Bad State?

If some people describe the Prophet ﷺ in a way that is irreverent, God, the Exalted, will deal with them. God, the Exalted, will certainly protect His perfect servant. Can He not defend the one He invited to the Station of *"two bow's-length or nearer?"*[80] Of course He can, at any time and from any threat:

Indeed, truth has come and falsehood perished. Surely
falsehood is ever bound to perish.[81]

So why are we losing? Why are so many people coming against us as Muslims? Could it be that we are not listening to the Prophet ﷺ as we should be? In turn, could this be because we are not patient? Don't be carried away by emotions. If you want to be moved by emotion, move against Satan. We make a mistake in looking outward. Instead, we must look inward. Each of us knows what we are doing on a daily basis. Look inside yourself and take stock of what you see. Allah said:

No bearer of burdens can bear of burdens can bear the
burden of another.[82]

In the end, each of us will be asked what we did, not what others did.

The Prophet ﷺ had a troublesome neighbor who would put rubbish in his path every morning. This went on for many years. Through all this, the Prophet ﷺ had never complained or mentioned it to anyone. Instead, each day he cleared away the

---

[79] Suratu 'sh-Shura, (Mutual Consultation), 42:40.
[80] Suratu 'n-Najm, (The Star), 53:9
[81] Suratu 'l-Isra, (The Night Journey), 17:81.
[82] Suratu 'l-Isra, (The Night Journey), 17:15

rubbish—filth of the most unpleasant sort—before making his way down the street. One day the Prophet ﷺ noticed that there was no rubbish left in the usual place. He made inquiries and found that the neighbor had fallen ill. He was concerned and went to visit and comfort this sick neighbor who had been tossing rubbish at his door for seven years. That is how you learn patience!

Do your work. Raise your family. Be someone who dedicates his life to the Lord, to the family and children. God, the Exalted, did not ask anything else of you. God, the Exalted, did not ask anyone to fight. What political fight is worth the effort? There is no *Jihad* today. Where is the basis for *Jihad* in this time? Today there are only political struggles borrowing the name, *Jihad*.

The worst characteristics that anyone can acquire are *hubb ash-shuhra*, love of fame and *hubb ar-riyasa*, love of power. This refers to everyone's underlying desire for fame and leadership. We would all love to be famous and powerful leaders. This is human nature for Muslims and non-Muslims alike. Everyone wants to be the chairman or CEO of a mosque. However, in reality, how can there be a CEO of a mosque, which is God's House? Look at all the titles we give ourselves! Secretaries, managers, treasurers: isn't it Allah's ﷻ house?

Love of fame is a big problem today—*Hubb ash-shuhra*. Too many of us want to be leaders heading up mosques or organizations. Every moment there are mounting problems. Wouldn't it be wiser to avoid problems, especially given the current climate? Don't be a leader. Leaders are responsible for the safety of those they lead. It would be better to be one in a flock of sheep. Let the shepherd deal with the problems and dangers.

One of the Prophet's Companions requested the Prophet ﷺ appoint him in a position of responsibility. The Prophet of Allah ﷺ

patted him on the shoulder and said, "O Abu Dharr! You are weak and it is a trust and thus will be shame and regret for the people on the Day of Judgment, except for those who fulfill it its right and perform their responsibilities."[83]

Who is best shepherd for us? Who do you think is better: the leaders who are sitting in Washington claiming to represent the Muslim community? Or is our leader is Sayyidina Muhammad ﷺ? Work to make him happy, not to make these would-be leaders happy! They say they are furthering the rights of Muslims. However, things really move forward through intention.

The Prophet ﷺ said: "Actions are only by intention, and everyone shall only have what he intended."[84] Safety is in making sure our intentions are pure and in agreement with those of the Prophet ﷺ.

---

[83] Muslim.
[84] Bukhari and Muslim.

SHADOWPLAY

In the Eyes of the Shaykh

Alhamdulillah, praise God, we are so fortunate that all of us are
students and disciples of Mawlana Shaykh Nazim ق. There is no
one higher or lower in the eyes of the shaykh, everyone is equal.
Everyone is equal in the love our shaykh has for us, but they may
not be equal in knowledge: the shaykh opens to some and not to
others. It depends on how much you listened and learned, or
whether you have been chosen to represent the shaykh in certain
areas.

Look at the Companions of our Prophet. Prophet Muhammad
ﷺ did not differentiate in the way he treated each of them, but he
gave some various sorts of knowledge and rank. And while he
made some senior to others, his love was the same for all. What he
gave Sayyidina Abu Bakr ﷺ he didn't give to Sayyidina 'Umar ﷺ,
and what he gave to Sayyidina 'Ali ﷺ he didn't give to Sayyidina
'Uthman ﷺ. He gave each one according to his capacity, but all
are Companions.

The *awliya* always look to their exemplar, the Prophet ﷺ, and
they use his example in their behavior towards others. He loves all
of us, but what he gave me he didn't give you and what he gave
you he didn't give me. Although there are many things we have
in common and share together, still there are things you know
that I don't and things I know that you do not.

Al-'Alim—The Knower

We don't know the wisdom of everything because God, the Exalted, is al-Mudabbir, The Arranger. He is the one that plans everything. From His attribute al-'Alim or al-'Aleem, the Absolute Knower, everything has been planned. Through that Attribute of Divine Knowledge that describes His Essence, He knows everything. When Allah's Will, *iraada*, manifests, the Attribute of Knowledge emerges and the plan of the universe is set into motion. Whatever eventually appears was already in the plan, just as an architect's drawings prefigure a building.

In the case of Allah's Plan, the fit between the drawing and the execution is much tighter than that of an architect's control, because Allah's ﷻ Plan virtually foreordains creation. A master plan for a city or a building might not come to pass because of financial or political circumstances. However, this is not the case with Allah's ﷻ plans. This is similar to Plato's description of the eternal archetypes, which serve as Divine templates for all created things.

Grandshaykh 'Abd Allah al-Faiz ad-Daghestani ق said:

Here is an important and useful secret. It can be knowledge for anyone. As much as he remembers and know, he will draw much benefit.

We can observe the universe, and know that it is filled with many creatures, all made by the Creator. What we must also see, however, is that the Creator and His creatures stand together. All things exist by the power of the Creator. If He Almighty did not support all things, they would vanish instantly. They have no existence outside of their Lord's Power. They are like shadows. If you hold your hand over a table, you can see its shadow. If you remove your hand, the shadow goes away. One is original, the other is not.

What God, the Exalted, sends through his Beautiful Name, al-'Alim, the Absolute Knower, must appear. The created instance must appear because it has already occurred in the heavenly sphere, which is timeless, but from that timeless place drives causation down into our plane of existence. The reality of the created entity is in the heavenly plan: the created thing is merely a reflection of the Divine master pattern, an aspect of al-'Alim. God, the Exalted, wants us to know that these reflections are coming to us from heaven. He wants us to know that it is His Plan governing the universe, and none other.

Once He sets something into motion, it cannot be changed. It is as though everything that seems so real to us here on Earth were actually being observed in a special sort of mirror. We are watching an image of something that happened somewhere else, a reflection of what has already transpired. But what is that mirror?

Jalaluddin ar-Rumi says in his poem *Lost in the Call*:

> Lord, said David, since you do not need us,
> why did you create these two worlds?
> Reality replied: O prisoner of time,
> I was a secret treasure of kindness and generosity,
> and I wished this treasure to be known,
> so I created a mirror: its shining face, the heart;
> its darkened back, the world;
> The back would please you if you've never seen the face.[85]

---

[85] Jalaluddin Rumi, *Love is a Stranger*, [Transated by Kabir Helminski], Threshold Books, Putney: 1993.

The Divine Wisdom in Iblees' Disobedience

God, the Exalted, commanded the angels "Prostrate to Adam." We know that God, the Exalted, created angels without sin. Paradise cannot accept sin, nor can it accept anything wrong. So since Paradise cannot accept something wrong, angels should not be able to commit sins there. So when Allah ordered them to prostrate what was their duty? It was to make prostration to Adam ﷤. However, Iblees refused. God, the Exalted, cursed him because through His Beautiful Name al-'Aleem, that plan had foreseen that Iblees would not prostrate before Adam ﷤ and Allah would curse him for it. If Iblees would have prostrated, he would not have been cursed, and Adam ﷤ would not have been sent to earth.

God, the Exalted, with His *'ilm al-mutlaq*—absolute knowledge—ordered Iblees to make prostration to Adam, but His Will was that Iblees will *not* prostrate, in order for God, the Exalted, to curse him.

Had God, the Exalted, so desired He could have taken the soul of Iblees, just as He takes the soul of any human being or a jinn, and Iblees would have died; but He did not.

The Station of Buddha

Our master Mawlana Shaykh said that, indeed, Buddha was a prophet. He was looking for truth and reality: he found these things. The Buddhist goal is nothingness. They reach for nothingness, the limit. This is similar to the limits expressed in modern physics. At certain limits, the measures of time, space and energy all approach nothingness. *Awliya* can interact with the emptiness—the void.

Similarly, Buddhists, reach for complete emptiness. However, the Buddhist ideal of void would not be empty for *awliya*.

85

Grandshaykh related a story about Sayyidina Bayazid al-Bistami. He set out on a mystical journey from his place of seclusion. When he reached the *bahr adh-dhulmah*, he was thrown into an immense ocean. Grandshaykh said he moved through that ocean faster then the speed of light. Bayazid al-Bistami moved with the speed of the mind, of reflection. He moved through that ocean seeking reality at speeds beyond human imagination. He passed through the *bahr adh-dhulmah*, the Ocean of Darkness, which however is not the one that Buddhists call the Ocean of Emptiness. Rather it is something else.

When Sayyidina Bayazid al-Bistami reached the edge of the universe he heard nothing but the *tasbeeh*, recitation of God's Praise *Hu: Huuuuuu*. He tried to count the number of beings doing that *tasbeeh*, praise, and he could not, even though Mawlana said with his power he was able to count all human beings. He discovered that all these beings reciting God's glorification were disciples of Shah Naqshband, the seventeenth Grandshaykh in the Naqshbandi lineage of masters, and so despite being a Grandshaykh in the lineage he was unable to interact with them. The reason is he had only reached a certain level, but not the level those students of Shah Naqshband had attained. So everyone reaches a certain level of nothingness, but it is not emptiness. Rather, depending on what you bring to that level you find that in reality, it is full of different *tajallis*—manifestations—coming from the different Divine Names and Attributes—each a different manifestation of Names emerging from the Essence.

That is *hadd ad-dunya*—the limit of the worldly life. No one can reach past the worldly limit if they don't believe in the Prophet ﷺ. They will attain an aspect of nothingness there but according to *awliya* that is not the highest level. So according to the level of a *wali*, he reached a level of nothingness, but according to the next level of *wali* (above him in the lineage, *silsila*, on a higher in level), that is not true nothingness. This goes for each level up to the level of the Prophet ﷺ.

That is the meaning of ascension—rising from level to level. At first one cannot see it, but after acquiring complete understanding of that level one can then proceed to the next. First the second and third levels were "non-existent," which means they are out of view. However, when one achieves the first level and realizes it completely he began to interact and become aware of a second level and he began to move up to that level. The entire structure of the levels is always ascending, because the Prophet ﷺ is always ascending. And to where? To the reality of Huwa, which is the ultimate reality that cannot be known. So below that there are different levels of nothingness. The *wali* interacts with these different levels depending on his capacity.

The Absolute Unknown, Huwa, is the name of the Divine Essence. Whatever level you might reach, there is always that highest level above all. There must always be a level above that you cannot understand—that you cannot reach in your ascension. You stop at the door that seems empty, but in reality if you continue, you find that it contains much more than in the preceding level. Then you keep asking for more and you keep going up.

Naqshbandi Shaykhs Withhold Unveiling Their Students

Many *awliyaullah* stop, but in Naqshbandiyya they don't open the *maqaam al-awwaam* or *hijab al-awwaam*, the Station of the Common Folk, the thick veil that you cannot see through. Naqshbandi saints open from the back, proceeding though the 70,000 veils between you and the Prophet ﷺ. They don't want you to be busy in desire and busy with what you see or experience., so they don't open the common veil. That is why in other Sufi paths, *tariqats*, they say "we are seeing this and we are seeing that" along the way. As a result, they become happy with what they have and come to a stop.

On the other hand, you see many Naqshbandis who feel they didn't achieve anything in their lives. But when they reach the time of death, the shaykh comes, Grandshaykh comes and the Prophet ﷺ comes: a white hand emerges, and written on it is God's Divine Name, Allah. Some *awliya* see it in this *dunya*, the worldly life.

Other shaykhs in other *tariqats* let you see such appearances in this life. These experiences can become distracting and stop real progress. The traveler becomes satisfied with a lower form of Paradise. Such a thing in the Naqshbandi Tariqat would invalidate the contract signed between the seeker and his shaykh.

They are disciplined in that, in reaching a level of perfect conduct. That is the story of the disciple of Grandshaykh Khalid. Allah gives them and gives everyone, but those who are with the Prophet ﷺ will ascend with the Prophet ﷺ. If you connect with Buddha, you will be connected with Buddha, not to the level of the Prophet ﷺ.

WILL AND SURRENDER

Noah and the Flood

Allah ordered Prophet Noah ﷺ to build the Ark on a mountain in the forest where no ocean existed. People were coming to him saying, "Are you crazy, why are you building a ship here?" But he didn't listen to them, because he knew he was executing Allah's ﷻ Plan. If he put forward his own *iraada*, his will, he knew that would change everything. That is why submission is always recommended to believers and that is why *awliya* always submit to Allah's ﷻ Will. They don't put their will over Allah's ﷻ Will.

There is a general will and there is a partial will. God, the Exalted, gave us that partial will to check how much we would rebel. That small will of ours is like an atom compared to the general will, but still we manage to be rebellious.

So what happened to Prophet Noah ﷺ? When God, the Exalted, told him to build a ship far inland from the sea, outwardly there seemed only a slight chance that water could reach that level during a flood. Nevertheless, God, the Exalted, caused a gigantic flood to sweep the planet and reach the spot where Noah ﷺ had constructed the ship. This flood was a much greater than the tsunami we saw recently. God, the Exalted, wants people to know this secret coming to us through the hearts of Sayyidina al-Mahdi ﷺ and Mawlana: the recent tsunami was to give us a taste of the flood in the time of Prophet Noah ﷺ. The tsunami of 2004 is like an ant beside an elephant when you compare its strength with the one that happened in time of Prophet Noah ﷺ. That tsunami in which half a million people died showed us what happens when people are not righteous. Perhaps a bigger one is coming. It will be a huge flood like the one that came in the time of Prophet Noah ﷺ showing everyone that it is not difficult for God, the Exalted, which takes away everyone except the believers.

It might do well for us all to consider the power of such events and how they relate to past catastrophes. When Allah moves His Hand, all of nature does His bidding. Floods have dotted human history. Every moment *awliya* can see that floods can come as the result of Allah's ﷻ Divine Justice, affecting people who are deviating and going astray; on people who are harming others; on people who are giving suffering and pain to others; and, on people who are destroying the peace on earth, killing innocents.

Strangely, most of humanity still manages to ignore the warning rumblings from nature. It would seem that unless we are directly affected by the disaster, the significance of the event escapes us almost entirely. Surely, a simple scientific explanation could be offered for any natural event. Or could it? God, the Exalted, can show us things that we would never have pictured in our minds. In most cases, the event has to come crashing down over our heads before we take proper notice. However, a prophet, such as Noah ﷺ, felt it, understood it, and took action. In contrast, despite all the media coverage, the meaning behind the 2004 tsunami has gone largely unheeded. Of course, those who died or saw their villages wash away felt it, but no one else felt it outside the area impacted.

As the Prophet ﷺ said, when describing the Last Days, there will be many earthquakes affecting the whole planet. Look what happened in Kashmir. Millions and millions are suffering without shelter from that huge earthquake. I am mentioning these examples to emphasize the difference between the obedience of Prophet Noah ﷺ and the disobedience of Iblees.

Allah ordered Noah ﷺ to build the ship and to carry in that ship all those who believe. And what happened?

> Noah called out to his son, who had separated himself (from the rest): "O my son! Embark with us, and be not with the unbelievers!" He said: I shall take myself to some mountain that will save me from the water. (Noah) said: This day there is none that is saved from the commandment of Allah except him on whom He has had mercy. And the wave came in between them, so he was among the drowned. Then the word went forth: "O earth! swallow up your water, and O sky! Withhold (your rain)!" and the water abated, and the matter was ended. The Ark rested on Mount Judi, and the word went forth: "Away with those who do wrong!"[86]

Noah ﷺ said to his son when he saw the flood coming, "Come and get aboard the ship with us." The son refused saying, "No, I am going to a very high mountain to protect me from the water." Noah ﷺ said to his son "There is no one protected from Allah's ﷻ Order except for those on whom He bestows mercy." At that moment, even though Noah's ﷺ son was up on the highest point of the mountain, the flood sent its waves up and swallowed him. Like all the others not on his father's ark, he was one of those who drowned. What happened to the water? Similar to what happened recently in 2004.

> And the word was spoken: "O earth, swallow up your waters! And, O sky, cease [your rain]!"[87]

Gheeth al-mai. The ocean flowed inland with a huge flood, but just as suddenly sucked all the water back into the sea bed. Everything became normal. Those huge waves of the tsunami

---

[86] Surah Hud, 11:42-43.
[87] Surah Hud, 11:44.

91

were coming back and forth. After some time, I don't know how many hours or days, the earth swallowed the water back completely, and everything appeared as before.

Gheeth al-mai means "swallow the water." That is giving us an example and a warning to watch for what is going to come. This has given us a small foretaste of what is to come. The real dose that is coming will be more than the flood of Prophet Noah 氹.

Noah's Disobedient Son

The son of Prophet Noah 氹, disobeyed. What happened to him? He drowned. Why wasn't Iblees drowned? He was disobedient as well. Why didn't God, the Exalted, take Iblees' soul and finish him? How could Iblees have stayed in Paradise if sinners are not allowed there? On the Day of Judgment, we will ask God, the Exalted, to have mercy us and to send us to Paradise with the *shafa'a* of Sayyidina Muhammad 鸞. While our faith may be weak and incomplete, the Prophet 鸞 is going to take us with his *shafa'a* and his mercy to Paradise. We know we could never get there with our *'amal*, our deeds, because we are all sinners. If it was based on our deeds, we would end up like Prophet Noah's 氹 son.

> And Noah cried to his Lord and said: "My Lord! Lo! My
> son is of my household! Surely Your promise is the
> Truth and You are the Most Just of Judges." He said:
> "O Noah! Lo! He is not of your household; lo! He is of
> evil conduct, so ask not of Me that whereof you have no
> knowledge. I admonish you lest you be among the
> ignorant." He said: "My Lord! Lo! in You do I seek
> refuge (from the sin) that I should ask of You that

whereof I have no knowledge. Unless You forgive me and
have mercy on me I shall be among the lost."[88]

Prophet Noah ﷺ said, "This is my son, he is from my blood; he is from my family." God, the Exalted, replied, "No he is not from your family. The one who is from your family is the one with good *'amal*, deeds. I am taking him and if you ask me again, then I warn you that you will also be counted among the ignorant." God, the Exalted, was frightening Prophet Noah ﷺ who replied, "O my Lord! Forgive me."

This is what happened to the son of a prophet. On the other hand Iblees, an angel, disobeyed God, the Exalted, but he was allowed to remain in Paradise. He was not thrown from Paradise to earth because Allah's Will was that he go and tempt Adam ﷺ. Allah wanted Adam ﷺ and his wife to descend to earth. That is His *iraada*, His Will, that they fall to earth and build a generation from which sprang the entire human race. God, the Exalted, gave Iblees permission to whisper to Prophet Adam ﷺ and his wife, our mother Eve. He gave them the idea to eat from the forbidden tree. Adam ﷺ listened to his whispering and ate from the tree, but what can he say to Allah for his disobedience?

Intercession of the Prophet

For human beings on Judgment Day, only those who fall under the *shafa'a*, intercession, of the Prophet ﷺ, will be in Paradise. If someone did not come under the Prophet's ﷺ mercy and shafa'a, then even if he repents and asks forgiveness, it will not be granted because of what he has done. Only with intercession can he go to Paradise, because Paradise does not accept sinners.

---

[88] Surah Hud, 11:45-47.

You have to have *adab*, good manners, and say "O God! All my good actions are from You and the bad ones are from me. O My Lord! It is my fault, forgive me." God, the Exalted, forgave Adam because he repented. However, Iblees did not; he said to God, the Exalted, "You made me do it." God, the Exalted, then ordered Iblees to earth and he asked, "Ok, but give me life to the end of time." He is speaking to his Lord, sending messages and receiving answers through the angels. Iblees, the one who is cursed in the Holy Qur'an, is speaking to God, the Exalted, and getting a response. He believes in God, the Exalted, but Allah's ﷻ Will is to bring the human race to earth and introduce His beloved Prophet ﷺ to humanity.

If the human race were to have stayed in Paradise, there would be no reason for God, the Exalted, to send His Prophet ﷺ to humanity, because they would all have remained pure and sincere, worshipping like angels. God, the Exalted, wanted to demonstrate the excellent character of Prophet Muhammad ﷺ and the importance of his role as master of creation in all these universes. That could not be seen in Paradise. Allah ﷻ wants everyone to know that it is because of Prophet Muhammad ﷺ, that you can enter Paradise. This was to show us that we enter Paradise through the Prophet's ﷺ intercession and not simply as a matter of course.

Know the Importance of Muhammad

Prophet Adam ﷺ knew that secret so he said, "O My Lord! For the sake of Muhammad ﷺ forgive me." Allah asked him how he knew of Muhammad ﷺ and Adam said, "Anywhere in Paradises you look, you see the name of Muhammad ﷺ. Even on Your Throne his name is written."[89]

God, the Exalted, wanted everyone on earth to know the importance of Sayyidina Muhammad ﷺ: that because of him He created creation; that because of him He is going to send us to our last station and highest rank .

God, the Exalted, wants to present the beloved one, Sayyidina Muhammad ﷺ, to be like a shining diamond that has no resemblance on earth or in Paradise—not anywhere. God, the Exalted, wants to present Sayyidina Muhammad to humans, jinn, angels—and to all other creation that we don't know about—that is why He sent them all to earth to continue life and to know about Prophet Muhammad ﷺ. He told His prophets and messengers in the Day of Promises:

> Behold! Allah took the covenant of the prophets, saying:
> "I give you a Book and Wisdom; then comes to you an
> prophet, confirming what is with you; believe in him and
> support him."[90]

A Special Taste

Because we do not live in his time, that special taste of love for Prophet Muhammad ﷺ is not in us. That is a problem. If we were to taste it, we would sense his presence, his light, his holy perfumed scent, and his magnificent appearances. We would feel him watching us and realize just how near he is to us. Nowadays only *awliya* are inheriting that from the Companions. We are not. If Prophet Noah ﷺ cared so much for his son, can you imagine how much the Prophet ﷺ cares for his Ummah?

---

[89] Hakim in *al-Mustadrak*, Bayhaqi in *Dala'il an-nubuwwah*, Tabarani in his *Kabir*, Abu Na'eem in his *Hilya* and ibn 'Asakir in *Tarikh Dimashq*.
[90] Surat Aali-'Imran (Family of 'Imran), 3:81.

God, the Exalted, wanted us to know that *"La ilaha illa-Llah Muhammadun Rasulullah—*There is no God but Allah and Muhammad is his Messenger." The secret of that *tawheed,* Oneness, did not open yet and its reality will not open until Judgment Day. Some of its meaning will open now in the Last Days, when Mahdi ☙ comes and Prophet Jesus ☙ comes, so people can taste of it, but its reality will only come in Paradise. Now it is only a phrase that comes on the tongues of people, but God said, "The best of words is *La ilaha illa-Llah Muhammadun Rasulullah."*

May God keep these meetings always taking place and keep the love of Prophet in our hearts, love of Mawlana Shaykh in our hearts, of Grandshaykh 'Abd Allah ad-Daghestani ق in our hearts and love of each other in our hearts.

The one who knows all the prophets is Sayyidina Muhammad ﷺ.

The Messiah, Jesus son of Mary, was only a messenger
of Allah, and His Word which He conveyed unto Mary,
and a spirit from Him.[91]

Prophet Jesus ☙ is His Word, *"alqaaha ila Maryam—which He conveyed unto Maryam."* As for Prophet Adam ☙ he said, *"I breathed into him of My spirit,"*[92] No one can explain what that spirit, *ruh,* is. Is His *ruh* light? Is it the light that God, the Exalted, has sent into him, radiated into him—we cannot say from His Soul—but from His Light, His Order, His Word.

There is another tradition that says that God, the Exalted, has sent his *amr,* command, to Prophet Adam ☙. That relates to the

[91] Suratu 'n-Nisa, (Women), 4:171.
[92] Suratu 'l-Hijr, (The Rocky Tract), 15:29.

96

verse, *"The Spirit is by command of my Lord."*[93] The authority, the energy came from our Lord.

Bi-hurmati 'l-Fatiha.

---

[93] Suratu 'l-Isra, (The Night Journey), 17:85.

KNOWLEDGE FROM THE HEART

The Secret of the Path

[Talk before a large group of Muslims in Washington, DC. A female student introduces the shaykh:]

O my dear Lord, I ask that you grant me your love, I ask that you forgive us first, then annihilate us in your love.

O my Lord, tonight for the sake of Prophet Muhammad ﷺ, give us special attention, help us get out of our own world and get us acquainted with You,

O my Lord I don't want to think of anyone else, I want you to fill every cell of my body with Your Presence.

O my Lord, give us one drop form the love of the ocean of Prophet and annihilate us in His love,

O our Lord, help us reach the state of self-effacement and take away from us all those thoughts that connect us with material life,

O our Lord, help us remember our Lord even when we are busy with others, help us recite *dhikr* "Allah, Allah" at all times, and O our Lord, take away *an-nafs al-ammara*, *insinuating self*, and give us the peaceful self, *an-nafs al-mutma'inna*.

Oh My Lord... tonight I will cry and pray until morning and I ask that when it is time for me to die, let Your Name be my last word. I am a traveler here, far from city of the beloved.

Marwah! The path is full of difficulties and if you want to surpass them, you must purify your heart.

Awliya are Receivers

[The shaykh speaking:]

In the name of Allah, the Compassionate the Merciful. I am very honored to be here with you a second time.

I think Marwah speaks better than me and it might be that God, the Exalted, has opened to her heart and she has explained the secret of *tariqah* better than I can explain. I am not a lecturer so don't expect a lecture. I am like a transmitter. I can only say what comes into my heart. Sometimes I say what will benefit everyone and me as well, and sometimes I am not able to say anything. It's something like being in a radio station: signals are received and broadcast.. This sort of knowledge does not depend on reading books nor is it ever truly captured on paper.

Knowledge is what comes to the heart of the Prophet's 🌿 inheritors as he rises continuously in ascension. As she mentioned, those inheritors will send one drop from the ocean of the knowledge of the Prophet 🌿. That one drop is enough for the whole world. It is the source of all that has been discovered by scientists and written down in books. The full extent of human knowledge comes from just one drop from the ocean of the Prophet's 🌿 knowledge.

Levels of the Heart

This year is 1427 from the Hijrah. It is one, four, two, and seven. In the science of numerology, 1427 equals five. In that system, nine is counted as zero. If we add 1427 together it comes to five. If we add 1 and 4 it is 5 and 2 and 7 are nine. So 7 and 2 is really zero because in the science of numerology 9 is zero. And 4 and 1 is five.

The *awliyaullah* consider this the Year of the Heart, because the heart has five different levels: *Qalb, Sirr, Sirr as-Sirr, Khafa, Akhfa.*

Qalb is the first level of heart where we see and communicate with each other. Satan is present there; *an-nafs al-lawwama*, the lower self which *"does incite to evil"*[94] is also there. Additionally, the three different levels of the ego are contained in the first level of the heart.

The second level is the Secret (*Sirr*), which has to do with knowledge found only within the Sufi orders. These secrets were transmitted through Sayyidina 'Ali ؏ (there are forty that come from Sayyidina 'Ali ؏), (I will explain later about the two sides of *tariqah*, some come from Sayyidina 'Ali ؏ and one coming from Sayyidina Abu Bakr ؏), when the Prophet ﷺ said, "I am city of knowledge and 'Ali ؏ is its door."[95]

Then there is "secret of the secret" that combines the knowledge that is from Sayyidina 'Ali ؏ and Sayyidina Abu Bakr ؏. The next level is the "Hidden", which is knowledge from the Prophet ﷺ, and finally the last level, the "Most Hidden," that comes from Allah's ﷻ Divine Presence.

This is the Year of the Heart, and we might see many changes take place this year. The *awliya* can see into the future with the knowledge that the Prophet ﷺ has given them. I am not going into this subject, because it is only for saints to speak about future events.

Secrets Behind the Prophet's Migration

The Prophet ﷺ willingly submitted to the difficult journey from Mecca to Madina, and this submission opened many things that affected the future. During that time, he saw that Allah wanted him to pass secret knowledge to Sayyidina 'Ali ؏ and

---

[94] Surah Yusuf, (Joseph), 12:53.
[95] Tirmidhi.

100

Sayyidina Abu Bakr ⬧, knowledge that would later come down to us through certain inner paths.

So what is the essence of Islam? We say we are Muslims we are submitting to Allah's *Iraada*, Will. The Prophet went with Allah's Will. He saw that Sayyidina 'Ali ⬧ had to take his place in his bed in Mecca and Sayyidina Abu Bakr ⬧ had to be with him in the cave on the migration to Madinah. This enabled tests and transmissions for both of them. And for us? Our lesson in this is that you cannot meet and overcome obstacles without a guide. Here we are shown that even the Prophet ⬧, who went beyond a station which exceeded even Gabriel's reach, had to accept a guide to show him through the desert. Why then, would we not accept a guide to help us through life's many difficulties? Even the Prophet ⬧ accepted a guide.

During this time, the Prophet ⬧ tested Sayyidina 'Ali ⬧ to see if he would give his life for him. When the enemy was preparing their scheme to kill the Prophet ⬧, Gabriel came to tell him that Iblees had recruited forty conspirators to kill him. Iblees had told them that they needed to kill the Prophet ⬧, but they didn't want to do it. Iblees then devised a plan to convince the various tribes that if they all worked together in the conspiracy, no single group would be blamed.

'Ali and the Essence of Sacrifice

Sayyidina 'Ali ⬧ said, "I will give up everything for you, my life is for you." Later he became son–in–law of the Prophet ⬧. The Prophet ⬧ wanted 'Ali ⬧ to sit in his place, a symbolic throne, a place of authority. When you have a king or president sitting on a chair, what do you call it? It is called *'arsh*, the chair or throne, or the president's chair. Can anyone sit on it? No it is impossible. The only ones who can sit on it, are the children of that king. If the king becomes ill and dies, who succeeds him? His son, sitting on that chair. No one else has that right, because the royal inheritance is from his father. The Prophet ﷺ wanted to show the Ummah that he was giving that inheritance to 'Ali ؏, because he was the one who could carry that responsibility.

We say this with full respect to all the Companions: you cannot discriminate between them, because, the Prophet said, "My companions are like stars, whichever one you follow you will be guided."[96] However, he did bestow unique characteristics to each one of them. What he gave to Sayyidina 'Ali ؏ he did not give anyone else. So he wanted to bequeath him that inheritance. He wanted him to sleep on that bed and to feel that warmth and those good manners which compose the state of *Ihsaan*, perfect character.

This state was described by the Prophet ﷺ when the Archangel Gabriel ؏ came to him in the form of a man in front of all his companions and asked him to describe Islam, *Iman* and *Ihsan*. At that time the Prophet ﷺ explained the five pillars of Islam and he explained the six pillars of *Iman* which all Muslims know. When Gabriel ؏ asked about *Ihsan*, the Prophet ﷺ said, "It is to worship God as if you are seeing Him." It means you cannot lie within your heart while on your tongue you say something else—that is *nifaaq*, hypocrisy. You can be in the first level, *maqaam al-Islam*, the Station of Divine Law. You can even achieve the first levels of Islam and still lie and cheat. You can repeat the *shahada*, the testification of faith, saying "I accept Allah and I accept His Prophet," you can practice prayer, observe the fast of Ramadan, pay the obligatory charity and go on the pilgrimage at least once in your life, yet still commit sins. But in *maqaam al-Ihsaan*, the Station of Perfected Character, when you are "worshipping God, as if you are seeing Him," how can you do something wrong?

---

[96] 'Abd ibn Humayd.

So the Prophet ﷺ gave Sayyidina 'Ali ؏ special gifts, during the eight hours in which the murder conspiracy transpired. When the Prophet ﷺ poured this into the heart of Sayyidina 'Ali ؏, he became the manifestation of the Prophet's saying "I am the city of Knowledge and 'Ali is its door."

It does not take time to learn. What God, the Exalted, pours into someone's heart is real knowledge. You see many *awliyaullah* who never went to school, and their tongues articulate more meanings than the greatest *mufassireen*, interpreters of the Holy Qur'an or *muhadditheen*, transmitter of hadith, ever brought to light. Such enlightened ones are higher and know better. Many of our imams who came after Prophet ﷺ had that kind of teaching. The early history of Islam has many such examples.

Sayyidina Abu Hanifah, said, "*Wa law la sanataan la-halaqa Nu'man*—If it was not for those two years [I spent with Ja'afar as-Sadiq] Numan [Abu Hanifah] would have perished" He spent two years with Jafar as-Saadiq. Remember this is Imam Abu Hanifah: half or nearly half of Muslims follow his Shariah teachings.

Similarly Imam Shafi'i studied with Bishr al-Hafi, a great Sufi sage of his time, while Imam Malik studied with nine hundred shaykhs. He studied jurisprudence, *fiqh*, theology and hadith from 300 shaykhs, but the Sufi path, *tasawwuf*, he took from 600. These were teachers of the heart, they were granted the power by Allah "to say to a thing 'Be!' and it will be," not like university teachers, whose students spend their lecture time napping.

Abu Bakr and the Essence of Surrender

So why did the Prophet ﷺ take Sayyidina Abu Bakr ؏ with him to the desert? God, the Exalted, wanted to test his love for the Prophet ﷺ. It was written that he was to be the companion of the Prophet ﷺ on the journey from Mecca to Madina.

*He had no more than one companion when they were
hiding in the cave.*[97]

He took him first to the cave, which symbolizes the House of
the Prophet ﷺ. Every one of you has a cave—that is his house. So
that cave represented the House of the Prophet ﷺ, which today
has unfortunately been destroyed.

He took him to the other cave, Ghari Thawr. The Prophet ﷺ
had gone to another cave, Ghari Hira, every year of his life, for
forty days or more at a stretch, where he spent his time in
contemplation. God, the Exalted, prepared him to go to the cave.
In Qur'an the Lord addresses the seven youths who were fleeing
from their king:

*Fa-uw ila al-kahf—Betake yourselves to the Cave; your
Lord will shower His mercies on you and dispose of your
affair towards mirfaqa—comfort and ease.*[98]

God said this about Ashaab al-Kahf, the Companions of the
Cave. *"God will send His mercy on you."* We don't know how many
youths were there, but Holy Qur'an counts from three to seven.
Most scholars say they were seven. So God, the Exalted, said to
them, *"Run to the cave!"* and later the people were ordered to build
above that cave a mosque, meaning a dome. That explains the
holy hadith, where the Prophet ﷺ relates God saying, "My saints
are under My domes, no one knows them except Me." [99]

God, the Exalted, built domes above the heads of *awliya*. That
does not necessarily mean a physical dome, but a spiritual dome.
You have to run inside that cave to your "in." You have to run to
your "in" in order to reach your "inn," for everyone's heart is his
inn, his hotel, his motel. It means "don't look outwardly, look

---

[97] Suratu 't-Tawbah, (The Repentance), 9:40.
[98] Suratu 'l-Kahf, (The Cave), 18:16.
[99] Al-Ghazali, *Ihya 'uloom ad-deen*.

inwardly." Most people today look outwardly and they are busy cutting down everyone—no one looks inwardly. The modern world is reversed.

The Prophet ﷺ took Sayyidina Abu Bakr ؓ to the cave. Sayyidina Abu Bakr entered the cave first to check its safety and found it full of snake holes. After filling all the snake-holes with pieces of cloth Sayyidina Abu Bakr ؓ allowed the Prophet ﷺ to enter. The Prophet ﷺ laid his holy head on Abu Bakr's leg in order to rest. At that time Sayyidina Abu Bakr ؓ discovered one last snake-hole. To avoid disturbing the Prophet's sleep, he put his foot over the hole to prevent any snake from coming out.

A Snake's Love

The snake in that hole had been promised by its Lord in pre-history that he would see the Last Prophet ﷺ before he died, and Sayyidina Abu Bakr's foot was the final obstacle blocking the snake from a glimpse of the Prophet's ﷺ majesty and beauty. Just imagine—out of love that snake had been waiting 40,000 years to see the face of Prophet ﷺ. That is a snake. Where does that put us, whose lives might only last one hundred years? Look at us! We are not anxious, nor are we even trying our best to be like that snake that waited all those aeons with patience and dedication to see the face of Sayyidina Muhammad ﷺ and we know we shall die after a maximum span of one hundred years without seeing the face of Sayyidina Muhammad ﷺ in this life. It is not as important to see his face in the next life, because everyone will see him then. Rather one must ask to see in this life. How many awliyaullah have seen his face in this life?

That is the importance of the story of the snake. In spirituality one can explain a snake in a dream as symbolizing an enemy. But even the "enemy" Iblees has love for the Prophet ﷺ. It is related that Iblees approached the Prophet ﷺ by permission of God, the

Exalted, to speak with him ﷺ. He was not able to go to the Prophet ﷺ to ask him questions except after seeking permission from God, the Exalted, because Iblees wanted to see the Prophet ﷺ face-to-face. Even though he was accursed, he said, "I want to see Muhammad ﷺ." Remember Iblees was able to speak with his Lord.

How is it that Iblees can ask God, the Exalted, permission to see the Prophet ﷺ and we raise our hands and never such answer comes? That means Iblees is still a believer. That is why Iblees said:

> *Indeed, if You will but allow me a respite till the Day of Resurrection, I shall most certainly cause his descendants—all but a few—to obey me blindly!*[100]

He was asking sincerely to mislead the people.

This is a message for us: "Ask with sincerity." Iblees showed sincerity. He showed by his intensity of emotion that he was asking from his heart to mislead people. He went astray, so he wants others to go astray. When we ask, we don't really ask wholeheartedly from within ourselves, it is only from our tongue.

So that snake began to eat Sayyidina Abu Bakr's foot. A snake is not like cats, tigers and lions which snatch and shake their victims. Rather when a snake eats it moves, enveloping its prey and strangling it. It grinds you and crushes you. The lion doesn't grind you. He bites and goes, then comes back to finish you off.

The snake began grinding the feet of Sayyidina Abu Bakr ﷺ. Imagine how much pain Sayyidina Abu Bakr ﷺ was carrying yet he did not try to cry out! The pain of giving his life for his Prophet ﷺ was no pain for him at all. He did not feel that as pain; it was a joy for him. He was happy to be eaten by the snake so that

---

[100] Suratu 'l-Isra, (The Night Journey), 17:62.

the Prophet ﷺ would be saved. He did not care for his life. Perhaps he was even rejoicing in that pain.

As much as you love God, the Exalted, as much you feel pain, just as the more you love your beloved in everyday life the more you seek to be nearer to that lover, man or woman. So what you think of the love of *awliyaullah* for God, the Exalted,? As much as you reduce the distance between yourself and God, the Exalted, the pain of longing increases.

A Blessed Tear

So Abu Bakr ﷺ did not worry about his pain: he was happy giving his life for the Prophet ﷺ. But at some point it occurred to him that the snake might finish him off and then attack the Prophet ﷺ. Then he was crying, for he could do nothing to stop that. He was happy to be eaten or tortured or to give his life for the Prophet ﷺ, as did many Companions. But he was worried about this enemy reaching the Prophet ﷺ. It was at that moment that a tear of love fell from Sayyidina Abu Bakr's eye. Feeling the loving warmth of that tear on his cheek, the Prophet ﷺ awoke from his slumber and said, "O Abu Bakr! Don't be sad, for verily, God, the Exalted, is with us."

God described this in the Qur'an:

> and he said to his companion, "Have no fear, for Allah is with us."[101]

It means, "I am pouring into your heart the knowledge of before and after because of your love for me and your love for God, the Exalted. You gave up your life by putting your foot over that hole. I am giving you what you desire. A single one of your tears is sufficient to extinguish the whole fire of Hell."

---

[101] Suratu 't-Tawbah, (The Repentance), 9:40.

That tear that sprang to the eye of Sayyidina Abu Bakr ❀ is not resting. He was with his Lord. The Prophet ❀ had seen the pain that Sayyidina Abu Bakr ❀ was going through. He also saw the fear that Sayyidina Abu Bakr ❀ had for his safety. How many tears had the Prophet ❀ shed during his life? How many tears came from the eyes of his Companions? How many tears came from people today who are giving their love to the Prophet ❀ and to their guides? Don't think that these tears are for nothing: they are like pearls. If you measured the wealth of *dunya* against just one of these tears, the Scale would tip in the favor of the pearl. Sayyidina Abu Bakr ❀ received that inheritance in the cave.

The Prophet ❀ brought Sayyidina 'Ali ❀ and Sayyidina Abu Bakr ❀ together. Both of their lineages were inherited by Sayyidina Jafar as-Sadiq, who became the locus of the combined power from Sayyidina 'Ali ❀ and Sayyidina Abu Bakr ❀. This continues even today, for these two branches of knowledge are flowing like an ocean.

Divine Orientation

Such knowledge does not need to be in rooms confined by dimensions, nor in time, as in a one-hour speech. Such knowledge has no direction, no dimension, no confines. This type of knowledge emanates without a known orientation in this universe in which space has three dimensions and time is the fourth. This earth is not even like the head of a pin compared to the universe. Where is up and down, where is right and left?

Even the physical universe has no apparent orientation, up or down. Scientists have discovered that the background radiation from the Big Bang emanates evenly from every direction. In the same way, any way you face there is your Lord.

To God belongs the East and the West, and wheresoever
you turn, there is God's Face. Lo! God is All Embracing,
All Knowing.[102]

The heart can go in every direction while the eyes cannot. The eyes can only shift slightly to the left and slightly to the right. You can turn your head to some extent and shift your eyes in their sockets. But the *awliyaullah* have eyes that can see in all directions. Shah Naqshband, the shaykh of the Naqshbandi Sufi Order, could see everywhere.

The journey from Mecca to Madina was important because in it Sayyidina Muhammad ﷺ bestowed the inheritance of knowledge to Sayyidina 'Ali ؑ and to Sayyidina Abu Bakr ؓ. At the same time the Prophet ﷺ established his nation and founded his capital.

Protest Your Ego

The issue of the notorious Danish cartoons, while they were disrespectful to the Prophet ﷺ, has been blown out of all proportion. Many Muslims died for nothing because of the demonstrations made over this issue. Additionally, billions and billions of dollars have been wasted because of the boycotts, which not only hurt non-Muslims, but Muslim businesses as well. It is much as what happened with 911: the actions of a few Muslims hurt the many.

I had a meeting at the White House, so I brought up this issue. The solution is simple, but in order to address it we must first understand why some people blew the issue out of proportion. The simple reason is that Islamists are trying to fuel increased hatred for America and the West. Who will be victims? We will be.

---

[102] Suratu 'l-Baqara, (The Heifer), 2:115.

In that meeting I said, "Ask the scholars of the Muslim world one simple question: why protest about a picture, which has no meaning to Muslims?" Because the Prophet ﷺ has no image, *la dhilla lahu*. He does not even have a shadow when he stands in the sun. That means his form is only for us to see but in reality if they had a camera in his time and managed to take a picture, they would have found that his form does not exist. If you put an object in the sun, you see a shadow. This tells you it has a form. But something composed of pure light, while visible to our eyes, has no shadow.

O scholars open your minds! The Prophet ﷺ has no shadow. He came to us with a subtle visual form only in order that we could see him with our eyes. But in reality he has no existence as a form because he is a subtle human being.

So why are we angry about a cartoon whereas Abu Jahl said, "You are the greatest magician," and yet the Prophet ﷺ still extended his hands to him to save him from disaster. It is related that Abu Jahl conspired to harm the Prophet ﷺ (see page 38). When the Prophet ﷺ went to his house, what happened? Abu Jahl fell into the hole of his own making, because when he saw the Prophet ﷺ coming, from happiness he forgot the trap he had set and fell in himself. So what did the Prophet do? He extended his hand to pull Abu Jahl out.

Hypocrital Protests

From another point of view, let us say that we felt compelled to protest this disrespect towards the Prophet ﷺ. But why then, O Muslim scholars, are you not also protesting what they have done to the Prophet's house—the house in which he married Sayyida Khadijat al-Kubra ﺱ and where his children were born and brought up—Sayyida Fatima ﺱ, Ruqayya ﺱ and Zainab ﺱ and Umm Kulthum ﺱ? How strange. That house does not fuel hatred.

110

What did they do to it? They converted it into restrooms. All these restrooms near Safa and Marwa were built on the site of the Prophet's house. Therefore *awliyaullah* never use these restrooms. Where were the Muslim scholars when this outrage was perpetrated by the Saudi authorities? Why they didn't say anything? Why didn't they demonstrate? The answer: because it is not a political issue.

Similarly regarding the house of the Prophet's ﷺ birth—a very important blessed and historic site. Now they seek to destroy it. It is last of these historic sites left. They want tear it down and put up a hotel, and they have planned many restrooms in that hotel. Where are the Muslim scholars? Where is that renowned scholar who speaks on al-Jazeera?

The reason nothing is said is because it is not an issue against the West; rather it will show the Arabs as culprits. This is our problem. Today, where is the love for Sayyidina Muhammad ﷺ? Where are professors in universities? Not a single one will stand up and says one word. Where are the moderate scholars; where all these national Islamist organizations? Why are they silent? Because they receive money from one country which seeks to impose its ideology on everyone.

Everything is governed by money these days. No one wants to lose his chair, professors or otherwise. There are even many people today who claim that they are *tariqah* leaders, without valid authority. That is worst characteristic in Islam that the Prophet ﷺ specifically prohibited: Seeking fame and power—*hubb ar-riyasah* and *hubb ash-shuhra*. May God, the Exalted, take these two things away from our hearts.

May Allah bless you all and bless this evening.

DIMENSIONS OF OBEDIENCE

*Obey Allah; obey the Prophet and obey those in
authority.*[103]

The Five Pillars

We were speaking yesterday about Iblees. He would not make
sajda, prostration, to Adam, and therefore God, the Exalted, cursed
him. Iblees disobeyed one time. Many people don't ponder the
reason Iblees disobeyed and refused to prostrate before Adam ﷺ.
It is so simple to make *sajda*. Is it difficult? Say, *"Bismillah, Allahu
Akbar!"* and make prostration. Why was he prevented from
making that prostration?

Scholars have two opinions. One school holds that that Iblees
preceded Adam's creation by two thousand years and another
holds that he was in existence 70,000 years before Adam ﷺ. Iblees
had been very conscientious about making prostration, but when
it came to Adam ﷺ, he refused: he had no intention of paying his
respects to a new creation made of clay.

Consider the five pillars of Islam, as the Prophet ﷺ described
them: the testification of faith—*ash-hadu anna la ilaha illa-Llah wa
ash-hadu anna Muhammadan Rasulullah.* Immediately following that
obligation comes *salaat*, prayers, then *ita'uz-zakaat*, charity, then
sawmu Ramadan, fasting, then *hajj*, pilgrimage to Mecca. Why
didn't he say *hajj* first, *sawm* second or *sawm* first, *shahada* second?
Rather he said *shahada, salaat, zakaat, sawm, hajj* in that order. When

---

[103] Suratu 'n-Nisa, (Women), 4:59.

did the Prophet ﷺ made *hajj*? At the end of his life, in his last year, known as *'am al-fath*. This means that *hajj* is the crown of these five levels or pillars.

Shahada is to bear witness that God, the Exalted, is the Creator and Muhammad ﷺ is the Messenger of Allah, saying, "I bear witness that Allah is the Creator; there is no God except Him and I bear witness that Muhammad is His messenger." It means "I bear witness on both sides." What are we witnessing? I am saying here and now: *ashadu ann la ilaha illa-Llah wa ash-hadu anna muhammadun Rasulullah.* Say it. [Everyone repeats the *shahada*.] Ok, what did you see? What are you witnessing?

Nothing.

Unlike us, when the Prophet ﷺ said *ashadu an la ilaha illa-Llah*, he was seeing. When they call you in court to testify as a witness, they ask, "Did you see anything?" If you say "yes," they take your evidence into the record. If you say "no," they dismiss you from court. Your presence is no longer required. So when you make the *shahada*, on whom do you bear witness? To say, "I am bearing witness" means "I am seeing." Are we in that level yet? No!

So if we are not in the first level, which is to bear witness that God, the Exalted, is the Creator and Muhammad ﷺ is His messenger, how can you can go on to *salaat* where *salaat* is a pillar of this religion? And the Prophet said, "The best time is when I am in my prayer because that is when I am between the hands of My Lord." That is the time he is bearing witness.

So *salaat* comes <u>after</u> witnessing. The highest station of perfection was described by the Prophet as "The object is to worship God, the Exalted, as if you are seeing Him and if you aren't t seeing Him know that He is seeing you."

113

So imagine then that we are carrying over our shoulders all the dirtiness that can be carried and going to the Divine Presence. If we were going to an appointment to meet the king and carrying all kinds of dirtiness on our shoulders, what would they do with you at the door? They would tell you, "Y'Allah, get out!" So *shahada* is meant to clean you, readying you for prayer. That is why in the Naqshbandi Sufi order before we observe the *fard*, the obligation, it is an order from our masters to recite the *shahada* three times and seek forgiveness 100 times, *istighfaar*, and three times Surat al-Ikhlas, after which calling the *iqamah* that signifies we are ready to enter prayer.

Divine Adornment

> *O Children of Adam! wear your adornment at every*
> *time and place of prayer: eat and drink: but do not waste:*
> *verily, He does not love the wasteful!*[104]

What adornment is meant here? What dress is there other than what we wear?

It can be read, "O believers, wear your medallions and decorations in every mosque!" Medallions here means your full self-realization, which will lift you up to the enlightenment of the manifestations of the Beautiful Attributes of the Name of the Divine Essence, the hidden Essence of our Lord.

Adorn oneself with beauty, peace, submission, wisdom and patience? Let the manifestations of these Beautiful Names and Attributes carry you on that Ocean of the manifestations of the Name of the Essence, like a vessel that is sailing across a stormy ocean to reach the far shore. We are speaking about prayer to God, the Exalted. After bearing witness and *shahada* and preparing to go for prayer then *"wear your adornment"* means to take your inner

---

[104] Suratu 'l-'Araaf, (The Heights), 7:31.

beauty into the prayers and eliminate all your bad characteristics, those things that Satan and Iblees try to dress you with. *"They are the enemy, so beware of them. God, the Exalted, fights them."*[105] So then go to your prayers!

What has the first part of the verse, *"wear your adornment"* to do with eating and drinking? When you go to your prayers like that, what happens? God, the Exalted, says, *"eat and drink!"* This is not related to physical eating and drinking. I am going to the mosque adorned with all my decorations. Where I am going to eat and drink? In the mosque or when I am praying? What would I have to eat and drink?

God, the Exalted, is saying, "O My servant, eat and drink in the midst of your prayer. I am giving you permission to eat and drink." What are we to eat and drink during prayer? It means, "Eat and drink from the *futuhat ar-rabbaniyyah*—the heavenly mercy oceans that will open for you; drink from these oceans of sweetness. Wherever there are trees in Paradise, I am giving their fruit to you."

God, the Exalted, is saying, "Adorn yourself in every place of prayer, then go and eat" meaning partake of whatever you can from Allah's Manifestations upon you; His ever-increasing blessings and overflowing beauty, and every possible Beautiful Divine Name that you can reach. It means "keep these meditations in your prayers and Allah will open to you even more."

Note also the order here. He said, *"eat and drink"* Why didn't He say "drink and eat"?

The references to eating provide us with a literal starting point for our understanding. When you eat you become full, so what do

---

[105] Suratu 'l-Munafiqoon, (The Hypocrites), 63:4.

you do then? You drink a bit more, thus allowing you to eat yet more. That is why water comes after food. If you drink before eating, it will fill your stomach too much to allow for food. He wants you to have delicious food first and then to drink. Drink what? Water.

God, the Exalted, told Adam ﷺ to eat from every tree in Paradise. What kind of trees were they? The trees of knowledge.

> *And if all the trees on earth were pens and the ocean*
> *(were ink), with seven oceans behind it to add to its*
> *(supply), yet would not the Words of Allah be exhausted*
> *(in the writing): for Allah is Exalted in Power, full of*
> *Wisdom.*[106]

He said, "I opened for you Adam ﷺ every authority to partake." In doing so Adam ﷺ would adorn himself with the Beautiful Names and Attributes. Then he would open the water of youth, *ma' al-hayaat*, which is the spring that Sayyidina Khidr found when he and Iskandar Dhul Qarnayn set forth in search of the Fountain of Youth. Sayyidina Khidr found it first and God, the Exalted, taught him from His heavenly knowledge.

God, the Exalted, is saying, "Eat first, then I will bring you to the Fountain of Youth." This is what happened to Prophet Moses ﷺ, when he asked his man-servant, *"bring us our breakfast."*

> *And when Moses said to his servant: I will not give up*
> *until I reach the point where the two seas meet, though I*
> *march on for ages. But when they reached the junction*
> *between the two [seas], they forgot all about their fish,*
> *and it took its way into the sea and disappeared from*
> *sight. And when they had gone further, he said to his*

---

[106] Surah Luqman, 31:27.

> *servant: Bring us our breakfast. Verily we have found*
> *fatigue in this our journey*[107]

Merging Oceans

Moses said he would not stop searching until he reached the junction of the two oceans. These two merging oceans represent the inner and outer. It means I will not accept, I gave an oath, that I will never go back without finding the truth, where the ocean of *dhahir* and *baatin* meets. They are not going parallel, they meet at one point. I am not going to explain this now.

So Moses ﷺ said, "Now I want to eat."

> *He said: Did you see, when we took refuge on the rock,*
> *and I forgot the fish and none but Satan caused me to*
> *forget to mention it, it took its way into the waters by a*
> *marvel.- He said: This is that which we have been*
> *seeking. So they retraced their steps again.*[108]

His man-servant Joshua said, "What should I get you to eat? The dead fish has miraculously returned to the ocean." Prophet Moses ﷺ said, "This is the sign I was awaiting."

> *He said: This is that which we have been seeking. So they*
> *retraced their steps again.*[109]

What did he find there? Sayyidina Khidr.

> *Then found they one of Our slaves, unto whom We had*
> *given mercy from Ourselves, and We taught him from*
> *Our heavenly knowledge.*[110]

---

[107] Suratu 'l-Kahf, (The Cave), 18:60-62.
[108] Suratu 'l-Kahf, (The Cave), 18: 63.
[109] Suratu 'l-Kahf, (The Cave), 18:64.
[110] Suratu 'l-Kahf, (The Cave), 18:65.

If Allah doesn't bless you from His mercy, he will not open things for you from His *ma'rifah*, gnosis. And who did He give the mercy to? God, the Exalted, gave it out, for He is not in need it. God gave it to Sayyidina Muhammad ﷺ:

We sent you not, but as a Mercy for all the worlds.[111]

Prophet Moses ﷺ met with the Prophet ﷺ at that time. The spirituality of the Prophet ﷺ appeared. That is why God said, *"We had given him mercy from Ourselves."* The Prophet ﷺ is the gift of mercy to humanity:

Full of concern for you, for the believers full of pity, merciful.[112].

He is watchful and protective and very careful with each emerging event. Allah ﷺ described him ﷺ as Raufun Raheem; two of His Beautiful Names with which He dressed his beloved Prophet ﷺ.

Prophet Moses ﷺ was not able to be dressed with heavenly knowledge without being dressed first with the mercy for humanity that Sayyidina Muhammad ﷺ came with. When Prophet Moses ﷺ had been adorned with that mercy, Sayyidina Khidr ﷺ gave him the hidden knowledge that he was seeking.

So we make *shahada* bearing witness to God and His Messenger, and we hope before God that we are sincere servants. We cannot be one hundred percent sincere; only the Prophet Muhammad ﷺ can do that. But in making the *shahada*, you earn the right to take on the position of prayer.

We are beginners. We are like a young child who is wearing diapers. Our prayers are rank-smelling in comparison to the

---

[111] Suratu 'l-Anbiya, (The Prophets), 21:107.
[112] Suratu 't-Tawbah, (The Repentance), 9:128.

prayers of the Prophet ﷺ, his Companions and of the *awliyaullah.* We carry the stench of wild character.

So He said, "First bear witness." Attain to the Station of witnessing, *maqaam ash-shahada* and then you are allowed to be in the station of prayer. At that time you are able to comprehend charity.

Is it charity to give one-forthieth, or 2.5 percent of one's wealth. *Zakaat* is 2.5%? This is what the Qur'an orders—*ita'u 'z-zakaat.* What is *ita'u 'z-zakaat?* Charity. Now bring the understanding of the stations we were discussing before: the station of witnessing, *Maqaam ash-Shahada* and the station of worship, *Maqaam al-'Ubudiyya* and finally the station of servanthood, *Maqaam al-'Abdiyya.*

The station of servanthood is above the station of worship. The station of worship is general like *Maqaam at-Tawheed,* the station of affirming Divine Unity—*Maqaam al-Ahadiyya,* the Station of Oneness and Uniqueness. Similarly, *Maqaam al-'Ubudiyya* is for everyone. *Maqaam al-'Abdiyya* is only for Sayyidina Muhammad ﷺ and no one else. He is *la shareek laha,* without any partner, in his position as servant, *'abd.*

So what is that Station of Charity then that comes after the Station of Prayer? It means that we should share with the Ummah what we have. Allah is saying, "What I gave to you, share." The Prophet ﷺ said, "I am not sharing, I am giving it all. I will stand in front of You on Judgment Day with nothing, Ya Rabbee."

In this, we are shown how to love God, the Exalted, more than our parents, our family, our spouse and our children; more than everyone and everything. The Prophet ﷺ gave up everything to his Ummah—that is the meaning of charity.

Today we are taught the Five Pillars of Islam by parrots reciting things they do not understand. They mechanically say that this is *shahada, salaat, zakaat sawm, hajj*. This is for artificial, paper people, not for people reaching to high levels and asceticism. Some scholars say "There are no more *awliya*." They say "There used to be *awliya* but not any more." How do they dare? If you cannot see these *awliyaullah* it means you are blind.

Hidden *Awliya*, Heavenly Knowledge

Awliyaullah are among us even until Judgment Day: until Allah orders Archangel Israfil to blow in the Trumpet. They are hidden ones, but if you look for them you may find them. But if you don't seek them out, or even worse, refuse to admit their existence, you certainly will not find them, for how can you find something you claim does not exist?

People are digging down hundreds of meters to find diamonds. You say there are no diamonds? They are selling them in Manhattan and in Brussels. How are they finding them? Miners are digging very deep. Can we say that there are no diamonds because they are not lying about on the surface, already cut and polished? The *awliya* are hidden in every direction except down. You can find them — they are all around us, but you have to mine for them. They will not be given to you on plates of silver and gold. God, the Exalted, wants you to work hard; as hard as miners work to get diamonds. Where today are the Islamic scholars explaining the Qur'an in the most beautiful ways?

Today they are writing translations of Qur'an and making commentary and explanation. All this is expected, but go and look at their commentaries. They contain no heavenly knowledge. Heavenly knowledge does not come from study. It comes from *taqwa* — God consciousness. It doesn't come from reading books, or scientific research. God, the Exalted, must choose you. He made

120

this role for only certain people. When He adorns someone in this way that one needs nothing else: no degrees, no titles, no organizations.

Charity means to give and to share any manifestation that God, the Exalted, has chosen to grant you. In the Prophet's ﷺ case, he bequeathed his legacy first to his Companions and then to the *awliya*. That is charity. That is a huge legacy because the wealth of *akhira*, the hereafter, is infinitely more valuable than wealth of the world, *dunya*. The *awliyaullah* are giving from what God, the Exalted, gave them. The *awliyaullah* will refuse to enter Paradise until all their followers can enter Paradise just as Sayyidina Muhammad ﷺ will not enter Paradise until all his followers enter.

When we attain to bearing witness, *Maqaam ash-Shahada*, then the station of our prayers *Maqaam as-Salaat*, is in the Divine Presence. Then we give charity, we give up or share this blessing. The Prophet ﷺ gave everything. After you give up everything you come to *sawm*, fasting.

What is fasting? Is it merely refraining from eating and drinking? This is what they say. They say also fasting means to avoid backbiting and anything that is prohibited. What is fasting in its real meaning? When you bear witness that there is no creator except God, the Exalted, then you enter the Presence of God, the Exalted, where everything in His Hands. After that you give away everything that was given to you. Then you reach to the station that Adam ﷺ achieved. Adam ﷺ was bearing witness in Paradise that Allah's ﷻ was the Creator and he was eating from every fruitful tree save one.

But this is not about trees that we know of, apples trees and lemon trees—that is not what this is about. The trees of Paradise are the trees whose every leaf is an ocean of knowledge. It means that each tree is one of Allah's ﷻ Beautiful Names and that manifestation is coming from the Divine Essence describing that particular Name. The Names are linked together in a chain of meaning that leads higher and higher. The Beautiful Names are like trees with roots and branches that bind creation together in a living structure. New leaves and branches appear at every moment: the miracle of continuous creation.

This is what Adam ﷺ received. His charity was to share whatever he was receiving and he knew he would have children with whom to share. And to keep that *ni'mat*, favor, one must fast. Fast from what? Fasting for God means to be obedient to God, the Exalted. Fasting is to be in *ita'atullah*—the manifestation of obedience. Fasting is submission. Fasting means when God, the Exalted, wants His servant to fast, he must obey. When you reach the first three levels you have no choice but to obey; only thus may you attain the fourth.

When these four levels are fulfilled, then what? You must go for pilgrimage. The pilgrimage is not to go to Mecca and Arafat. The reality of pilgrimage is to worship in al-Bayt al-Mamour, the Heavenly House. The crown comes then: for whoever achieves true *shahada, salat, zakaat* and *sawm* is free to enter and explore every one of the Lord's Paradises. That is the access code to free the servant to do as he or she likes.

Stations on the Path

So who reached the station of perfect servanthood? Only Sayyidina Muhammad ﷺ reached the Station of *"two bow's-length or nearer."*[113]

When Iblees was prostrating to God, the Exalted, and the order came to prostrate to Adam ﷺ, he had already attained the fourth level, the Station of Fasting. He was bearing witness that

---

[113] Suratu 'n-Najm, (The Star), 53:9.

God, the Exalted, is Creator and Muhammad ﷺ is His messenger, the first station. He was making prostration in every part of creation, the second station, and he was giving charity to the angels, the third. And when the order for fasting came he obeyed that as well. What happened then? When he disobeyed the final order, all his previous levels vanished beneath him. When he disobeyed he became *mal'oon*, cursed.

When Prophet Adam ﷺ committed the sin and ate from the forbidden tree, he became naked. That means that the three levels he had achieved up to that point vanished. His point of failure was the fasting—to give up something for God.

And [thus] Adam disobeyed his Lord, so went astray.[114]

Adam ﷺ disobeyed His Lord and fell down. Why did he fall down? Because God, the Exalted, was opening a path between heaven and earth. Adam's ﷺ fall provided just that path, so that the human race had an upward route, leading above the earth.

This chain of events began with Iblees when he refused to prostrate before Adam. *"(Iblees) said: 'I am not one to prostrate myself to man'..."*[115] His reasoning was that to prostrate to anyone other than God amounted to *shirk*, idolatry. Then Adam ﷺ fell, and after the Fall, he repented and God, the Exalted, forgave him. Also, when Adam ﷺ fell, he became naked, which means that God, the Exalted, took everything away from him when he disobeyed Him.

At this point the difference between Adam ﷺ and Iblees becomes clear: Adam ﷺ repented, while Iblees did not.

Iblees did not repent, but he presented his case to God, claiming that God, the Exalted, had made him disobey. This holds deep wisdom. That is because Iblees knew that this was his job—

---

[114] Surah Taha, 20:121.
[115] Suratu 'l-Hijr, (The Rocky Tract), 15:33.

to fulfill the role of the evil one. In every play, story or drama there must be a protagonist and an antagonist, the evil character. He accepted his role, for he could not change it. If Iblees did not whisper in the ear of Adam ﷺ, all that followed, including opening a connection between Heaven and Earth, would not have been possible.

> *Then the two ate thereof, so their nakedness appeared to them, and they began to hide by heaping on themselves some of the leaves of the Garden. And Adam disobeyed his Lord, so went astray.*[116]

Nakedness after a fall refers to an exposure of bad characteristics. When Adam ﷺ disobeyed, it exposed his weaknesses. That is how *awliyaullah* can observe at people and see their bad characteristics. Nakedness here does not refer to literal clothes, for everyone has limitless outfits for every occasion and situation. When they look at someone, *awliyaullah* can identify them, not by what we observe with our physical eyes, but rather they look at their inner nature. When they look at the people around them, they see their faults. The Prophet ﷺ said, "Beware the vision of the [true] believer, for truly he sees with the light of God."[117] That is why they try to polish and clean them.

Sayyidina ibn 'Abbas ﷺ said that there are one 124,000 prophets and at the foot of these prophets there are 124,000 *awliya*. Whether you see them or not, they are there. They see our wild characters and they try their best to polish us. That is why any disobedience is like disrobing completely.

Adam ﷺ was disrobed by his disobedience. Look Allah's ﷻ mercy! Iblees was disobedient only once and he was punished

---

[116] Surah Taha, 20:121.

[117] Tirmidhi, Ibn Jarir, at-Tabari and a similar wording in Abu Na'eem and al-Munawi in his *Fayd*.

forever, while we, on the other hand are continuously disobedient, yet we can escape endless punishment through the merciful intervention of Sayyidina Muhammad ﷺ.

> *Thereafter, [however,) his Sustainer elected him [for His grace], and accepted his repentance, and bestowed His guidance upon him.*[118]

When Adam ﷺ and his wife found themselves naked, they began to cover themselves with leaves—the leaves of the fig tree. That is why God, the Exalted, swore an oath by the fig tree:

> *wa 't-teeni wa 'z-zaytoon wa turi seeneen wa haadha al-baladi 'l-ameen—By the Fig and the Olive, and the Mount of Sinai and by this land made secure.*[119]

The word *teen* has a special meaning. God, the Exalted, gave an oath by *teen*, "the fig tree," by *zaytoon*, "the olive," and by *touri seeneen*, "Mt. Sinai," and by *balad al-ameen*, "this land made secure." Notice how *Teen*, *zaytoon* and *balad al-ameen* end with the Arabic letter *nun*. Why?

> *Nun. By the Pen and that which they write (therewith), You (O Muhammad!) are not, for your Lord's favor unto you, a madman. And lo! Yours verily will be a reward unfailing. —And lo! You are of a tremendous nature.*[120]

God, the Exalted, is pointing out the importance of the letter *nun*. God, the Exalted, gave an oath by that letter *nun* and by the Pen—the one that records all history. Remember that people were saying *haasha*, that the Prophet ﷺ was *majnoon*, but Allah said

---

[118] Surah Taha, 20:122.

[119] Suratu 't-Teen, (The Fig), 95:1-3.

[120] Suratu 'l-Qalam, (The Pen), 68:1-4.

"no!" What is the significance of *nun* and how does it make this verse so special? We will leave this for another time.

Companions in the Train of the ProphetT

Sahabi is the brand name for a companion of the Prophet ﷺ. The Prophet ﷺ is like a train engine pulling all the cars behind it. The Sahaba and the *awliyaullah* are the cars of the train. The last cars are carrying the freight, and the first cars are the highest: closest to the engine. All *awliyaullah* are connected to the Prophet ﷺ. So those near the engine are getting more and those at end are still connected but they are farther.

The Station of Worshipfulness, *Maqaam al-'Ubudiyya*, is not just one level. If we think of it as one level, we are limiting the power of the Creator. The Station of God's Servant, *Maqaam al-'Abdiyya* belongs to the Prophet ﷺ alone. He is the highest of *'ubaad*, the highest of those who are performing worship, *'ibadah*. *'Ubudiyya* is an adjective while *'ibaad* is noun, in plural. And the Prophet ﷺ is the one above all *'ibaad*. He is the only one who reached that level. That level is always in ascension because God is great, *"Allahu Akbar."*

Ongoingly Greater

We don't jut say "Allah" and stop, but we continue and say *"Allahu Akbar."* Thus we keep reminding ourselves of God's Greatness, and all such reminders are made up of multiple steps. The phrase *"Allahu Akbar!"* is part of the call to prayer, *adhaan*. Even before reciting *adhaan*, you first perform ablution. Then one recites *"Allahu Akbar!"* Later in the *adhaan* you recite, *"haya 'ala as-salat; haya 'ala al-falah*—come to prayer; come to success." One then enunciates *"Allahu Akbar"* to begin the prayer itself, and then in each step of the prayer we repeat *"Allahu Akbar"* again. So we are always reminding ourselves of God's Greatness by saying "*Allahu Akbar.*"

That means that whatever we have reached there is something higher. And the greatness of the higher level means that the lower ceases to have meaning and disappears. When the higher level manifests, the level that preceded it vanishes because the level above it encompasses it completely: the level that preceded it is superseded by the level above. The level above it comes with a more defined explanation from Allah's ﷻ Name, al-'Alim or al-'Aleem. Then the next manifestation encompasses the first and the second and they become subsumed in the third. At that point you can no longer see the first and second levels.

Awliyaullah don't look back as they are ascending. As the Prophet ﷺ is ascending, he is pulling his Ummah with him. We ask God, the Exalted, to make us learn and understand the essence of the taste of Islam. It is not simple. The scholars of today have dropped these teachings, having been compromised by money and politics. They dropped these teaching because every human possesses the two characteristics of *hubb ash-shuhra*—the love of power and *hubb ar-riyasah*—the love of fame. They sell Islam for these two things. They repeat the phrase "we are doing *da'wah*—calling people to the faith," but in reality this is only words from their mouths.

What happened? When you are called you must come. This is submission.

What will God, the Exalted, do with you? He knows you are still in spiritual diapers. What can you do? Angels clean you and send you to Paradise. They dress you with manifestations and say "go on, enter." Because a newborn child knows her mother from her smell, and then he gets to know his father. He knows mother and father mostly. He runs to them. Where are we going to run?

We are going to run to the one we know. Who is the one we know? Sayyidina Muhammad ﷺ. So when we run to him what do you expect from the one described as "mercy"? Will he tell you to go away?

That is why if human beings understood the mercy of Sayyidina Muhammad, he would appear to every human being, but from his compassion and mercy he will not appear. One only need call him saying, *"Ya sayyidee Ya Rasulullah,"* and he is present. *Awliya* are with him, spiritually present. They don't need books and they don't need teaching. *"Qaala wa qeela,—*he said, she said," is for academic people. At that moment he tells them what they need to know. Where are these *awliya* today? They are hiding. Some people say every believer is a *wali*— it that were true then why does everyone still listen to Satan?

A *wali* is someone who has polished and cleaned himself: he avoids falling into the traps laid by Satan. Remember the verse:

> Behold! verily on the friends of Allah there is no fear, nor
> shall they grieve.[121]

Remember the hadith "My saints are under My domes, no one knows them except Me."[122]

Didn't He say "no one knows then except Me"? Few are those who ask why He said it this way. Some imams say that all *mu'mins* are *awliya*. If that were the case, then why did the Prophet ﷺ say that the *awliya* are few? So that is not correct.

Subhanallah, if God, the Exalted, opened things up so that His servants could see all the invisible things going on around them, they would go out of their minds. There are an infinite number of jinn servants all around us who could, and in some cases do,

---

[121] Suratu 'l-Anbiya, (The Prophets), 10:62.
[122] Al-Ghazali, *Ihya 'uloom ad-deen.*

interact and talk with people. So the 'ulama of today who cannot see do not know of what they speak.

Prophet Muhammad's Manifestation

One time I was with Grandshaykh, in 1969, around forty years ago. He was speaking about the Prophet ﷺ and suddenly he looked at the wall to his left and said, "Ya Sayyidee Ya Rasulullah." I immediately kissed the wall. Then Mawlana said to me, "O my son, you kissed the Prophet ﷺ."

On another day, Grandshaykh showed me the same vision in a different manner. He was describing the earlier event, but this time, there was no wall there when the Prophet ﷺ appeared and I kissed him. It was as though Grandshaykh could play back the event to me in this special way. *Awliya* can describe things to you by summoning live recordings of the feelings and tastes of earlier experiences—just as though you were reliving the events. They can access a video and audio recording from incidents in past history. They can place you in that incident so that you experience a "live broadcast." What does live mean? It doesn't mean a live TV broadcast, which is still only audio and video. It means they are bringing it from a place where the event is still happening. You feel the pain and joy of the experience in all its living depth.

But today you have to look long and hard to find the *awliya*. It's like mining for diamonds over two miles deep under the Earth. Why are we not mining for *awliya*? I am asking this simple question? Why are we not looking for *awliyaullah* in all corners of the globe? Is it prohibited or prevented? No. It is, in fact, our duty, just as mining companies search for a diamonds to sell on the world market is to find them and they will guide you to the hereafter, *akhira*. This is not a quest for money, cars, children, wives or husbands. The undertaking means you give your life to God, the Exalted, because He owns it. Every cell in your body, every breath you take, every gift you have is His. He is going to call you one day, and then you must return this trust. Do you want to give back these gifts all covered with dirt and grime?

In the worldly life, *dunya*, when you go to court, you bring a lawyer with you, do you not? You bring your own legal counsel to defend you. If you have no lawyer, what do they do? They assign you a lawyer, called a public defender. If need be, they even postpone the session until they find a lawyer for you.

On Judgment Day do you not need a lawyer when it is far more difficult case than one in a court? If there is no lawyer, God, the Exalted, will appoint a lawyer for you. And God, the Exalted, knows that you cannot find a lawyer because you didn't look for a *wali* in *dunya*. So he will appoint a lawyer for you and that will be the Prophet ﷺ. At least you are given that chance.

Subhanallah, today they treat Prophet ﷺ as if he is nothing.

Respect from God

People shout *"Allahu Akbar!"* When they hear a rousing Islamic speech they shout this word. Why are they saying this? It is usually not an expression of God's glory. Rather it is said as an expression of egoism, as if saying, "O God made us great!" or "O God made him great; a great speech."

In reality, we are all *asghar*, smaller. As much as you can make yourself *asghar*, so God, the Exalted, will raise you up.

> *Honor, dignity and respect are for God, the Exalted, His Prophet ﷺ and for the believers.*[123]

Seek respect from Allah ﷻ, not from people. The respect of people is worthless and goes with them to their graves. But if

---

[123] Suratu 'l-Munafiqoon, (The Hypocrites), 63:8.

Allah gives His respect, you move like thunder: people listen to you when you have such support.

Consider that among the 124,000 *walis*, even the last one is capable of bringing every person in this *dunya* to be a believer. One! Do you think that God, the Exalted, created this *dunya* and left it? Is there no *mudabbir*, arranger, one who is a conductor who takes responsibility for everything? There is, not only one but many. Find them. Don't say there are none, that they only existed in the past. That is ignorance and blindness. They were here before and people wrote about them in books. Today we also write in books about *awliyaullah* that exist today. But out of jealousy, many do not accept them.

Paper Credentials

Three days before Shaykh Sharafuddin's passing, he wrote in his will that "after me my successor is Shaykh 'Abd Allah al-Fa'iz Daghestani ق." That way, everyone knew who the next Grandshaykh would be.

Today many people go to Mawlana Shaykh Nazim ق and come back with a big paper. They frame it on the wall and display it on the Internet. Do you know what Grandshaykh did with his certificate of authorization, his *ijaza*? As soon as his shaykh died he tore it up and burned it. He said, "I don't need people to know that my shaykh left me this inheritance. I need only My Lord. I am not interested in showing off. Whom God, the Exalted, wants to send to me he sends. I don't care."

Today everyone writes a resume to introduce himself or herself. Then they repeat it aloud. That is for this world. In the afterlife you need a resume for God, the Exalted. God, the Exalted, will send you whom He chooses. Allah has even written the name of the person who will eat a specific morsel or that bite of food; if it is not written it cannot be eaten. No one can eat someone else's portion because God, the Exalted, is the One who gives provision, whether it be *'ilm al-manawiyy*, spiritual knowledge or physical knowledge.

When Grandshaykh finished his last seclusion in Madinat al-munawwara in 1967, I was in Damascus waiting to greet him upon his return. He told us that in one of his visions during his seclusion the Prophet ﷺ appeared to him and told him, "O my son; don't run after people to call them to the Path. From now on don't go out of your house. I am sending the quality people to you." And never again did he move from his house until he passed away.

God, the Exalted, will send whomever He wishes. No one can eat that grape if it is destined for someone else. Even if he takes the grape and puts it in his mouth, someone will come and take it out before he swallows it. So if he is truly clever he will say, "yes, eat it my brother; it is yours." This knowledge has no end, but the *awliya* are hiding it. Today, there are no containers to hold this knowledge—no one can understand it any more.

Bi-hurmati 'l-Fatiha.

MANY-SIDED MERCIES

Divine Provision for Men and Women

[A talk addressed to university students in Berkeley, California.]

I am only a student and I am learning from my teacher whose name is Mawlana Shaykh Muhammad Nazim ʿAdil al-Haqqani ق. He is 85 years of age and lives in Cyprus. What I saw and I learned I cannot express because those fountains are always pouring forth, like a waterfall, always flowing. And the hearts of such people are like waterfalls: giving always and they are not asking to take anything, asking only to give.

Sufis around the world like to give rather than take. If God wants to give something to them, He gives. It is up to our Lord to give or not. He is the Most Generous. According to our Islamic belief He provided food to the Virgin Mary ﷺ in her seclusion, without her going out and without anyone bringing it to her.

> *Right graciously did her Lord accept her: He made her*
> *grow in purity and beauty: To the care of Zachariah was*
> *she assigned. Every time that he entered (her) chamber*
> *to see her, he found her supplied with sustenance. He*
> *said: "O Mary! Whence (comes) this to you?' She said:*
> *'From Allah. for Allah Provides sustenance to whom He*
> *pleases without measure."*[124]

The Prophet Zachariah ﷺ used to visit his niece, the Virgin Mary ﷺ, in her niche and every time he went there he found

---

[124] Surat Aali-ʿImran, (The Family of ʿImraan), 3:37.

something strange happening. He didn't understand what was happening. *"He found her supplied with sustenance."*

The point was not how this was being done, but rather that God was providing for the Virgin Mary ﷺ. The significance of this is that God was giving her provision without her seeking it. God was giving everything to her because she was sincere. She gave herself up to the Lord.

> *Behold! a woman of 'Imran said: "O my Lord! I do*
> *dedicate unto You what is in my womb for Your special*
> *service: So accept this of me: For You hear and know all*
> *things."*[125]

When Elizabeth, Virgin Mary's mother, was pregnant with her, she said "O My Lord I am giving my oath to you that I am giving that child to You," meaning "to Your service." Who donates their child? No one. It means "I am giving myself to You and Your service by giving You my child."

Remember Abraham ﷺ, when his Lord asked him to give up his son. He asked him to slaughter his son. And when his son understood this, he said, "O my father. Who is more generous, you or me?" And his father said, "I am of course; I am giving you to my Lord." His son said, "No, my father you are not giving yourself, but I am giving myself." At that time his son was thirteen years of age. So the one who gives his life to his Lord gives more. When her mother gave her the Virgin Mary she said, "I am giving up this girl, I am giving her to You." God, the Exalted, didn't differentiate between a boy and a girl – He accepts the service of either. God, the Exalted, sent to her the Holy Spirit to become pregnant and to bring forth Jesus ﷺ.

---

[125] Surat Aali-'Imran, (The Family of 'Imraan), 3:35.

And call to mind, through this divine writ, Mary. Lo!
She withdrew from her family to an eastern place and
kept herself in seclusion from them, whereupon We sent
unto her Our angel of revelation, who appeared to her in
the shape of a human being in all respects. She
exclaimed: "Verily, 'I seek refuge from you with the
Most Gracious! [Approach me not] if you do fear Him!"
He said: "No, I am only a messenger from your Lord, (to
announce) to you the gift of a holy son. [126]

Sincerity is what counts, for male or female. There is no difference between a male and a female, except through one issue. It is like this; give me this [he picks up a drum]. You drum it a little bit. Stop. Now you drum on your *oud*. [dun, dun] Now both of them. That is female and that is male. Or that is male and that is female. Both of them give a musical sound. Both are musical instruments. To our Lord there is no difference between the two. That one has a certain specialty and the other has a certain specialty. Each instrument makes its own sound. That one cannot do the work of the first and the first cannot do the work of the second. If they unite they will bring forth a symphony of sound, instead of just a single note. A garden filled with a variety of flowers is far more beautiful than a garden filled with only one type. All these men and women together produce a garden of beautiful flowers.

Lesson for a Czar

There was a Sufi shaykh who used to put his students in seclusion. Shaykh Jamaluddin al-Ghumuqi al-Husayni, one of the masters of our Naqshbandi lineage, would put one man and one woman in a room in seclusion together for forty days. Some people became jealous. They went to the czar of Russia and

---

[126] Surah Maryam, (Mary), 19:16-19.

complained that he was putting men and women together, which was contrary to certain Islamic regulations. The ones complaining did not understand that the essence of Islam is to treat everyone equally. You must not look for the worst explanation for every situation, but rather seek the best.

So they called him to court. This is a true story. A royal messenger came and told him to come before the czar, because they had accused him of coming against the rules of Islam and the rules of Christianity. They charged that the shaykh was putting people together in seclusion who were not related: not man and wife nor brother and sister.

Men and women here are symbols, representing unity in diversity. You look from one to another to another and your eyes shift to the next and then to the next. Just like when you have many different flowers, your eyes will be restful and happy.

So what happened? Shaykh Jamaluddin al-Ghumuqi al-Husayni sent the czar a box and he told the messenger to return and tell the czar, "I am coming." The shaykh was famous in his country. So the messenger came with the box and said "The shaykh is coming to your presence." The shaykh had instructed the messenger they must not open the box before he arrived.

Eventually the shaykh came to the czar's court and told the helper to open the box. Inside it there were burning coals and sitting on top of the coals was a layer of sulfur. Seeing that, the czar threw it away, afraid it was going to explode.

The shaykh said, "The one who can keep fire and sulfur from exploding is able to keep men and women in the same room, just as here in that box."

So that is expression of sincerity to the Lord. When one is sincere, then miracles can happen. The Virgin Mary ☙ had great sincerity. She received more than her uncle Zachariah ☙, who was one of the Lord's prophets. Why did she receive more? To God there is no difference between a lady and a man. God only looks at our hearts, as the Prophet ﷺ said, "Truly God does not look at your pictures but He looks are your hearts."[127]

When God sends His Attributes to our hearts, he sends from His love. Servants receive gifts from His Beauty, His Patience and all of His other Attributes. All of these divine characteristics manifest in each person in a different was. Each one of us possesses something holy, that thing which God gave to us. That holiness gives us our very existence. Holiness is power: the energy and the spirit which makes our lives possible. If that is taken away, you become nothing. We then go to our graves. What is left? Nothing except the soul. That which God has given us as a trust at one time will be taken back.

Punishment or Paradise?

One day Prophet Muhammad ﷺ was sitting and suddenly he began to laugh. He was known to have smiled a radiant smile most of the time, but this time he began to actually laugh heartily. His companions were surprised and one of them said, "O Prophet of God, why you are laughing?" They wanted to know the reason. You cannot laugh in a group of people; people will look at you strangely, they will wonder what you are doing.

He said, "Just now, I saw a vision." I am not going to explain how that vision is seen, for that is a miracle. He saw that two people had been brought into the presence of their Lord to be questioned about what they had done in their lives.

---

[127] Muslim.

This is an important point. Did God create us just to punish us or did He create us to be in Paradise? If He created us to punish us when He knows we are weak; He knows we are selfish. He knows He threw Satan on our shoulders. Why? Can He not take away Satan and cause him to die. In every belief: in Christianity; in Islam; in Judaism; in Buddhism even; in Hinduism; the influence of evil is taken into account.

Can't He take it away? Or does He like to make life like *Fear Factor*? Does God produce TV shows in Hollywood? However, in reality God loves us. He didn't create us to punish us.

Do you think He is going to take us on Judgment Day and say, "You did this and did this and did this. I am very happy about this and now I am going to throw you into hellfire." Is that our Creator?

Two of God's Names are ar-Rahman and ar-Raheem—the Beneficent and the Merciful. That is why the Prophet 靐 was laughing. He saw the interaction between these two people and their Lord.

One was a tyrant and the other was a simple person living under the rule of that tyrant. And the tyrant took his house, took his things, and even further was backbiting him.

So God said to the one who had been oppressed, "What do you want?" He replied, "This one was a terrible tyrant. He took everything from me; he was backbiting me and spoke bad about me in this way and this way and that way." God asked the other, "Did you do that?" The tyrant could not deny it. He said, "Yes." God said, "Then give him all your good deeds so that he may forgive you!" Even though he was a tyrant, he did have a few good deeds, which he promptly gave to his former victim. Then

God asked the oppressed man, "Are you satisfied now?" He said, "No, that is not enough. I want more."

So then God ordered the oppressed man to look up. There he saw huge cities made out of silver hovering above them. God asked, "Do you know who these belong to?" The man said, "I am not sure, but surely they must belong to Muhammad ﷺ or to Jesus ﷺ or to Moses ﷺ or to Adam ﷺ or to Noah ﷺ." God said, "No, if you want them they belong to you. If you want them pay their price." The man replied, "O God, I don't have anything with which to pay. Money does not work here. What is their price?" God said, "Only one thing: forgive your brother. Forgive the one who gave you harm!"

So the man looked and compared God's offer to his former life. He said, "I forgive him." God said, "Then all that you see is yours. Take your brother and enter there."

The Prophet ﷺ said, "I was laughing at the Lord's mercy."

That mercy can erase all kinds of bad actions and evil in one instant. And perhaps that is the secret of Iblees' mission. God left him among people because He wanted him to have a job. He didn't want anyone to be jobless—He gave him that job and Satan was happy with it. So on Judgment Day Satan might even say, "Give me my reward for doing that dirty job."

God's Infinite Mercy

I want to emphasize that God's Mercy is huge and without end. That is why Satan came to one saint and asked him a special question. The saint was Muhyideen ibn 'Arabi, a famous mystic from the Sufi tradition like Jalaluddin ar-Rumi. Rumi is famous for his poetry of passion and compassion. Ibn Arabi is famous for his heavenly revelations and knowledge. There is a big difference between the two, for each saint has his specialty.

Satan came to ibn 'Arabi and said, "God said in Holy Qur'an *'My mercy encompassed everything'*[128] and I am something from that everything. Am I not under that mercy? I am part of that everything? If so, do I receive mercy or not?"

Think about it? What could Muhyideen ibn 'Arabi say? He didn't say "yes" and he didn't say "no." He was worried. If he said "yes" then God would ask him "why?" And if he said "no" God would also ask him "why?" He felt like Pharaoh when the Red Sea was closing in on him after Moses' passage.

> *And We brought the Children of Israel across the sea,*
> *and Pharaoh with his hosts pursued them in rebellion*
> *and transgression, till, when the (fate of) drowning*
> *overtook him, he exclaimed: I believe that there is no God*
> *save Him in whom the Children of Israel believe, and I*
> *am of those who surrender (unto Him). What! Now!*
> *When hitherto thou hast rebelled and been of the wrong-*
> *doers?*[129]

Pharaoh said, as he was drowning, "Now I believe in what the people of Israel believe. I accept your messenger Moses." Archangel Gabriel came and said, "Now this one is saying 'I believe in Moses'? Now! After years and years of tyranny against Moses and his people?" So he took mud and threw it in his mouth to prevent him from saying, *"I believe in what Moses brought, what the people of*

---

[128] Suratu 'l-'Araaf, (The Heights), 7:156.
[129] Suratu 'l-Anbiya, (The Prophets), 10:90-92.

140

Bani Israel believed in" out of fear that the mercy would reach him.'[130]

God scolded Gabriel, and said to him, "Is he going to take your place if he believes and is he going to take anything from Me and my Paradises?"

Even Tyrants can be Guided

Look how God shows His mercy. When someone believes it is finished. That is to show that tyrants lose their minds and that causes them to act as they do. But when you build bridges with them you find they soften up and begin to understand what a prophet might have been saying:

> *But speak to him mildly; perchance he may take*
> *warning or fear (God).*[131]

That is what I realized in my travels and meetings with different rulers. They are leaders. When you talk with them, then they soften and listen and become convinced. You cannot argue with them and force them. People today try to force them by holding demonstrations. This only hardens their hearts. You have to build friendship with people. Jesus ﷺ built friendships with people; Moses ﷺ built friendship with people; Prophet Muhammad ﷺ built friendships with people.

That is what I think you are learning here in these institutions: to become people of friendship and to build these realities and bridges for people to walk on. You are not learning to become harder and more rigid and authoritarian. You are learning in order to build your knowledge. This school, I don't know how many students it has. You have a library here. How many books are in it? Perhaps many thousands? Books all aim at the same

---

[130] Abu Dawud At-Tayalisi, Tirmidhi, Ibn Jarir.
[131] Surah Taha, 20:44.

target: to find the truth and reality. There is nothing else. A scientist is looking for a discovery to find a correct formula. A priest is looking to find the reality of his existence. A doctor is looking for a discovery to cure people. Everything is taking us to find the reality of our Lord. Millions of books in libraries around the world are calling people to reality. The search begins with sincerity. Go look at hearts! If hearts are good, then everything is smooth and good. If hearts have problems, then everything is going to be a problem.

A Believing Leader

There is a country in the Far East that has suffered a thirty-year civil war. There are rebels in the northern part of the country fighting the central government. Finally the rebels agreed to come to the table to negotiate a peaceful solution. I was visiting there at that time. The vice president of that country sent me a message saying, "I have a problem. We came to dead end, the other party from the rebellious province left and went back to their hotel. They don't want to sign a peace agreement. We are deadlocked." He called me. Look at his belief. It was certainly not from belief in me. No, it is belief in the Lord that saves you.

He said, "What do I have to do?" I asked, "Do you have belief in your Lord? If you have belief, then go and meditate on this matter." He asked, "Alone?" I said, "No, take the president with you." And later I heard that he took the president, the cabinet and everyone and they were meditating and praying in the mosque to solve that problem. Where do you find someone like that here? They have belief.

He called me back in thirty minutes and said, "They came back and signed the agreement." And with that, thirty years of bloodshed came to an end. It was finished, and the killing stopped.

That means you must be in meditation with your Lord at all times. He created you because He engraved you with certain attributes. Every person is a piece of art. Every artist loves his art. You think God, the Exalted, dislikes His own works of art. You are His artwork. That is why, in Islam, the Prophet ﷺ completely prohibited backbiting. This is because when you seek to criticize someone, you don't necessarily know that person. You certainly don't know what is in her or his heart.

Sufism is the subject that opens up your inside to you. It teaches you to not just look outside. People today only look outside. If there is an invitation to a buffet, people are looking at the delicious food, but they only check the outward appearance of the food.

My teacher said to me, and I will never forget it, "Don't eat in a restaurant." I didn't ask "why?" It isn't respectful to always ask "why". He said "Don't eat in restaurants," so I don't eat in restaurants. Later he said to me, "I told you not to eat in restaurants. Do you know why?" I said, "You know better, my master." He said, "Because when you sit in restaurants, and especially when people sit by the glass, homeless and hungry people may look in at you enjoying your meal. They are capable of producing negative energies that can travel through the glass and harm you. There you are, eating a good meal that cost more money than they will have in weeks. Maybe their only shelter is under a bridge. In these circumstances bad energies can begin to flow."

They asked Junaid once to describe poverty. He said, "I will but give me some time." He got up and left his association where many students were attending. When he came back the next day he began to speak on poverty.

They asked him, "Why did you leave and not speak yesterday?" He answered, "How could I speak about poverty when I still had money at home? I went home and distributed that money to the poor. Now, and only now, can I speak truly on the subject of poverty."

ENDLESS KNOWLEDGE

Three Levels of Perfection

[A talk in a mosque in which a class of university students are present to observe and learn about Islam.]

First of all, before we begin, I would like all of us to remember one of our Shaykh's representatives in the Bay Area, Shaykh Mazhar Jamil, the father of brother Adam Jamil. May God, the Exalted, bless his soul, we remember he opened this first place for us in the Bay Area. Recite Fatiha for him.

Professor, how are you? Thank you for the honor of allowing our students here. You are trying to do your best and we are trying to do our best and we hope that both sides will do the best. And we ask our Lord that whatever is best for our world will happen. How many students do you have? [Twenty-two.] Twenty-two equates to two plus two equals four, and four is a favorable figure. The heart is divided into five levels. The first four of these levels are the Heart, the Secret, the Secret of the Secret and the Hidden. The last, the fifth, is the Most Hidden. These are called *qalb, sirr, sirr as-sirr, khafa, akhfa*. We will not go into that another time.

Tonight we will try to explore some aspects of spiritual knowledge. Since your students are taking a course in the religion of Islam, I would like to tell them that Islam is divided into three different parts. They may not have studied or heard about this particular aspect of Islam.

Three Levels of Religion

Once, in response to a question from one of his followers, the Prophet explained that religion can be divided into three different categories. The first category is the one that everyone knows and it might be that you are already teaching it: the five pillars of Islam. The first pillar is to bear witness that Allah ☀ is the creator and that Muhammad ☀ is His messenger like other messengers, and he is the Seal of the Messengers. The other four pillars are prayer, fasting, charity and pilgrimage.

The questioner then asked the Prophet ☀ if there was not more to it than that, and the Prophet indicated that, indeed, there was another level called *Iman*, or faith. Many people do not focus on faith, or the question of belief itself. The Prophet went on to explain that to have *iman* is to believe in God, in His prophets, from Adam ☀ to Jesus ☀ and including Muhammad ☀. Furthermore, *iman* includes belief in the existence of angels and the revealed holy books, including the Psalms of David, the Torah of Moses, the Bible of Jesus and the Holy Qur'an of Muhammad ☀. Finally, *iman* includes belief in the Last Day, the Day of Resurrection, in the afterlife and belief in Destiny. These are the six pillars of *iman*.

At this point, still not satisfied, the questioner persisted with his questioning. He asked what is *al-ihsan*, the highest level of perfection? The Prophet ☀ answered that at the highest level of perfection your everyday behavior would reflect excellent standards of morality and character, and that when you worship God ☀, you would do so as though either you were seeing Him or He is seeing you.

From this we can see that religion is not only the outward practices of Islam. That religion that Muhammad ☀ brought consists of Islam, *Iman* and *Ihsan* – Divine Law, faith and moral excellence. Many people can go to churches, shrines, mosques or temples and pray, but in their hearts there are things that are still negative. Things remain that might not be good for themselves or others. This is where the second and third levels come into play. In any religion, while praying, it is good to have a pure heart, not just towards the Creator, but for all of His creation as well, including our fellow humans. We are His subjects, His creation, His citizens. He owns us. All religions say that.

It must be emphasized that the most important issue that Prophet Muhammad ﷺ and all the other prophets were focusing on was how to behave well. How to pray is between you and your Lord but how to behave is between you and others. If you don't respect others it means you are not respecting the Creator.

Allah's Veils of Mercy

Allah loves not that evil should be noised abroad in
public speech, except where injustice has been done; for
Allah is He who hears and knows all things.[132]

Allah is saying that He veils our sins. One of His Beautiful Names is as-Sattar, the Veiler. He does not want us to expose each others' faults. If God veils your sins, then why would you expose the faults of your brother? God does not accept that. He tries to make everyone happy so that we can live in love and harmony.

God regards us with mercy and compassion. He did not create us to punish us. Why would He create us for that? That would not be justice. Do you think that a father and a mother would bring children into this world just to torture or kill them? Or do they bring them to life to care for them? Many people think of God chiefly in terms of punishment. God is the Merciful One. He will, if He chooses, extend His mercy even to a tyrant. He is the

---

[132] Suratu 'n-Nisa, (Women), 4:148.

Forgiver, the Merciful and ar-Raheem, the Beneficent. His Essence is indicated though these Attributes.

The Prophet ﷺ is asking us to use our minds and think about this. We are not so cheap. We are very expensive and very valuable. God has modeled every person with His Hands to make them perfect. We are like pieces of art: you cannot say to an artist "that piece of art is bad." That would be humiliating to him or her. One painting is good for one person, while another is good for another.

Bedouin Asks a Question

Once, when the Prophet ﷺ was giving the Friday service, a Bedouin came and stood by the door of the mosque. He was a simple, rough man of the desert. When he addressed the Prophet, he used none of the usual honorary titles: not Our Master, nor Our Prophet. He called out to the Prophet ﷺ directly, without ceremony. This upset the companions, but they said nothing and watched to see what would happen.

The Bedouin demanded, "When is Judgment Day?"

This was the first time that he had appeared before the Prophet ﷺ, and it was a difficult question involving a long discussion. So, the Prophet ﷺ did not answer and continued his speech.

The Bedouin again demanded, "When is Judgment Day?"

The Prophet ﷺ still continued with his speech, and the companions were becoming frustrated.

When he called out to the Prophet ﷺ a third time, the angel Gabriel came and spoke in the Prophet's ﷺ ear. Then the

Prophet ﷺ addressed the Bedouin, "That is a long journey which needs a lot of preparation and many provisions."

This means: "you need to do the best in your life so that when you are questioned at the Judgment, you will be able to answer for yourself."

The Bedouin answered, "O Prophet of God! I have not prepared much of prayers and fasting. All that I have prepared is love of God and love of you."

When the Bedouin said this, the companions were all listening with the utmost attention to what the Prophet ﷺ would say, because this was a very important question. The answer would show what the Day of Judgment would be like. Would it be a day when God would run after us through a jungle with a machine gun? Would it be like "Fear Factor" on TV with worms to eat? At this point everyone was listening very carefully.

The Prophet ﷺ addressed the Bedouin directly and said, "You have answered the question. For you, this is enough. You will be with the ones whom you love." The barefoot Bedouin never stepped inside the door but took this answer and left.

The companions, who were engaged in advanced devotions, praying all night and fasting often, were amazed at this response. The Prophet ﷺ said the Bedouin had enough, just like that! [133]

At that moment Sayyidina Abu Bakr ؓ stood up and took his *jubbah*, cloak, and whirled. [Shaykh showed us by covering his face with one end of his *jubba* and turned].

---

[133] *Sahih Muslim, Musnad* Ahmad, *Sahih Bukhari.*

When he whirled, it was like a great turbine engine. He went to such a high speed that it generated a burst of air, just like a jet engine. He whirled so fast and with such intensity, that the spiritual force pulling him up surpassed the force of gravity holding him down. This is the origin of what the whirling dervishes practiced in later centuries. In Islamic history, there are many such miracles, where the laws of physics are surmounted in highly sophisticated ways at the bidding of a saint.

To return to the main topic: religion has three parts. Most people only practice the five pillars. Few go on to the advanced levels of faith and moral excellence.

A powerful and useful daily practice, one that can improve our lives tremendously, is to worship God as though you are seeing Him or He is seeing you. This has a number of affects and, importantly, can be the road to moral excellence. Consider the implications: how could you always carry your dirty habits and negativity with you everywhere in the sight of the Divine Countenance? Would you not be ashamed? How could you cheat and backbite people if you were aware, in a very real and personal way, that someone, not just anyone, but the One who created the heavens and the earth was watching your every misdeed? Your prayers would become hollow, a bit like eating plastic fruit. You would try to chew them, but then quickly spit them out.

Paper and Taste

In Islam there are two kinds of knowledge. There is '*ilm al-awraaq*—the knowledge of papers, of academics. Then there is the knowledge of taste, '*ilm al-adhwaaq*—the knowledge of faith. The difference is that the knowledge of paper is dry and the knowledge of taste is juicy. Both types must balance with each other. If they don't balance then you cannot progress. In Islam, we deal with things largely relating to the body when we fulfill the obligations of the five pillars. Beyond the five pillars, the knowledge of faith deals with the spirit. When you combine these two in the right way, you approach the third level, *ihsan*, moral excellence.

Consider the physics of subatomic particles. The mass of the atom is held in the nucleus, and the charge is held in the electrons orbiting the center. Each element is not complete until both mass and charge are combined, a body and a spirit. This perfects the element, and gives it its own particular characteristics. Both things must be balanced, or the atom flies apart. Similarly, in religion, we must reach for balance: feeding both the body and the spirit in the right proportions. Reaching such a balance can bring physical and spiritual health.

God has created the universe with a technology so sophisticated that it would take countless engineers to simulate even a fraction of it in a computer program. It requires hundreds of programmers years to create games to go on Playstation and Gamecube. Look how many different program languages there are today. Think about all the millions of computers in the world. How many engineers and years of work does it take to create and maintain them? And yet, each one of us has trillions of cells in our bodies. Who programs and regulates these entities? No computer on Earth could match this degree of complexity. Our cells are microscopic compared to our bodies, our bodies are small compared to the Earth, and the Earth is less than a pinpoint compared to the universe. Who creates and maintains such a vast structure? Such a One deserves praise and worship. His greatness is beyond all imagination. This wonder, this respect, is part of the religion of taste. This is not the religion of habit and custom. It is not a mechanical, outward observance of certain practices and rituals. Religion, in this sense, is to taste the Greatness of the Creator.

Such a realization can transcend all the apparent differences between the world's great religions. How could it be that a superpower capable of commanding the entire universe, could not, after all is said and done, be sending us one message? Islam, Christianity, Judaism, Hinduism, Buddhism, Zen, all these different beliefs must, at some level, have converging meanings. A unity of truth binds these systems together. There is no basis for disputes between these different faiths. There have been people from all these traditions who sought and found enlightenment. It is our duty to follow that journey, to follow their paths.

Islam doesn't teach politics and fighting, regardless of what now goes on in many mosques. It is the same for Christianity and Judaism. The object of all should be to know our Lord. There is a saying in Islam: "Whoever knows himself, knows his Lord." I will ask you a simple question. How many of us in this room know how many hairs we have on our heads? If you don't know yourself, something this simple, how will you your Lord?

You say you have 250 million hairs on your head? I don't believe you, we'd better count. [everyone laughs]

So if you don't know yourself how do you want to know your Creator. There is a way to know but you have to move through all these obstacles. They tried to kill Jesus, because he was showing people the truth. It was the same with Moses ﷺ and Muhammad ﷺ. When anyone brings truth, people will try to kill him. This is because people do not like the truth.

Twin Pitfalls: Power and Fame

There are two things that Islam teaches us to avoid. If you can avoid them, you will be safe: love of fame and love of power. These two desires can destroy you and everything you hold dear. It is good to know your limits and stand by them. Why do I have to jump higher and farther? Let me sit here, being still. Then, I won't hurt myself or anyone around me. If I sit quietly, I will remain happy and stay at peace. People hurt themselves when they try to do more than has been assigned to them. If I am a student I take notes in class and then go home and study. Why go protest in the street and make trouble? If you find your limits and remain within them, you will find peace within yourself.

You will find that Sufi teachings while found mainly in Islam, are also found in Christianity and in Judaism. All teach human beings to remain within their limits. Why seek to become president and end up being criticized till the end of your days? For what? I would rather go home and sleep peacefully.

Tonight, your professor will go home and read his students' papers. This one gets an "A," this one a "C." Why bother? Everyone tried his best: why not give them all "A+." [everyone laughs]

This is religion—to love and laugh. This is Islam. This is Christianity. This is Judaism. This is Buddhism. I say all religions share love and laughter. If there is no love, then there is no religion. Everything is created with love. If there were no love, we would all disappear in an instant. Had there been no love between Adam ﷺ and Eve, would we even be here? Love is a central aspect of being human. So let us love each other. That is the message of heavens. That is why God sent messengers and the Holy Spirit Archangel Gabriel to the world to show us what he wanted. He is saying I don't want anything more. You cannot do more. Love Me and love each other, but don't love Satan. If you love Me I will be happy. But Satan will object, saying, "O my Lord, why can't they love me?" Was not Satan created by our Lord or was he created by someone else? He was created by our Lord. O professor, did not the Creator create Satan?

[Professor, "Well, yes, actually Judaism and Christianity agree that Satan was created by the Lord."]

So repent and then you will be safe. Satan would not repent. When we do something wrong we must repent. When we apologize and repent, do you think God will not forgive us?

Say: "O my Servants who have transgressed against their souls! Despair not of the Mercy of Allah. for Allah forgives all sins: for He is Oft-Forgiving, Most Merciful."[134]

God is saying this to every Muslim. If we do not follow this teaching, we are in danger. *"Obey God, obey the Prophet 🌿 and obey those in authority."*[135] That order is in the Holy Qur'an and every Muslim is obliged to obey it. Obey God, for if you do not, you will end in a major problem. Everyone in this nation needs to obey its authorities. God is ordering us to obey. Disobedience, lawlessness is wrong. When we disobey, we must ask forgiveness.

It is a big honor to be here with the professor and his students. We hope for many more meetings like this in the future.

Bi-hurmati 'l-Fatihah.

---

[134] Suratu 'z-Zumar, (The Groups), 39:53.
[135] Suratu 'n-Nisa, (Women), 4:59.

13: WASTE NOT

Hydrants of Flowing Knowledge

Don't look at me, I don't know anything. Whatever Mawlana Shaykh wants me to say, I say. I ask my shaykhs for support. They are the ones with all the wisdom and the knowledge. If you are humble enough to say that your teacher knows everything and that you know nothing, then wait to see what might open for you. In practical terms, we all think that we know a great deal already. However, compared to what God, the Exalted, gave to the Prophet ﷺ, what we know is barely a drop in his ocean of knowledge.

The knowledge of the prophets cannot be measured—*'Ilm an-nabi la yuhsa. 'Ilm ul-'ulama yuhsa*—whereas the knowledge of the *'ulama*, of scholars, can be measured. That kind of learning is finite, it is severely limited. If you have a tap and it is dripping, you can count the drops, one, two, three. But if the faucet is open at full power, can you count the drops? No, finished! They are rushing by too quickly. This is the difference between the knowledge of *awliya* and that of *'ulama*. If there is a fire and the fireman come and opens the hydrants, the water gushes out and they are able to dowse the flames. The knowledge of *awliya* is like such fire hydrants. *Awliya* can reach their followers from far away. They can put out fires that threaten their followers and overcome negative energy and bad conduct even from the other side of the globe

But the *'ulama* don't have hydrants like this: they have a tap that is dripping, drop after drop. Slowly, one drop after another emerges from the tap. What good will that do you if your house is on fire? It won't help at all. That is the difference between the knowledge of *awliya* and the knowledge of scholars. If you put all the scholars together, their knowledge is measurable and limited, because it is one drop plus one drop plus another drop. Look at the hydrants—on one street you can see many of them. Imagine how many hydrants there are, on the streets between San Francisco and Concord. There are thousands of them, all of them taking water from one reservoir. For the *awliya*, that reservoir is like a huge ocean of knowledge whose source is the Prophet ﷺ. Each of the *awliya* is like a hydrant, some large, some small. If the *wali* has a large capacity for transmitting knowledge, then he is like a giant fire hydrant moving rivers of water. This happens when a *wali* needs to reach many followers. That is why you have the immense hydrant of the Sultan al-*awliya*—he reaches the world.

If you connect all these hydrants you can measure their capacity relative to the Prophet's ﷺ knowledge. You can count the hydrants because you can count the saints, but the knowledge flowing through these hydrants cannot be measured. It is moving too fast, and there is too much of it to count. But the knowledge of the *'ulama* you can count, because it goes slowly, drop after drop.

It is very difficult for people like us, who have a lot of involvement in *dunya*, to understand this kind of heavenly knowledge. Heavenly knowledge of this order is only given to the Prophet ﷺ and he, in turn, gives it to *awliyaullah*. Ordinary people can understand some of what the *'ulama* know because it is easy access to that kind of limited knowledge. Hydrant knowledge is for a huge demand when a fire has to be put out. That is why God, the Exalted, gave the *awliyaullah* authority through the Prophet ﷺ to reach their followers at anywhere and any moment.

Consider the following hadith, narrated by Imam Ahmad. Remember that Wahabis or Salafis accept what Imam Ahmad recognized. In that hadith, Imam Ahmad quotes the Prophet ﷺ saying "If you are in a forest or a jungle and you get lost, then call on Allah's ﷻ servants." The servants mentioned here means the *Budala*, a special group of saints. Ask them to reach you with their support and they will reach you. If you are at a meeting or a lecture and you call on them, they will come and support you. Even if you merely recite the alphabet: a-b-c-d-e-f, people will be happy. Even if you don't say anything, they will be happy. This is because the attraction, *jazbah*, that these saints will put in the ears of people will be put in their hearts, even if you say only a-b-c. To the listeners' ears it will sound like music. Each of them will hear according to his own needs, and they will be happy. The *awliya* you have called upon will enter their hearts and fill them.

Anyone who sits and asks support from the *awliya*, they will bring light through his words. Anyone who thinks he is academic and prepares a speech will sound like a tape recording, it will be dry, and you can gauge his knowledge. However, the knowledge of the *awliya* cannot be measured.

Value the Drops

> *Verily spendthrifts are brethren of the Evil Ones; and the Evil One is to his Lord (himself) ungrateful.*[136]

The *mubadhdhir*, literal one who wastes, waste time and substance. It means to waste your money or throw too many things away or avoid giving the poor or homeless. This is to waste what Allah ﷻ has given you. From His point of view, those who waste are the brothers of devils because they are wasting the favors, *ni'mat*, that He gave them.

---

[136] Suratu 'l-Isra, (The Night Journey), 17:27.

This can take many forms: wasting food, money. Look at the waste all around us, and then think about how many children are starving in this world! Allah said they are the brothers of the devils.

That is an important point. If you waste the energy that Allah ﷻ gave to you in ways that are not worthy, you are under that curse, you are the brother of devils. Your energy was meant to be given back in worship. Always, He is looking and weighing us, checking everyone of us. He has sent angels to watch us, to see if we are wasting the energy that He has bestowed on us. Are we wasting our time in listening to what is not necessary to be listened to and leaving other things unattended? If you look and see people doing wrong, then learn what to avoid from those bad examples.

Someone was once asked how he learned to gain so much control over himself. He said, "I watched those who are not disciplined and from them I learned discipline." When you observe, let nothing be lost on you. Absorb the lesson: don't wasted what God, the Exalted, has given you.

On another level, God, the Exalted, is sending on us the manifestations of His Beautiful Names and Attributes. He sends these to every person, each according to his destiny. He wants you to take that manifestation and learn the secret of every Name or Attribute, that the Lord has sent you. For each of us, that Divine Name is like a hydrant, gushing with heavenly meanings.

God's Munificence is Akbar

When God, the Exalted, sends such things, He doesn't send them in little in drops. He sends according to His generosity. What is His generosity? It relates to His greatness. He is *al-Kareem*. That generosity cannot be described except as *karamun akbar, al-Kareem ul-Akbar*. There is no possible description of His generosity and its greatness. It is beyond whatever you think of as generosity. God's generosity is beyond all measure. If you were able to accept His generosity, you could become a hydrant of knowledge as well. If you don't become a fountain, a conduit for heavenly knowledge flowing to Earth, then you fall under that curse, the fate of those who waste. The *awliyaullah* know that if they are not acting as hydrants, then they are going to be the brothers of devils. They know that they would be wasting what God, the Exalted, has sent through them to humanity. How do you say that today? Outsourcing. God, the Exalted, is outsourcing heavenly knowledge to the *awliya*.

Outsourcing Angels

Today, businesses everywhere are outsourcing, because labor is cheaper overseas. They are building huge business empires by outsourcing data collection, software development and customer service centers. Similarly, God, the Exalted, is telling us that He is sending us work to do. He is opening up ways for you to dispense heavenly knowledge. "Build your empire," God says. "Become a fountain! I am outsourcing all my angels to help! They will be under your service. They will bring you the heavenly manifestations I am sending, the angels will carry them down to you."

Recall the Isra and Mi'raj, the story of the Prophet's ascension that I wrote about in *Angels Unveiled*. When God, the Exalted, ordered the angel Gabriel to take the heavenly steed, the Buraq and go to the Prophet ﷺ, he traveled accompanied by four archangels. They came bearing heavenly gifts accompanied by countless angels carrying special clothes with which to decorate the Prophet ﷺ. These were not worldly clothes, nor even heavenly ones, but were in fact different manifestations of the Divine, the best preparation for approaching the Divine Presence.

You cannot go to the Divine Presence of God, the Exalted, with your dirtiness. You have to be dressed as though you were going to your wedding, where the bride and groom are wearing their best. As an obedient servant of God, the Exalted, the Prophet was dressed with extraordinary Divine manifestations during this preparation. He was raised to the Station of *"two bow's-length or nearer."*

The angels are outsourced. They are there, just waiting for you to call. To call for them is by not wasting, Do not waste this chance by turning your face towards *dunya* and turning away these heavenly powers!

If you turn your back on this, it means you don't need these gifts from heaven. However, consider the opposite: by refusing such gift and wasting this chance, the alternative choice is terrible. If you turn away from the angels, Satan is waiting to bestow his own variety of gifts. That is why God, the Exalted, said:

> *Verily spendthrifts are brethren of the Evil Ones; and the Evil One is to his Lord (himself) ungrateful.*[137]

This means that those who are not wasting their lives and gifts are the brethren of angels. Those who are accepting this cosmic outsourcing, if we can use that word, are the brethren of angels, the opposite of the brethren of Satan.

Therefore waste, in this important sense, refers to the refusal of Allah's best gifts. When we fail in this, we spend our lives looking for enjoying material life and material wealth, we are not looking for a heavenly life and heavenly wealth. We are wasting heavenly life and heavenly wealth. That is why those who are wasting heavenly life and heavenly wealth are the brothers of devils.

---

[137] Suratu 'l-Isra, (The Night Journey), 17:27.

Awliya understand that they have to respect the knowledge that God, the Exalted, opens to His servants by moving towards their Lord. Then He will come to them quickly running. In the hadith, "Whoever comes to Me walking, I will come to him running." Don't waste your time and energy and your life. Your time is limited. Your energy is limited. After a certain age it is gone. Your time might be twenty years, it might be seventy, it might be more, but whatever it is, don't waste your time and don't waste your life. Don't waste period. "*And remain conscious of Allah and Allah will teach you.*"[138]

Have *taqwa* and God, the Exalted, will teach us from His heavenly knowledge. That is what Mawlana opened to us today.

This lesson should remind me and everyone here that we always need the support of *awliya*. That is the key point of this topic. When they send support, they send what you really need and what is of genuine benefit. However, if you want to make yourself a big professor, then they send knowledge only in drops.

May Allah make this blessed meeting, *bi-hurmati 'l-Fatiha*.

---

[138] Suratu 'l-Baqara, (The Heifer), 2:282.

OF CLAY AND LIGHT

The Honored Clay

God, the Exalted, ordered us to obey him, to obey His Prophet ﷺ
and to obey those who are in authority. Obedience can teach us
discipline: in most cases, we have little or no discipline. We begin
life with absolutely no control at all. Out parents try to teach us.
This state in children is called in *tasawwuf, at-tifl an-nafs al-
madhoumah. Madhmoumouah* means disliked: the childish acts of a
growing son or daughter must be curbed by the parents. They say,
do this, don't do this, don't do that. They try to discipline the
child's behavior, because they know that left alone, things will
soon get out of control. It is human nature to be rebellious, even
against our families. This is because each one of us thinks that we
know what is best for us.

God, the Exalted, knows this because He created us. From
Adam ﷺ, the seed of self will and rebelliousness was woven into
our very natures. We are made of earth. Adam ﷺ was created
when God ordered Gabriel to go to Earth and to bring back the
clay from which He began to construct the first man. God, the
Exalted, added more elements to the clay: water; fire and air. This
is an interesting point. God created the Earth and the heavens,
each with its own appropriate native elements. What is the *hikmah*,
the knowledge and wisdom behind this mixing of elements:
introducing some clay from Earth into Paradise?

What are we to understand from this? It means that God, the
Exalted, is saying, "You are earthly, O human beings, and you

have been created from this *dunya*; from dirt. Don't raise your head up with pride. Bow to Me in *sajda*, prostration, to Me."

In Arabic dirt is *turab*: something that doesn't have value. It is such that if you go and tell someone you need that mountain of dirt, people will give it to you for free. It has no value. They say, "Give us diamonds" they have value.

God, the Exalted, wants us to understand that for us, such humility is necessary. He has honored us, but we have nothing by which to be honored. There is knowledge hidden behind that fact the He ordered Gabriel to go to earth to get Adam's 🕊 clay. Surely God, the Exalted, has given a singular respect to Earth.

The Prophet 🕊 said, "Truly Allah made me the Seal of prophets while Adam was between water and clay."[139]

That means that God, the Exalted, took mud, mixed it with water, and shaped Adam 🕊. What water? What kind of water? Ordinary water? Heaven doesn't have ordinary water. Only Earth has ordinary water. God, the Exalted, honored the clay by bringing it to heaven and mixing it with the water there. He said:

> *Verily We have honored the children of Adam. We carry*
> *them on the land and the sea, and have made provision of*
> *good things for them, and have preferred them above*
> *many of those whom We created with a marked*
> *preferment.*[140]

God, the Exalted, brought us to the heavens, the place of Resurrection. He wants to send the *baraka*, blessings, of heavens to Earth. That is why He ordered Gabriel to bring the mud of Paradise, create Adam 🕊 in Paradise, honor him, then send him back to earth. When Adam 🕊 died, his *baraka* went to the Earth.

---

[139] Ahmad in the *Musnad*, Bayhaqi in *Dala'il al-Nubuwwa*.
[140] Suratu 'l-Isra, (The Night Journey), 17:70.

That is the secret of that honor, for Adam ﷺ was in Paradise for a long time. Every time Iblees went and looked at Adam ﷺ, he did not understand what he was seeing. He saw the outward form of clay, but not the *ruh* or soul.

Infusion of the Divine Spirit into Adam

When you want to dilute a very expensive perfume, essence of rose for example, you take one drop and add it to a bottle of plain liquid such as water, oil or other substance. So what happens to that bottle that is full of that plain liquid? One drop of essential rose oil permeates the entire bottle of another liquid.

Similarly, when you take a cup of water, warm it stir in one spoonful of honey, and drink it, you have a medicinal cure. There is a verse in the Holy Qur'an and hadiths of the Prophet about the importance of honey. The Prophet ﷺ used it as a cure for various ailments. Scientists in Egypt have recently discovered that when they add honey to water, the water becomes like honey. It changes the entire formula of the mixture to honey. It is no longer water— rather it possesses all the basic characteristics of honey.

One drop of perfume added to oil changes the oil into perfume. God, the Exalted, ordered the clay of the Earth brought up where the *baraka* of heaven could honor it and change it into something else. He placed the light of Sayyidina Muhammad ﷺ— the light of creation—in that clay and said:

> *When I have fashioned him (in due proportion) and breathed into him of My spirit.*[141]

When God, the Exalted, sent that *ruh* from the *bahr al-qudrah*, the Divine Ocean of Power, He blew it into Adam ﷺ. Adam ﷺ was honored thereby and the Prophet ﷺ said, "I was a prophet when

---

[141] Surah Sad, 38:72.

164

Adam was between water and clay." So we must ask ourselves what kind of water was it? That is the water of Kawthar—the water of *ma'rifah*, gnosis: *"We have given you the Kawthar."*[142]

The Fount of Abundance

Kawthar has two meanings. One is a river in Paradise that belongs to our Holy Prophet ﷺ and the other meaning is "infinite knowledge that never ends." That is: a fount of knowledge that is in everlasting ascension. God, the Exalted, molded Adam ﷺ with the river of Kawthar and molded him with special knowledge that belonged to the Prophet ﷺ. He adorned Adam ﷺ with it and, because the Prophet ﷺ is in continuous ascension, Adam ﷺ is rising higher and higher as well. This is how God, the Exalted, has honored Bani Adam ﷺ—human beings.

Therefore, God, the Exalted, created Adam ﷺ by combining the elements of heaven and Earth, of light and clay. As soon as Adam ﷺ stepped on earth, that honor blessed the whole earth. They say that when Prophet Adam ﷺ came down he put his first footstep on a mountain in Sri Lanka, Mt. Serendip. There are many mining concerns there, digging for gemstones on Mt. Serendip.

As soon as Adam's ﷺ feet touched the Earth, it was transformed from a dry lifeless orb into a paradise of rivers, trees and fruit. His children multiplied across the Earth: like that drop of rose oil I described earlier. That is how Adam ﷺ carried wisdom to Earth as part of the honor that God, the Exalted, bestowed upon him. Mawlana is now opening this secret to us—the Divine Plan by which earthly clay was enraptured to heaven and then sent back, having been granted distinction. That piece of heaven that came back with Adam ﷺ is the place between the Prophet's grave

---

[142] Suratu 'l-Kawthar, (Abundance), 108:1.

and *minbar*, pulpit: it is called *ar-Rawdah*—the Garden. That means that when you step in the *Rawdah* you are stepping into heaven. Do you think anyone who steps into heaven will ever leave? That is why they tell you "Try to pray two *raka'ats* in the *Rawdah*" because anyone who enters heaven will never touch hellfire.

The Hajara 'l-Aswad, the Black Stone, which is part of the original foundations of the Ka'ba, is from heaven. And the people kiss it because the Prophet ﷺ kissed it. Sayyidina 'Umar ؓ said to the stone, "If I didn't see the Prophet ﷺ kiss you I would not kiss you, for you neither give harm nor benefit." Then Sayyidina 'Ali ؓ said to him "Don't say that. That is a stone from Paradise and it will be one of your witnesses when you greet it."[143] That is why we say "*Allahu Akbar, Allahu Akbar*" before it. Because it is from heaven, the stone is holy. Similarly, the *Rawdah*, the area where the Prophet ﷺ is buried, is also holy.

This means that a heavenly element is in us. The Prophet ﷺ said, "All of you are from Adam ؑ and Adam ؑ was from soil."[144] But that soil, *turab*, has been honored in heavens and then sent back. That is one way in which God, the Exalted, has honored human beings.

Adam on Earth

If someone has lived in heaven, can he then be taken to hellfire? All of us were in heaven with Prophet Adam ؑ, in his loins. When he was sent down to Earth, we all came down with him: all his children, grandchildren and ancestors. That is why God, the Exalted, said:

---

[143] Reported by Imam Ghazali, *Ihya 'ulum ad-din*, and, Hajjah Amina Adil, *Lore of Light*, volume 1, p.24, with additional wording.

[144] Ahadith with slight variances in wording are found in ibn al-Marduwayah, al-Hakim and al-Bazzar.

Verily We have honored the children of Adam. We carry
them on the land and the sea, and have made provision of
good things for them.[145]

The land mentioned here is the land of heavens. Because
Gabriel ﷺ carried that earthly mud all the way up to the heavens.
God, the Exalted, honored us more than most of creation –
because He honored us in heaven and provided us with good
things. Provision here means *ma'rifatullah*—gnosis. The angels
were created in heaven, but human beings are especially honored
because they were originally earthly but were then taken up to the
heavens.

Many people take these verses to mean that God, the Exalted,
is saying that He carried human beings on earth and through the
oceans. Why would God, the Exalted, say "I honored you by
carrying you on the land and on the seas"? No, rather it means,
"I honored you to be on Heaven's ground and I honored you
there at the ceaselessly outpouring Fount of the Prophet ﷺ."

The verse continues:

And We have preferred them above many of those whom
We created with a marked preferment.[146]

God has made man higher than many of His other creations.
Which other creations? There are other creations that we know
nothing about. Where are they? Allah's ﷻ spoke of creations here
on earth that we cannot see. Adam ﷺ and his descendants were
honored above these other creations and allowed to move about
freely across the face of the Earth. God, the Exalted, mentioned
this in the Holy Qur'an and He counted the sons of Adam ﷺ:

---

[145] Suratu 'l-Isra, (The Night Journey), 17:70.
[146] Suratu 'l-Isra, (The Night Journey), 17:70.

He does take an account of them (all), and has numbered them (all) exactly.[147]

Ahsahum means they are under His control and He has numbered them one-by-one. Allah doesn't need to count them but He appointed angels to count them one-by-one, noting each human being.

That means no one can be away from Allah's ﷻ Observation and Presence. We are under His control, because they are under Adam ﷺ. Allah had created everyone's seeds, placing them in the loins of Adam ﷺ and He moved them about as He willed. That means they were carried by Adam ﷺ, just as the passengers were carried on the Ark of Prophet Noah ﷺ, described in Qur'an as *"al-fulk al-mashoun—the fully-laden ship."*[148] In that sense, Adam ﷺ was like a vessel, and that is why He said, *"We carried them on the earth and in the sea."* That is also why Grandshaykh said:

> Adam ﷺ did not eat from the tree, but the children of Adam ﷺ that were in his back[149] pushed him to wrongdoing and they caused his hands to move and take the fruit from the tree.

That was the means by which mankind was sent back to Earth. That mud belongs to where? To Earth. So God, the Exalted, sent it back, but honored it in the process.

Between Water and Clay

Earth was honored through Adam ﷺ. When the Prophet ﷺ said, "I was a prophet when Adam ﷺ between clay and water,"

---

[147] Surah Maryam, (Virgin Mary), 19:94.

[148] Suratu 'sh-Shu'ara, (The Poets), 26:119; Surah Yasin, 36:41; Suratu 's-Saaffaat, (The Rangers), 37:140.

[149] "in his back" is a metaphor meaning the sperm that he carried containing the essences of all his descendants.

what did he mean? A prophet for whom? It means Allah gave him the authority through his prophecy, which means through his existence. The Prophet ﷺ was in existence at Adam's creation. That is why the Prophet ﷺ said, "O Jabir! The first thing that God, the Exalted, created is my light."[150]

The beginning time of the Prophet ﷺ is unknown. That is why the Prophet ﷺ said in a hadith:

God, the Exalted, took one hand of light and said, *"Koonee Muhammad*—be Muhammad!" and it became Muhammad ﷺ.[151]

And the Prophet ﷺ said:

God, the Exalted, put my light into the Ocean of *Qudrah*, Power, and it was turning and turning for as long as He wished. And when God, the Exalted, wished to create creation, He divided that Light into four parts and from the first made the Pen, from the second the Tablet, from the third the Throne, then He divided the fourth into four parts [and from them created everything else]."[152]

This is why the Prophet ﷺ said:

I am the master of the Children of Adam and I say it without pride.[153]

And he said:

I was honored to be a prophet when Adam was still between water and clay.[154]

---

[150] Abdur Razzaq in his *Musannaf.*
[151] Mentioned in ibn Qayyim al Jawzi's *Mawlid al-'Arus.*
[152] *Op. cit.*
[153] Tirmidhi.
[154] Similar hadiths are narrated in al-Bayhaqi, Tirmidhi, Abu Na'eem.

And Allah said:

To you (O Muhammad) have We granted the Fount (of Abundance).[155]

That means that the Prophet saw the water which God, the Exalted, used to create Adam ﷺ. He fashioned him from clay and the Water of Youth and Life, the same water that Sayyidina Khidr and Dhul-Qarnayn went forth in search of. Sayyidina Khidr found it and Dhul-Qarnayn could not.

God, the Exalted, informed the Earth's clay with a beautiful presence. When he sent is back, it changed the entire Earth, changing it from a normal planet to a heavenly natural, place. We are honored by the presence, and He said, "*We have honored the sons of Adam.*"[156]

May God, the Exalted, forgive us and bless this meeting and bless those of us who have passed away, may they meet with Mawlana Shaykh Nazim ق and the Mahdi.

Bi-hurmati 'l-Fatiha.

---

[155] Suratu 'l-Kawthar, (Abundance), 108:1.
[156] Suratu 'l-Isra, (The Night Journey), 17:70.

THE KEY AND THE DOOR

Power of the Spirit

The Prophet ﷺ is explaining here that the physical body is governed by the laws of the Earth, but the spirit is governed by the law of heavens. The body is from earth, from dirt, from clay, from mud, and the spirit is what?

> *They ask You (O Muhammad) concerning the Spirit (of inspiration). Say: "The Spirit (cometh) by command of my Lord: of knowledge it is only a little that is communicated to you, (O men!)"*[157]

When asked about *Ruh*, the Spirit, Allah ﷻ told Sayyidina Muhammad ﷺ, "Don't speak about the *Ruh*; don't tell them. They cannot understand. Tell them only that it is from Allah's *amr*—*amrillah*."

Amrillah has countless meanings. *Amrillah* means that no one has the right to know more, it is not our concern or business. It is something that is from Allah's Order, Allah's Knowledge, Allah's Power. Wherever it is, it is Allah's Manifestation. In any event, it is not the business of human beings. It is enough for us to understand that whatever we have been given is from "the little." Had it been otherwise He would have said, *qaleela*, little, but He said, *illa qaleela*, "from the little," which is understood to mean "you have not been given anything."

---

[157] Suratu 'l-Isra, (The Night Journey), 17:85.

171

There are two opinions of the scholars concerning ar-Ruh. One is that ar-Ruh is the soul, that spirit that Allah has put in us and the other is that ar-Ruh is an angel. Allah said:

The angels and the Spirit ascend unto Him in a Day the measure whereof is fifty thousand years.[158]

The Ruh and angels go in ascension to a place where one day is like fifty thousands years of our earthly years. In this sense ar-Ruh is an angel. That is why God, the Exalted, said in the Holy Qur'an, *"of knowledge you have been given from the little."* So ar-Ruh, the Spirit, is governed by the heavens, and the laws of the Creator who created the heavens supercede those of the earth. Earthly powers are nothing in the face of heavenly powers. Therefore, the soul controls the physical body. We do not perceive with ordinary vision that the soul organizes, controls and sustains the body.

Awliya, such as Mawlana Shaykh Nazim ق, can see the true situation because they have been dressed with certain heavenly powers. Through the power of the Beautiful Divine Names and Attributes that Allah has adorned them, they can see the soul and its relation to the physical body. As such, they share in the heavenly world, manifest it laws, and perceive from that perspective. We ordinary people, locked in our bodies, see only a small part of reality, limited as we are by the confines of own bodies. We are not in close contact with the heavens and are continuously distracted by the cares and noise of this world.

The special powers of the *awliya* hinge on their heavenly orientation. For example, when they wish to move from one place to another, they use the power of the soul rather than that of their feet. They can move with the soul outside of the body. For most of us, the body is a cage. However, you can free the soul through worship, in the manner that God, the Exalted, has taught us and

---

[158] Suratu 'l-Ma'arij, (The Ascensions), 70:4

172

as explained in the hadith of the Prophet ﷺ, "My servant continues to draw near to Me with voluntary worship so that I shall love him."

If you can accept Him in a certain way, God, the Exalted, will be your feet and your legs and move you about with the speed of a thought. Some souls can travel at velocities greater than the speed of light. The times of the earthly world and the heavenly are hugely disproportionate. So it might have been a duration of one minute, or one second during the Prophet ﷺ ascended through this universe, into the heavenly sphere and from there to the Divine Presence—and then returned! God, the Exalted, might have stretched time during that journey, so that what appeared a few moments on Earth had, in fact, compressed years, centuries or millenia of experiences into the Prophet's ﷺ epic journey. In that realm and rapidness of experience, he was enjoying the ecstasy and highest level of knowledge in the Universe. In those few moments, in that ʿibadah, worship, he might have lived the experiences of million or billions of years. Who can say?

Invitation to Ascend

This sort of power is beyond anything we can conceive of. When the awliya follow the footsteps of the Prophet ﷺ, do you think that they follow him only in Shariʿah? Of course, you have to follow him in Shariah, you have to pray and fast. But he also invites us to follow him in his ascension—he is in miʿraaj all the time. He invites all awliya to follow him. He says, "Follow me; keep tight hold on my jubbah, my cloak. Hold my hand and I will take you with these powers that God, the Exalted, gave to me. We will travel to a place where time and space dissolve."

Gravity and clocks cannot control heavenly beings. A little bit of fuel in a rocket's engine can take you beyond the gravity of Earth. Imagine then, where heavenly power could carry you.

Unlike nuclear power, heavenly power has no restrictions. When *awliya* travel up through the layers of the universe, they are dressed with the manifestations of each layer. They have no earthly fears or concerns, they leave all that behind when they follow the Prophet ﷺ on his ascension.

Many Islamic scholars say today that every Muslim is a *wali*. This is not so. If every Muslim were a *wali*, we would be holding on to the Prophets ﷺ robes while he ascended. We would always be in *'ibadah*. However, we are not, we are involved in all *dunya* matters, the affairs of the Earth.

Beyond the Pillars

As a Muslim, I have to believe in God, the Exalted, in His angels, in His Books, in His messengers, in the Day of Judgment and in destiny. However, Allah did not stop there. The Five Pillars of Islam and the Six Pillars of Faith are not enough. If you stop at this and believe it is enough, the Prophet ﷺ said it is as though Satan were robbing you. Like a jar with a hole in it, the contents will drain out. How can we stop this loss? We need something like a savings account. Like people with only a checking account, we are spending our five prayers every day and saving nothing from them. We need savings accounts to save us from Satan.

Many people prefer to close their eyes to this reality or are simply unaware of it. They miss the significance of what Sayyidina Muhammad ﷺ described to the archangel Gabriel ﷺ as narrated by Sayyidina 'Umar ﷺ where he explained that Islam has other dimensions besides the pillars. Above everything else, God, the Exalted, wants us to perfect our manners: this is the highest level, known as *al-Ihsan*. Put simply, if you pray, but have bad manners, it is not going to work.

Satan cannot enter a mosque, because it is a place where God, the Exalted, is worshipped. Satan has a long reach, but God, the Exalted, doesn't let him in a house of worship. *"Say! I seek refuge in the Lord of mankind."*[159] When we go outside the mosque, it is a different matter. Outside we become angry with everyone: we carry jealousy and hatred with us. If someone is shouting outside a mosque, there is a different quality to the sound. It can block you from hearing *dhikrullah*, recitation of Qur'an or the Jumu'ah prayer. This can erase your prayers. This is why the Prophet ﷺ said, "Try to worship God, the Exalted, as though you were seeing Him."

This is an important aspect of worship. You have to worship God, the Exalted, as if you were seeing Him. You have to know you are between His hands. This is not like seeing your brother or your father. They don't know your heart. They are not at the level of *awliya*, the level of sainthood, people who are able to read hearts. Some people can read hearts through the inheritance they receive from the Prophet ﷺ, the *awliyaullah*. Very few people have that gift.

The Prophet ﷺ said, "The best time for me is in prayer, when I am between the Hands of Allah in that Presence."[160] So in prayer you are in that Presence. It is at these times that Satan comes and whispers. If you are not in the Divine Presence, then you are with Satan. Ordinarily, we are not in that presence, if we were, it would be impossible for Satan to approach us. Now make an account of yourself to see how far you are from the presence of God, the Exalted.

Clearly, we ordinary people are not seeing God, the Exalted. But what did the Prophet ﷺ say? "If you are not seeing Him, then

---

[159] Suratu 'n-Nas, (Mankind), 114:1.
[160] Lit. "Allah made the coolness of my eyes in prayer." Bukhari.

He is seeing you." So, that special moment of your prayer, when God, the Exalted, is seeing you, that prayer should be clean. If it is not clean then, we are losing the prayer. In order not to lose it, God, the Exalted, sent us Sayyidina Muhammad ﷺ as mercy for humanity. The Prophet ﷺ has mercy for everyone and through this mercy he is teaching us, so that we can improve ourselves.

Keys to Paradise

One of these teachings can take us very close to this ideal. We cannot be perfect, that is impossible. However, the Prophet ﷺ is giving us hints about how to be nearly perfect. Sayyidina 'Umar ﷺ said that the Prophet ﷺ said, "Everything in this life, and in the hereafter, has a key." You cannot open anything without a key. Even the prayer has a key. What is key for prayer? It is the *adhaan*. That key is the opening of the way to the Presence of God, the Exalted.

That is why it is very important to observe the *Sunnah*. Many people are leaving the *Sunnah* and doing the *fard*, the obligation, and then running away. The key is the obligation to clean yourself. The Prophet ﷺ was praying the *Sunnah*. There is a *Sunnah*, before the *fard* in every prayer. In one school of thought there are even two *raka'ats* before the Maghrib prayer. It is as if someone were preparing a gift, then wrapping it nicely and then presenting it. That *Sunnah* has to be done for it is the key. Sayiddina 'Umar ﷺ related from the Prophet ﷺ that everything has a key. Don't leave the *Sunnah* behind. It is a key for the *fard* prayer to be pure in the presence of God, the Exalted.

So everything has a key. What is the most important thing that Muslims are running for in all this life? What is the one goal? It is to be able to enter Paradise. Everyone is trying to worship to enter Paradise, *jannah*. Consider this. This view of prayer and its rewards is for common people, for us. There are special people

176

who are worshipping for the love of God, the Exalted, not solely to enter Paradise.

So the Prophet ﷺ said to his Companions, *"Miftah al-jannah,* the Key to Paradise, do you want to know what it is?" All the Sahaba were waiting to hear about the key to Paradise. Is it prayer alone? But the Prophet ﷺ is giving us some secrets; things that might serve as keys for us. God said:

> *We have not sent you (O Muhammad) except mercy for*
> *all creation.*[161]

What is the Key to Paradise? The Prophet ﷺ said two words only: *"Hubb al-masakeen*—love of the wretched."[162] Who are the wretched? "Wretched" means the poor, the homeless, the depressed and the sick. Those are the *masakeen.* You might have money but you have no luck; you are sick. Or you have money but no friends. Or you have money but no children. Or a man has money but no wife, or a woman has no husband. That is *masakeen.* So the Prophet ﷺ said the Key to Paradise is to love such people.

The *masakeen* are those who are important to God, the Exalted, because they are in difficulty. You have to befriend them. When you are kind to them God, the Exalted, will give you the Keys to Paradise.

Love of the Poor

And the Prophet ﷺ didn't end with *hubb al-masakeen.* He continued, *"wa hubb al-fuqara*—love of the poor." In general, the majority of people are *masakeen.* They are depressed, sick, cannot get married or have some other problem. If you can love these people, who are poor in some sense, then you will learn to humble yourself. Even if you sit on a big throne, or you own a company or

---

[161] Suratu 'l-Anbiya, (The Prophets), 20:107.
[162] Al-Ghazali, *Ihya 'uloom ad-deen.*

a chair, and you cannot normally sit with such people, recall that God, the Exalted created them, and they are just like you.

And the Prophet ﷺ didn't say "Muslim." He said "the poor" in general. Why are they the Key to Paradise? They have one interesting characteristic in common. *Sabrihim*—they have patience.

In many cases they cannot do anything about their conditions. You see them under bridges—homeless—unable to do anything, yet they are happy. They go to garbage cans and try to find food. Could we do that? No, not one of us can do that.

What is Allah's ﷻ last Attribute? He is as-Saboor. He has the greatest patience. He has patience for all His servants. He has patience for His creation. If He is not patient with us, then He would have destroyed the creation a long time ago. The poor are *"julasa'ullah yawm al-qiyamah*—they are the ones in Allah's Presence on Judgment Day." So when you love them you will be with them, it is very simple. The Prophet ﷺ said, "Love them, and they are the Key to Paradise." They will get you in from outside, because they are in that Divine Presence.

God, the Exalted, revealed to Isma'eel ﷺ, "Look for Me among those whose hearts are broken."[163] How many have had their hearts broken. When someone has a broken heart, he feels he wants to be alone with his Lord. People are like that. You can see them mostly in their homes or in their mosques; they only want to think about God, the Exalted. They are asking God, the Exalted, to heal them. "Find your Lord through these people who have broken hearts. If you want Me, find Me there," He said. Isma'eel asked, "Where I can find these people?" God, the Exalted, revealed to him, *"al-fuqaraa as-sadiqoon, was-sabiroon*—They are the poor, the veracious ones, the patient ones." Who is poor here?

---

[163] Al-Ghazali, *Ihya 'uloom ad-deen.*

Poor can mean simply having no money. But there is another meaning of *fuqara* in Arabic. The *fuqara*, the dervishes. They are those who gave up the world because they wanted more of Allah's ﷻ love in the Hereafter. They are not poor in the literal sense: they know themselves to be poor in the presence of God, the Exalted.

The Prophet ﷺ went in Isra and Mi'raaj. Who went in Isra and Mi'raaj other than the Prophet ﷺ? And at that place at the edge of all creation he said:

> *Say (O Muhammad): "I am but a man like you: It is revealed to me by Inspiration, that your god is One god."*[164]

Even though the Prophet ﷺ was that near to the Presence of God, the Exalted, he felt he as though he were nothing compared to that Greatness. That is why Imam Suyuti in his Quranic commentary doesn't say what square-headed people say today: that the Prophet ﷺ said, "I am nothing but a human being." Go beyond that and understand that the Prophet ﷺ is trying to humiliate himself in the presence of his Lord.

Imam Nawawi, in his *Explanation of Sahih Muslim*, explains this verse to mean that when He saw the Lord with the eyes of his head and realized the immense greatness of the Lord he felt shy. He humbled himself in that Presence. Regardless of what anyone says today about purifying Islam for *tawheed*, the only one who is testifying to *tawheed* is Sayyidina Muhammad ﷺ, who reached the Station of *"two bow's-length or nearer."* He, and he alone, bore witness there.

---

[164] Surah Fussilat, (Elucidated), 41:6.

LIGHT OF THE GUIDE

The Inner Search

[A talk to an interfaith group in Oxford, England]

I have just traveled 5,000 miles from San Francisco to go to Morocco to attend a conference and continued on today to be at this meeting in England. I was very surprised when I came and saw the sign on this building—"Friend's House." This means that it is a building that has everyone under one under one roof. Its walls enclose all of us. There are no differences between us here: we are all from one father and one mother. And that is why its name gave me a sign that the people who are attending here and even those who are not attending, are people—friendly and searching for reality.

To find reality, we must be ready to accept it—we must be like that screen up on the stage. Because the screen is white, it can receive any color on its surface and reflect back a full range of hues. If it were black, then we would not able to see anything: the projections of light would be absorbed instead of glowing before us as visible images. Imagine what would be possible if our hearts were this transparent! If our hearts were this pure, we could reflect back a clear image of the universe. We would bring that reality into ourselves and become part of it. We are clearly in the universe and part of it, why not clean our hearts enough to receive its many colors? How can we do this?

I would like to share with you some things I learned from my master.

There comes a point in many peoples lives where they wish to find a spiritual guide. They sense, at some level, that without a guide they would encounter insurmountable obstacles and wander far away from the light. Life can be a confusing and distracting experience, even in the best of times. Many people sense this: they realize that they are traveling in circles; searching and searching; reaching nothing. This first step is a big one. It takes a certain amount of humility to admit that you need an experienced guide—to admit that you are lost and need help. After all, we reason, "Why isn't this life enough in-and-of itself?" Life should be full and every day should be meaningful: family, business, friends, possessions—aren't all these things sufficient? However, in an instant, things can be taken away from us or, more likely, change into something else and lose their taste.

If you were to visit a strange land, filled with high mountains and deep ravines and dark caves, wouldn't you hire a guide to take you through the passes and avoid the more dangerous and slippery paths—a guide who knew the way and had walked there before?

Seeking Reality

People all over the world, at different times, have returned to the inward search. Buddha, when he tasted pain and suffering, sought out realities. Hindus, up to today, are trying to reach realities. Moses ﷺ never reached India or Southeast Asia. Likewise, Jesus ﷺ and Muhammad ﷺ never traveled to those parts of the world. So it means people from there are looking to find reality. Answering such questions is where the role of the guide becomes important: "Why do we exist?", "What is the point of existence?", "Do we merely live to eat and drink?", "Are we here just to get married and have children? Or are we trying to find something higher?"

I was lucky because I came to know my spiritual guide at the age of twelve. He is our master and master of many people here. We call him master or guru: Shaykh Muhammad Nazim Adil al-Haqqani ق, may God, the Exalted, bless him and give him long life, well beyond his 85 years.

About guidance, Mawlana Shaykh Nazim ق once said:

Everyone is created as a creation which can be lighted. If we take a piece of iron, it cannot be lighted, but a candle may be. And each one of the sons of Adam ﷺ, of mankind, is in a condition suitable for lighting.

In our time, those people who are carrying Divine Lights through the Prophet Muhammad ﷺ are still in existence. Therefore, we are in need to follow a holy person, to catch one of them, in order to acquire Divine lights…

Everyone across the globe and the centuries wants to know where we came from and where we are going. There are different methods for finding this guidance. That is why Buddha withdrew from the worldly life and began his meditations. He sought reality and tried his best to move beyond the physical plane. He was the son of a king. He left his family and his kingdom to seek that energy that everything was created from. I am mentioning Buddha as an example, because here was someone looking for the source of reality 2,500 years ago. Just as Buddha was looking for reality, so Jesus ﷺ and Moses ﷺ and Abraham ﷺ and Sayyidina Muhammad ﷺ brought the world closer to reality through religion.

The Heart's Swift Time

What we call reality is what we can see and measure in the universe. We work within the limitations of time, space and energy. Everyone thinks there is a past and a future. But I will say in spirituality there is no past and no future. In fact, there is only the moment we are living in—that is the moment that counts. Because that moment is like the second hand that clicks, moving forward. So what was present, as the second hand of the clock moves forward, becomes past and what was future becomes present. Everything is contained in that instant.

Sufis approach these mysteries with the view that reality never changes. There is a Universal Reality that exists in every one of us. It is a kind of energy that makes it possible for things to appear in creation. Scientists know that the speed of light is 300,000 kilometers per second, a universal constant. What scientists will not tell you is that the speed of the mind is faster than the speed of the light. If I am thinking now "I am on the moon" at that moment, in a fraction of a second I can, in a very real sense, travel to the moon. And if you think you are on the Sun and close your eyes and meditate on this, you might find that with deep concentration you sense its heat. You might also see its light and even penetrate to the source of the solar engine itself. That is faster than anything science contemplates, even faster than light. The sun is far from us, 160,000 kilometers away. If you close your eyes and see yourself in the presence of the Creator—standing, bowing and prostrating—you will feel that Presence immediately as long as your heart is clean like that white screen. Your heart will reflect that image of the Divine Presence; the meditation will carry you there at that instant.

Our focus should be on how we can clean our hearts in order to move forward. A pure heart is like a flying carpet: it can defy gravity and carry us to otherwise inaccessible places. A polished heart is a passport to the wide expanse of the universe. You will notice I am referring to the heart, and not the mind. The mind has its uses, but it is a slow and plodding thing compared to the heart. The heart has wings, and if we learn to use them, we can fly. If you can focus, you can expand the present moment into an extended, vertical experience and climb into the upper realms of the universe. All that is important is the moment you are in, because it is in that very moment that the door leading to the rest of time and space is located. As soon as that moment ends, the next one comes.

Meditate and be present with the moment. The moment you are living in is what counts: when you die all the moments will be gone. You may meditate and focus on a future goal, but in a sense there is no future, there is only the one present.

This is what a guide can bring us: a sense of the present and a way to feel the presence of our Lord, the ruler of space, time and travel. The guide knows the rules of travel and has already studied the maps and scouted the trails. The guide understands the seasonal changes, the risks, the hardships and the signposts of the path. The guide knows that the path leads to the Divine Presence, now matter how roundabout the way may seem.

The Creator—a Beginning

I was speaking to a group in the San Francisco Bay area near Stanford recently. They were young students, in their early twenties. I explained that before discussing anything with them, I wanted to express the presence of the Lord. By this I meant the presence of a superpower. Without belief in a creator, we cannot have a solution. So one of them was very clever, his name was Theo, and he asked, "What do you think about Darwin's Theory?"

I answered, "Of course, we all know about Darwin's Theory. It proposes the evolution, of everything, even humans, saying we developed from monkeys. It is not a discovery, it is a theory. Therefore it has a question mark beside it. Why do we have to involve ourselves in it? If we are coming form monkeys why are they not producing any more human beings from their line? Why did they stop? Or are they producing more and more men and women somewhere in the world?"

He looked at me and said, "You are right, if they once produced men and women they would still be doing that." I said, "Why worry about it, since that is problem of Adam ﷺ and Eve. That is their problem. Let them go to the monkeys and discuss that question of where they came from."

Heaveny Hearing

We have to establish a base that there is a Creator. This is a fundamental element, a starting point for our development. I know most of you are lovely, spiritual people because you have come together in this house in tolerance and friendship. Look around you at all the people from different nationalities and backgrounds, all peacefully listening to the music.

This particular kind of music is the melody of the instruments. [Shaykh Hisham taps a drum]. What do you think about the music that is being made by us, by human beings? And certainly here, this evening, everyone is happy with it, it is very nice. What do you think about the music that the angels make—the sound that the angels create with their movement? Yes, the angels that are around us in this huge universe make their own form of music. Their movement is a heavenly movement, a spiritual movement. People might say, "Why can't we hear it, but we can hear this [he drums]?"

What are these? [Shaykh points to his ears] These are our ears, but in reality what we hear is what reaches our eardrums. The inner ear is what turns the vibrations in the air into what we sense as sound. Our ears, both inner and outer, receive, focus and translate the vibrations into voices, music and even noise from great distances. If we can hear all this, then why can't we hear the angels? It must be because our eardrums are only able to decode only a limited range of vibrations. The inner ear relays the vibrations to the brain at very specific frequencies. Our ears are not able to decode all the other kinds of signals transmitted throughout the universe. Our ears are like a satellite dish. As the signals enter the dish, the small bulb in the center gathers and decodes them to give pictures or sounds.

Satellite dishes are like ears that can pick up all sorts of signals coming from the cosmos. If our ears could be adjusted in a certain way, we could decode these signals and also hear the angels.

The practice of mediation is the special tuning that could help us to hear the angels. I have met many people from different backgrounds and beliefs who can hear voices when they purify their hearing. Whether they are Muslims, Jews, Zen Buddhists or Hindus, some people are able to clear their receivers to the point that their ears have no limitations or fuzziness when receiving signals from great distances. Ultimately, these signals emanated from one point: call it what you will, the Big Bang, the Source of creation, the Creator. The signals are coming from the Creator, a superpower, a source of energy informing the entire universe. What would we be missing if, throughout the span of our lives, we ignored these signals? What would we lose if we pursue only material things, our pleasures and possessions? An important part of our lives should be spent in the pursuit of understanding the influences that come to us from the center of the universe, the life and the light that endlessly flows towards us.

To lose this chance is a great loss indeed. I am not speaking of hell and punishment. Is God going to send us to hellfire? How can a creator create and then say "I am sending you to hellfire?" What is the point of that?

Part of our challenge is to love the Creator that we cannot directly see. That is the easy part. But the great difficulty is to love each other. To extend our hands to help each other, to visit each other, to throw away hate from our hearts to throw away anger and negative energy from our hearts. When we look inward, not outward, we begin to realize that we are seeing our own faults in those around us. In fact, that is how we are able to recognize them in the first place.

The Inn-side Story

Grandshaykh Nazim ق, quoting his Shaykh, said:

Our Prophet ﷺ says, "Happiness is for him who is occupied with correcting his own faults, for it keeps him from looking to another's faults." Clear? It is a very big sin to look to others' faults, and to try to harm people. All troubles, all unsolvable problems, come after looking to another's faults. A bad habit indeed!

When we look in we find the inn, with the double 'en', the house where we stay you find everything. And what is that inn? You find the house, the place you belong, the reality, that place which centers your existence. That is why God, the Exalted, said:

Neither heavens nor earth contain Me, but the heart of My believing servant Contains Me.[165]

How can you contain the Lord in your heart? The Lord is found inside you where "The house of the believer is the house of the Lord."[iv] God created us from one father and one mother and then established us in many nations. We must try to know and understand each other. This most difficult of tasks must be approached with sincerity and piety. If we do not know one another, suspicion and anger can grow. It can begin with simply listening to one another, and trying to detect the common threads

---

[165] Razi, Suyuti, Jarrahi, Ibn 'Iraq.

of speech known to all. One such language is music because the human response to harmony and rhythm is inborn.

That is why we encourage students around the world to play music that can help them focus more inwardly than outwardly. Music can transcend cultural differences. Listen to these beautiful sounds now and watch the graceful whirling dance of Shaykh Ahmad Dede and his group. Why do they whirl? Everyone knows that Jalaluddin Rumi was the master of masters and he was whirling with his students. Why was he whirling? Is it as a show or a movement or a meditation or a demonstration of power and energy? Why are we whirling? Many people might ask this question, they might ask Shaykh Ahmad also. People from all over the world travel to the Mevlana festival that takes place in Konya each year. But many people don't know why Rumi was whirling.

Why Whirl?

Once a Bedouin from the desert came to the Prophet Muhammad ﷺ when he was giving his Friday services. He had no clothes, possessed nothing, and came barefooted and naked. He asked the Prophet ﷺ, "When is the day of resurrection?" The Prophet said, "It is a long journey. What have you prepared for it?"

He looked at people are around the Prophet ﷺ and saw all kinds of people who were intent, struggling to remember God, fast and observe the prayers. And he was standing at the doorway and asking, "When is Resurrection Day?"

The Prophet ﷺ asked, "What have you prepared for that day?" He said, "I have not prepared much, neither of prayer nor fasting. I have only prepared one thing." Everyone was waiting to hear what that man would say. He was an illiterate man with no clothes except to cover his private parts, and no shoes. Everyone wanted to know what he would say.

He said, "What I am preparing is my Lord's love. This is what I have in myself. I love Him and I love you and I love all prophets who came before you."

So what do you think the Prophet ﷺ said? He said, "It is enough! You don't kneed anything else. Out of happiness on hearing this, Sayyidina Abu Bakr ؓ was whirling in the presence of the Prophet ﷺ.

Jalaluddin Rumi, who was a great scholar said in his famous poem, and I am translating:

> I don't know myself.
> I don't know what I am.
> It might be many people know what they are
> but I don't know myself.
> I don't know if I am a Muslim,
> I don't know if I am a Zoroastrian;
> I don't know if I am a Christian or a Jew.

So he was whirling. What happens when one of you turns? What happens to his clothes? They move up, turning in a speed that is equivalent to the speed of his body. It is enough.

If he reaches a higher speed it will create more energy. If he keeps whirling at a higher and higher speed, up to 500 mph or 800 kilometers per hour, what will happen? Like an airplane he will fly. Because when you turn it creates energy. When you create energy it pulls you up; there is no more affect of gravity to pull you down. You will no longer be attracted to earth—rather you will be attracted to heavens. So when Jalaluddin Rumi was taken up with a speed that took him up to the heavens. We are not Jalaluddin Rumi else we would ascend as well. That is what the companions did after they heard the Prophet tell the Bedouin, "It is enough." That is why it is said in Arabic *"yuhshar al-maru ma' man ahab*—every person will be resurrected with the one that he or she loves."

When you love the Lord you will be resurrected in His Presence. When you love the Creator you will be with the Creator—that is the hadith. But loving the Lord is easy, because your Lord created you with His Love to you. How will you not love Him? But loving His servants is more difficult. When you achieved the Presence of the Lord, you will love the creation. If you love your wife or mother or father or son or daughter you seek to be with that family in the Divine Presence. If you hate people and introduce hate around the world you will be far from God's mercy. Those who are creating hate towards any country or towards any people are doing something wrong. You are trying to take advantage of a political issue to fight everyone.

We are Sufi people, we forgive everyone.

I was at a Sufi conference and one professor spoke and said something which made me so happy. His 90th birthday is coming in May. That is Bernard Lewis. He said, "The Sufis teach people around the world to tolerate each other." And that is what is wanted. But the Sufis, more than that, not only tolerate everyone they also accept everyone, and that is a far higher station.

Whatever we see or hear we try to digest. It means everyone here is like a flower in a magnificent garden. When you look at a garden made from only one variety of flowers it doesn't give much taste. But when you look at garden with hundreds of different flowers and colors it keeps you looking and looking and you wonder, "Who made this?"

May God forgive us all and guide us all.

ASCEND TO THE LIGHT

Obey Allah, obey the Prophet ﷺ and obey those in authority among you.[166]

Countless Stars

[A talk given at a home in the French countryside]

If you can put off the light a little bit. Look up! Can you count these stars?

[Shaykh Hisham points up to an array of stars painted on the ceiling.]

We are beginning a journey and we will be very happy if that journey brings us to a good place. Everyone here is happy when hearing music. That music has been created by human beings. Everyone here is very happy to hear this music of praise, for it encourages us to feel closer to Our Lord by reminding us of the Greatness of the Divine Presence. So, as we put the lights off, all these stars appear, showing their existence. I challenge anyone to count them. Although they have been painted by a human being, I ask anyone here if he or she count them all? Shaykh Amanullah, do you know how many there are? Shaykh 'Abd Allah, can you count how many? Shaykh Jamaluddin, how many? Can you count them? I can count them. I know how many there are. They are 1,271,000. If you do not believe me, go count them.

---

[166] Suratu 'n-Nisa, (Women), 4:59.

This means we cannot count them. Today, astronomers have estimated that this universe contains at least six billion galaxies, and every galaxy contains eighty billion stars. So, when we look up at night, we see the stars. Why only at night? Because, the darkness of the night signifies that when we isolate ourselves from the life of this *dunya*, this world. Then you can begin to see the light that God, the Exalted, has created in the Universe.

When you are not seeking the desires and pleasures of this world and begin to focus your whole heart and mind on the Divine Presence, then the light of these different manifestations which appears in these stars will be displayed to you, and you can begin to see that and identify them. When you leave *dunya*, the worldly life, *akhira*, the Afterlife, opens. When you enter the afterlife, visible light disappears and another light emerges. This is similar to the changing light around the time of dawn. As the distant stars fade away, the local star, the Sun, floods the sky with its light. This means that when you leave behind *hubb ad-dunya*, love for the world, *hubb al-akhirah*, love of the hereafter begins to appear, like these stars appear at night. The more you begin to reflect on the afterlife, the light that only appears faintly will drop. When the sun shines, your heart will open up, and the light of God, the Exalted, *"Allah is the light of the heavens and the earth."*[167], enters as the Prophet ﷺ said, Allah said [in a holy hadith], "Neither My heavens nor My earth can contain Me, but the heart of my believing servant contained Me."

Guides in Ascension

Everyone is searching for the reality through his journey or her journey for the Hereafter. Someone will find these stars. There are a limited number of stars, limited amounts of light. Some will find the moon, which represents a higher capacity for light. Others

---

[167] Suratu 'n-Nur, (The Light), 24:35.

will seek a guide who, like today's astronomers, tries to see to the edge of our galaxy and beyond. They are not able to see that tremendous without a special telescope. In a sense, the guide is like a spiritual Hubble telescope: with his heart's vision he can guide you through the darkness of this world to bring you not only to see the stars, but to take you forward into a higher level of enlightenment. He can take you to the real light of the Sun that never sets; a sun that is always shining.

The guide who is using his heart's vision is always in the presence of the Divine and so always knows how to guide you. He doesn't leave you with the stars, but takes you to the higher level of enlightenment by taking you to the sun that never sets. Such a sun has no sunset, it is always up. The light that comes from Sayyidina Muhammad ﷺ, that unique light that God, the Exalted, manifests to the Prophet ﷺ is, in turn, radiated on to humanity. God, the Exalted, manifests Himself through His Beautiful Names which pass through the Prophet ﷺ to us. This is how we can all share in the light that the Prophet ﷺ conducts to us directly from the Presence of His Lord ﷻ. The extent to which you share in this light depends on how far you accept the guidance of your master, shaykh or guru.

People who try to use their minds alone will fall down. If you want to go to a hotel, a restaurant, or any particular place, you may ask people hundreds of time to give you directions. Today, they are doing on-line maps to guide people to their destinations.

The same voice is heard in cars equipped with the latest GPS systems. Why do we believe that lady or that man on the guide tool? Blindly we go, we never ask a question: "Take a left! Take a right!" And if you pose a question, they don't answer you, because they know you are wrong. And if you don't listen to them and take a wrong direction, they immediately say, "Turn back!" or they change the routing. This is because they have are using the mind given them by their creator.

In contrast, a spiritual guide will use the heart, rather than the mind, as the primary orientation. If he tells you, "Go this way, you are not happy" you begin to think, "no, this way is better," or "that way is better." You begin to think and think and think and think until finally you fall.

How many times during our life with our guide, Shaykh Muhammad Nazim Adil Al-Haqqani ق have we failed, and how many times did he say "go this way," and we went the other way. The important thing is to listen and obey. "*Isma'oo wa a'oo, fa idha awaytum fantafi'u*—listen and take heed. After you have taken heed then you will benefit." Prophet Muhammad ﷺ and all other prophets followed that way without fail. Archangel Gabriel comes to them, and they listen and obey. Never in the Holy Qur'an, did Prophet ﷺ, pose a question to Gabriel. He was always listening and obeying. He is the role model, the perfect one, the Seal of Messengers, the faultless human being.

In an authentic chain of transmission, the guide was trained by his guide and, in turn, his guide was trained by his, and so on all the way back to the Prophet ﷺ. Such a chain must be unbroken through the generations—every link must be strong and true. In our Naqshbandi-Haqqani Sufi Way, between the Prophet ﷺ and our Shaykh, there are thirty-eight individuals. This line goes to the Prophet ﷺ through Sayyidina Abu Bakr ﷺ And then from one guide to another, all along the chain, each inheritor transmitting knowledge, which is beyond all description to his successor. To even begin to understand what they are opening for us would take many sessions.

Ongoing Ascensions

The Prophet ﷺ made the ascension to the Divine Presence during his lifetime. But the Prophet ﷺ did not have only one ascension. Rather he is in continuous ascension, in every moment, and as he is ascending he is acquiring new knowledge, and he is giving this ever fresh and growing knowledge to the Community through his inheritors. That is why this knowledge cannot be found in books. What was written before is not as fresh as what emerges today. There is much good knowledge in books, but it is not going to take you to the sun, it might take you to the stars. Because the sun is always *mutajaddidah*, in a continuous explosion, a renewal of knowledge.

A star might die, and you still see its light. But, in reality that star no longer exists; it already died. There is no more star, but because it is traveling through that lightspeed frame—that distance through time—because the light is moving in a speed of 300.000 kilometers per second, so that light is still coming, but it source has been extinguished.

The Sun, on the other hand, is always *mutajaddidah*, always boiling in a nuclear reaction of energy, a continuous formation of new energy. This is a good description of *awliyaullah*, the saints, they are always in a continuous formation and evolution of knowledge that comes to them as the Prophet ﷺ ascends eternally upwards. This is because they are ascending with him. As they receive from him, they pass it along to their followers.

If you eat this date here on the table, you will be happy. If it had been sitting here for a year, however, you wouldn't like it. It would be old and rotten. You want a nice fresh date. *Awliyaullah* are like that. They bring you fresh knowledge.

Throughout history, those who were looking for different ways to achieve enlightenment did so in forms appropriate to

195

their times. But we are in the here and now. We need knowledge that works for these times. That's why the Prophet ﷺ said, "I'm fresh and alive in my grave."

That means he reaches the Ummah immediately. He is alive "Whenever someone makes *salawaat* on me, God, the Exalted, returns my soul to me and I make *salawaat* back to that person."[168] This means, as Imam Suyuti said, "The soul of the Prophet ﷺ never left his body."

Look at this old tape recorder. Maybe it's based on old technology and out of date. Some people might like using vintage machines like this. Of course, it's ok, but it has its limitations. Maybe it can hold only an hour of recordings, while a new iPod can hold hundreds of hours. You can still enjoy old recordings, but with the new MP players, the sound is better and the capacity is superior. In spirituality, you need the higher capacity. The *awliyaullah* of yesterday are "on my head." But, the knowledge being given to *awliyaullah* today is so much faster than what came in earlier times.

Modern *Awliya*, Modern Powers

Look at this cup. You can fill it with only a few milliliters of water. Now this bottle, on the other hand, can take several times what you put in the cup. If you go to the shaykh who has the knowledge of one cup, it's going to be one cup. There was no technology in his time to make a bottle. Today we have big plastic bottles. You didn't have plastic bottles before. God, the Exalted, gives *awliyaullah* today strong powers that can stretch your heart with one drop from their vision. They can make your heart bigger than the universe and fill it with heavenly knowledge. Yesterday's

---

[168] Narrated by Abu Hurayra in *Sunan* Abu Dawud, Ibn 'Asakir, *Mukhtasar Tarikh Dimashq*, Ahmad, *Musnad*, Abu Nu'aym, *Akhbar Asbahan*.

awliyaullah didn't have that sort of power, they cannot stretch as far today's *awliyaullah* can stretch. And, don't say "Oh, what you are saying? We have a lot of big *walis*!" With respect, of course, we have big *walis*. But, big *walis* of yesterday are different than big *walis* of today.

Yesterday, there were no cars. They were using camels and horses. Is it not so? There was a certain speed of travel. They didn't have planes or rockets. Today, there is a higher level of science, which Prophet ﷺ didn't mention directly. It was kept secret, hidden in the Holy Qur'an and the Holy Hadith, because it had a certain time to be opened. It is open today for *awliyaullah*. This is why today's scientists are finding that information in the Holy Qur'an and Holy Hadith anticipated many of today's scientific breakthroughs. The Prophet veiled them fourteen hundred years ago and didn't mention it to the Sahaba or to *awliyaullah* from before. Today, however, he is revealing these secrets to the *awliya*.

The Nine Points

There are some things that Mawlana Shaykh Muhamamd Nazim 'Adil Al-Haqqani ق, may Allah ﷻ give him long life, allow us to speak of. But, there are also things that he doesn't allow. Grandshaykh, Shaykh 'Abd Allah al-Faiz ad-Daghestani ق, may, God, the Exalted, bless his soul, allowed certain things and not others. This is because people's hearts cannot fill more than one cup. And also, that's why you sometimes cannot give more, or else people will not be able to understand—it becomes too much. Say, for example the knowledge of Central Asia. There was a master known by the name Gurdjieff. He was looking to find reality, and he developed a system based on the Enneagram. In the course of his journeys he visited many of these Central Asian saints, and learned certain things according to his capacity.

Eventually he came up with the idea of the series of the nine points. He didn't know at that time, around eighty years ago, where this system of nine points originated. He categorized them as different levels of spiritual attainment. The object was to achieve a high level of balance and equilibrium. He arranged these in a linear fashion: by different levels of attainment. But why linear? Were Gurdjieff alive today, I would ask him, "How did this linear structure come into existence?" The origin of a straight line is what? It is a dot. If you look at that dot with your ordinary vision, all you can see is a small a dot. If you look at it with a magnifying glass, you see a bigger dot. If you put it under a microscope, it becomes a universe. This means, everything comes from a circle. The dot is a circle.

So, the Enneagram in reality is not a line, but a circle. So, when you put it on a circle, then we will be able to understand the relationships between the points. In the midst of these nine points is the center, the place that radiates energy out to the edge of the circle.

But where did the idea of the nine points come from in the first place? From here. Look at your hands! You will see two numbers on each hand. One side reflects the other. You can discern the number eight and the number one. The numerals are Arabic. One hand reads as eighteen, the other hand, a mirror image, says eighty one. In numerology, you would combine these numbers as eight plus one, or nine. The other side yields the same sum, adding one and eight. Similarly, eighteen plus eighty one equals ninety nine, and nine plus nine equals eighteen again, and one plus eight gives us nine, yet again. The origin of the Enneagram is encrypted in each of our hands. This system of nine is written on each one of us. We'll explain this another time. All the reality and knowledge that you want to know about your personality is in the hands. That's why people, palmists, can read hands.

Look at the numbers! What are these numbers? In which language? Does anyone know? [Audience: Arabic] Aha... that's wrong! It's Hindi, Indian. And the Arabic numbers are what we are using here in the French language, or in the English language. I will leave it here, and we'll explain next time.

Wa min Allah at-Tawfiq. Bi-hurmatil Habib Al-Fatihah.

THE GREAT GIFT

Salam alaykum wa rahmatullahi wa barakutuh—peace be upon you and God's Mercy and Blessings. *Alhamdulillah,* praise God we are very happy that we are celebrating the Prophet Muhammad's ﷺ birthday. All praise be to God who guided us to this, for we would never have been guided if not for the guidance of Allah.

The Light of Mercy

Over the last month, I have been traveling in the Far East, Morocco and Europe. *Subhanallah,* I found that in every country there are preparations for the Milad an-Nabi. The Prophet ﷺ was described as *"rahmatan lil-alameen—mercy to all creation."*[169] I am now asking myself, what is the meaning of mercy to all creation?

What is the meaning of *rahmat* then, since God, the Exalted, is *arham ar-rahimeen*—the Most Merciful of the merciful. *Rahma,* mercy, is coming from one of the Beautiful Divine Names and the Prophet ﷺ was dressed with that name. This means that anything that gives us something in our life, or the hereafter, anything that we feel around us, is mercy. If we breathe the air in the room it is mercy; if we eat it is mercy; if we speak it is mercy. Since He is mercy to all creation, it means that God, the Exalted, want Him to be the carrier of the mercy. It means we are enjoying *Muhammadun Rasulullah* in every moment of our life. That is one way to express the meaning of mercy to all creation.

It is not enough to say simply *"He is a mercy to humanity."* Mercy to humanity for what? It means that if it were not for him

---

[169] Suratu 'l-Anbiya, (The Prophets), 21:107.

200

God, the Exalted, would not have created anything. It means that for him Adam ﷺ was created. The Prophet ﷺ said, "I was a Prophet ﷺ when Adam ﷺ was between clay and water." The Prophet of what? If he was a Prophet at that time, it means he was present, in order for Allah's Beautiful Names and Attributes to be manifested on Sayyidina Muhammad ﷺ before the creation of Adam ﷺ.

A famous contemporary scholar, Shaykh Jesus ﷺ al-Mani al-Humayri, has written concerning the book *al-Musannaf*, a very famous book of hadith by the scholar ʿAbd ar-Razzaq as-Sanʿani. He began that book with the hadith about the first thing that God, the Exalted, created, which was the light of the Prophet ﷺ.

There is a great deal of controversy surrounding this hadith today. The hadith had been lost, but now a copy has been located in India. It explains how the first thing that God, the Exalted, created was the light of the Prophet ﷺ. Then God, the Exalted, created Adam ﷺ to carry that light. That is the meaning of the verse in the holy Qur'an concerning this original light.

How long ago did the universe start? How long ago did the Big Bang occur? The scientists say about sixteen billion years ago. How can we speak about the greatness of the Prophet ﷺ who was created before the Big Bang? Sayyidina Muhammad cannot be described by any human being. The only one who can describe Sayyidina Muhammad ﷺ is the Creator, and He alone. God, the Exalted, said:

We have honored the Children of Adam and we provided for them from good things.[170]

Islam is Mercy. Islam is Light. The Prophet is the connection, the bearer of both, from time before time, the Prophet ﷺ brings the

---

[170] Suratu 'l-Isra, (The Night Journey), 17:70.

light of mercy. Before the Big Bang, before Adam, before the foundations of the Universe were laid, the Prophet ﷺ was given the light of mercy for all humanity. While these gifts are unique, singularly the destiny of the Prophet ﷺ, his very existence and position represent an invitation to all of humanity.

The Divine Invitation

When God, the Exalted, caused the birth of the Prophet ﷺ, what kind of decoration did He make? Today just now they gave me an invitation to go to a conference, written in a very nice way. When God, the Exalted, asked Sayyidina Muhammad ﷺ to come to *dunya*, what kind of invitation he did he give to his mother, what kind of roses did He send for that birth? What kind of decorations did he put in heaven for that event, for the honor of Sayyidina Muhammad ﷺ?

Allahu Akbar, God, the Exalted, is Greatest, the Highest, and He gave greatness to the Prophet ﷺ by raising his name with His own Name. He gave Sayyidina Muhammad ﷺ an exalted level: not something low. You cannot say *La ilaha illa-Llah* without saying *Muhammadun Rasulullah*.

Consider Judgment Day. We will arrive at that point where: "Adam ﷺ and everyone other than Adam ﷺ will be under my flag on the Day of Rising."[171] We will present ourselves to Sayyidina Muhammad ﷺ and he will login into his computer just like the computers of today. Imagine the things he might see in his computer files, records on each one of us. "O, you were a good one, while that one was busy defaming me, rejecting celebrating my birthday!"

I was in London and we had a big concert, whirling dervishes and so on, and we had the Naqshbandi chanting group playing

---

[171] *Musnad* Ahmad.

and singing and the time finished. The time finished but the audience jumped up and said "continue!"

There is a hadith about Judgment Day in Imam Bukhari's *Adab al-mufrad*. It relates that on Judgment Day God, the Exalted, will give Prophet Muhammad ﷺ permission to go into *sajda*, prostration. In prostration Allah will inspire him to make invocations that would never have been opened before— completely new invocations.

If we read the *Du'a al-maathuraat*, that we learned from prophet through the 124,000 Sahaba, all of them learned different invocations. That means that God, the Exalted, Who is the Creator, al-Khaliq, in every moment is creating new creation. There are levels being created, there are attributes being manifested as levels are being created—there is no stop to creation.

That is why when He goes into prostration, He will be doing invocations that no one has been given before. Then God, the Exalted, will say, "raise your head, *sal tu'ta*, and ask, you will be given." The Prophet ﷺ will raise his head and say, "O my Lord, give me my nation, *Ummattee*." And Allah would grant his intercession immediately for one-third of the Ummah. There would be no account for one third of humanity.

Who will the Prophet take into Paradise with no account? Perhaps he will take the lovers, perhaps others.

Then He will go into prostration another time and make an invocation that has never before been given. Then God, the Exalted, will say "raise your head and ask, you will be given, *sa'l-t'uta*."

Then He will go into prostration a third time and take whoever has an atom's weight of faith into Paradise. Sinners or lovers and non-sinner and non-lovers.

And then all of the remaining souls will be allowed to enter Paradise.

We are *Ummatan marhoumah*—a community granted mercy. When we celebrate his birthday we are celebrating his love for us. Our love for him is like epsilon before infinity. We are the atom and he is the universe.

O Muslims, don't look at the past! There is no past. Don't look at the future! There is no future. There is only the present. When you look at the watch and it clicks forward one second, that moment becomes past and the one future becomes present. So everything is present. There is nothing you can say was my past or this will be my fit in the way of Sayyidina Muhammad ﷺ or in the way of your desires?

Oh Muslims! Don't think that God, the Exalted, gave the Prophet ﷺ a small gift.

God, the Exalted, sent Gabriel ؇ to invite Sayyidina Muhammad ﷺ to Paradise in a very special way. He dressed the Prophet ﷺ in order to raise him beyond the physical structure of the universe. He raised him to the Station of *"two bow's-length or nearer"* Is *qaaba qawsayni* in our universe? In this universe where there are six billion galaxies and in each one 80 billion stars? Is it In the universe or outside? It must be outside the universe for God, the Exalted, cannot be in something created. Therefore, He took Sayyidina Muhammad ﷺ beyond creation. He reached *"Qaaba qawsayni aw adna—two bow's-length or nearer."* Two bow's length is one hand or two hands. God, the Exalted, said *"aw adna."*

For you speakers of Arabic here, what is the meaning of *adna*? It means "less." There is no description of how much less. Less might be one centimeter, or one inch or one millimeter. So Sayyidina Muhammad ﷺ was very close to the Divine Presence. This was an invitation to Paradise like none other, before or after.

God, the Exalted, gave the Prophet ﷺ directly from His Grandeur, from His Greatness and from His Beautiful Names and Attributes. Don't think there are only ninety-nine Names and that is it. This is what people are reciting. In reality, God, the Exalted, created universes with an infinite number of names and attributes.

Have real love of Muhammad ﷺ in your hearts. Then fear nothing. Those who love Sayyidina Muhammad ﷺ are the *awliyaullah*: they have nothing to fear in this life and the next.

TIME OF THE MAHDI

Two Kinds of Faith

The Prophet ﷺ told his Sahaba that the Mahdi ؏ is coming. It is related that when the Prophet ﷺ said to his Companions that the Dajjal, the Antichrist, was near, they actually thought that he was lurking in a nearby palm grove. [172]

> 1400 years ago, in explanation of Surat al-ʿAsr, the Prophet ﷺ said, "If my Ummah will be on the right path it will be given an age by God, the Exalted, of one day and if it deviates then it will be given a life of half a day *and verily a day in the measure of God is like one thousand years of what you reckon.'"* [22:47][173]

Therefore, within sixty years we expect Mahdi ؏ to come, as will Prophet Jesus ؏ and the Dajjal.

This year is very heavy and carrying a lot of issues that are going to change the way the world is. Leaders and outlooks will change. *Awliyaullah* are ready for Israfil to blow the trumpet. It means to blow in excitement, happiness, that God, the Exalted, has given permission to Sayyidina Muhammad ﷺ to give permission for Sayyidina Mahdi's appearance. *Awliyaullah* are expecting in the very near future that Mahdi ؏ will appear to everyone.

---

[172] Ibn ʿAsakir in his *Sahih*.
[173] Al-Munawi cites it in *Fayd al-Qadir* from Shaykh Muhyi al-Din Ibn ʿArabi.

That is why Mawlana recently said, "I am reaching over eighty years and I received a promise that I would be with the Mahdi ﷺ and the *awliyaullah* in Arafat. We were all asking with one voice for the Mahdi ﷺ to appear because there is too much *dhulm*. Earth cannot carry any more or it will explode."

There are basically two kinds of people: those who have faith and belief in spirituality and spiritual knowledge, and those who use only their minds. Like these intellectuals who only believe in what their minds tells them.

Sufi people are waiting for information that comes to them from the Prophet ﷺ. The Jews are preparing for the Messiah, the evangelical Christians are preparing for Jesus and some Muslims believe and are preparing for the promised Saviour to come. Such leaders have been inspired for that. Just as the Christians and Jews preparing for an expected savior, the Muslims should be as well. We must prepare for the Mahdi.

Predictions of the Last Days

Sayyidina al-Mahdi ﷺ has been described in over 40-50 hadith of the Prophet ﷺ. All of them authentic, from the Sunni traditions. No one can deny these hadith. In 1980, when the false Mahdi ﷺ appeared in Mecca and they took al-Haraam, the Hijazi people began to ask about al-Mahdi ﷺ and said to the Saudi government "you never told us about Mahdi."

You find a lot hadith about Mahdi ﷺ in ibn Majah and in Abu Dawud but not in *Sahih Bukhari*. The scholar Muhammad 'Ali Sabouni compiled these hadith of Mahdi ﷺ in one book and of these I put many in my book, *The Approach of Armageddon*. In one of those sayings, the Prophet ﷺ said, "If this world has just one day remaining Allah will extend that day until a man comes. He is from me, (or from my family). His name is like my name, (i.e. Muhammad), his father's name is like my father's name (i.e. 'Abd

Allah). He fills the earth with equality and justice, as it has been filled with injustice and oppression."[174]

That is one among many hadith he gave. Sayyidina Al-Mahdi ﷺ will appear before the appearance of the Masih al-Dajjal, the Anti-Christ. Most of these signs that the Prophet mentioned have already occurred: you can see read about them in my book. The biggest recent sign was anticipated when the Prophet ﷺ said, "The Hour will not be established until a fire emerges from the land of Hijaz which will light up the necks of the camels in Basra.[175]

When they asked the Prophet ﷺ to bless Najd he said, "Oh Allah bless us in our Sham and in our Yemen." They repeated the request to bless Najd two more times and on the third time the Prophet ﷺ said, "Over there will come forth earthquakes and dissension, from there will come two horns of Satan."[176] Ibn 'Umar ﷺ related, "I saw the Messenger of Allah ﷺ pointing to the East and he then said, 'Look! The dissension is from here, the dissension is from here. From there will arise the horn of Satan.'"[177] where directly east of Madina is Najd and Basra, Iraq.

And the Prophet ﷺ said, "One of the signs of the Last Days is to see the barefooted naked Bedouin competing to build high buildings."[178] And now the biggest high rises are where? In Riyadh. They are bigger than the World Trade Center; even bigger than the two towers in Malaysia. That is why you see between these Arab princes trying to say "my building is higher." All this is happening now. It foretells the coming of the Mahdi. And when he appears, he will first move from Mecca to Madina. First people will make *baya'*, initiation, in Mecca and then move to Madina

---

[174] Tirmidhi, Abu Dawud.
[175] Bukhari and Muslim.
[176] *Sunan Abu Dawud.*
[177] Bukhari and Muslim.
[178] *Sahih Muslim.*

where he makes takbir that everyone will hear. With the power of only saying *"Bismillahi 'r-Rahmani 'r-Raheem"* he will move to Sham, as the Prophet ﷺ said, "How will you be when the son of Maryam (Jesus, Jesus) descends upon you and your Imām (Mahdī) is among you (leading the prayer)?"[179]

The Imam is Sayyidina Mahdi, not those imams who wear jeans today standing in every mosque. He is from that line of the twelve imams, and he will appear in *minaratun bayda*, the white minaret, at the Ummayyad Mosque in Damascus. He will make *takbir* from there and that *takbir* will stop a huge war that will be taking place around the world at that time. That is according to the hadith "The Hour will not appear until there will be two enormous groups fighting each other in a colossal battle, (and) their issue is one."...[180]

Samuel Huntington has written that we are seeing a clash of civilizations, which is actually a clash of ideas, and no one knows what the outcome will be. However, the Mahdi ؑ will come in the middle of that fire and pull that secret out. Everything will stop when he pronounces:: *"Allahu Akbar, Allahu Akbar Allahu Akbar."* Then, with the second *takbir*, with *"Allahu Akbar, Allahu Akbar Allahu Akbar,"* every believer will find himself in Damascus with Mahdi. Then, the third time he repeats *"Allahu Akbar, Allahu Akbar Allahu Akbar,"* he will declare an expedition to retrieve the *amanaat*, the trust, of the Prophet ﷺ in Istanbul. After succeeding in this, Mahdi ؑ will declare that the Dajjal has appeared in the area of a big mountain near Sham called Douma. That mountain is the *hadd*, the limit, beyond which the Dajjal cannot pass because at that time Sayyidina Gabriel will lower his wing and block him at that spot.

---

[179] Bukhari and Muslim.
[180] Bukhari and Muslim.

I want to emphasize we are people who don't carry weapons, we don't even carry a knife. Sayyidina Mahdi ؏ does not come with anything, he does not carry weapons, he only uses *Allahu Akbar* that cuts through every difficulty. Make sure you don't carry a weapon, even a knife. I have never carried a knife, though it is a *Sunnah* to do so. Mawlana Shaykh Nazim ق used to carry a knife when he was younger but now he does not. But his knife was something small like this. With the coming of the Mahdi, physical knives will be useless.

I Left Two Weighty Matters

The hadith "I have left among you two weighty matters by holding fast to which, you shall never be misguided: Allah's Book and the Sunnah of His Prophet."[181] Is one side of an equation. The right side is balanced against the left side, another hadith: "I have left among you …Allah's Book—a rope extended down from the heaven to the earth—and my mantle (*'itra*), the People of my House."[182]

Since the common term in both is the Holy Book, it means the Prophet ﷺ is saying, "my *Sunnah* is the way" and "the way is my family." It means my family is the *Sunnah*.

This means that anyone not following the family of the Prophet ﷺ is not following the way of Prophet ﷺ. That is why I mentioned that verse yesterday:

Say: "If ye do love Allah, Follow me: Allah will love you
and forgive you your sins: For Allah is Oft-Forgiving,
Most Merciful."[183]

---

[181] al-Bayhaqi in *al-Sunan al-kubra*, al-Hakim, Malik in his *Muwatta*.
[182] Tirmidhi and al-Hakim.
[183] Surat Aali-'Imraan, (The Family of 'Imraan), 3:31.

What, in this instance, does "follow me" mean? It means that if you hold onto the rope, you go on the ascension. Hold the rope of his family and you will be ascending with him as he is always in *mi'raj*. That is why the verse says:

> *O Prophet! Truly We have sent thee as a Witness, a Bearer of Glad Tidings, and Warner, and as one who summons [all men] to God by His leave, and as a light-giving beacon.*[184]

He is calling people to his way, and holding up a lamp of light.

Consider what *shaahidan* must mean. The usual explanation is that the Prophet ﷺ is a witness on people: he can see what they are doing. Could it really have so limited a meaning? In the larger sense, witness here refers to perceiving the creation of the light of Muhammad ﷺ, seeing the manifestation of the Beautiful Names and Attributes that created the whole universe. He is witnessing the Big Bang, He is witnessing the creation of Adam ﷺ, He is witnessing *'uloom al-awwaleen wa al-akhireen*—the knowledge of the Firsts and the Lasts.

He is not witnessing in the petty sense of seeing the shortcomings of humanity. He sees and knows the unseen. Where our eyes fail us, his eyes see beyond. Where light eludes us, he brings more light.

May God, the Exalted, forgive us and give blessings for this Mawlid and dress us with His Beautiful Names and Attributes.

Bi hurmati 'l-Fatiha.

---

[184] Suratu 'l-Ahzaab, (The Confederates), 33:45.

NOT ALL KNOWLEDGE TASTES THE SAME

Imam Bukhari

Bismillahi 'r-Rahmani 'r-Raheem—In the name of God, the Compassionate, the Merciful.

I was recently in Bukhara where there is a school there called al-madrasah Mir Arab. It was named after an Arab emir. That area is also famous for Imam Isma'il al-Bukhari. He is known for compiling the most reliable and widely accepted ahadith of the Prophet ﷺ Sahih al-Bukhari. He was named Bukhari because he originated from Bukhara. His masjid was there, in the Mir Arab School. He is buried in Samarqand, but his school was in Bukhara.

They told me a story there about how many people could fit in his mosque. After the Soviet Union collapsed they rebuilt it along the lines of the original and it could hold five thousand people. But the courtyard of the mosque and the rest of the school can fit another ten thousand people. They say that in the time of Sayyidina Isma'il al-Bukhari, the congregation would swell to twenty-five thousand. When he would read the hadith everyone could hear clearly. Of course, they had no microphones then. Today a sound system is indispensable at any large gathering. But al-Bukhari had no such device and yet everyone, all twenty-five thousand souls, could hear every word he said.

God, the Exalted, sends His loyal servants what they need for each occasion. However, no such provision is made for those who are not interested. God, the Exalted, gives things to those who are on the way of Shari'at an-Nabi that He does not give to others. God, the Exalted, gives according to the progress and accomplishment of the 'abd, the servanthood. If Allah's ﷻ 'abd is going on *siraat al-mustaqeem*, the straight path, and His knowledge is being spread, He will give the power of hundreds of microphones to that person's voice. Such a voice could reach from east to west. Imam Bukhari reached all twenty-five thousand people at his association. How could this be?

This is the reality of the hadith *qudsi*, in which God said:

My servant continues to draw near to Me with voluntary worship so that I shall love him. When I love him, I am his hearing with which he hears, his sight with which he sees, his hands with which he strikes and his foot with which he walks. Were he to ask (something) of Me I would surely give it to him; and were he to ask Me for refuge, I would surely grant him it.[185]

He said "approach Me through <u>voluntary worship</u>," He did not say "approach Me through obligations." There are obligations, which you must observe. But it is better to do them out of love rather than by force. You are obliged to observe the prayers and fasting. But *nawafil* means voluntary. If you don't do them you are not written as a sinner, but also you are not written as a lover. The one who does the *nawafil* is a lover of Sayyidina Muhammad ﷺ and God, the Exalted, loves the Prophet Muhammad ﷺ.

If you observe the voluntary practices, God, the Exalted, will love you for following the Prophet's ﷺ example. Such things as wearing a beard, a head cap, doing the *Sunnah* prayers before and after the *fard* obligatory prayers such as Dhuhr and Asr; praying Salat ad-Duha, or *tahajjud*; visiting your neighbors, all add up to a powerful affirmation of the ways of the Prophet ﷺ. If you do them God, the Exalted, will love you as in the holy hadith: "When God, the Exalted, loves you, He gives you hearing He did not give to

---

[185] Bukhari.

anyone else." He will give you a heavenly form of hearing. What does that mean, heavenly hearing?

Extended Hearing

There are two kinds of hearing: *dunya* hearing and heavenly hearing. The Prophet ﷺ said on his Lord's behalf, "When I love him, I become his hearing with which he hears…"[186]

"I will be the ears he hears with." This does not literally mean that it will be Allah's ﷻ ears doing the hearing, but that He will give His servant heavenly ears. What could this mean? It means that should He grant it, you would be able to hear things you cannot hear with your ordinary ears. How is this different from *dunya*, worldly hearing? What are the special characteristics of this type of hearing?

Think of a satellite dish. So many signals come from all directions and not all of the signals will be picked up by any given dish. We are like these dishes: our ears and awareness are tuned in to only certain channels. The signals are there, "floating" through the air, but they are all encrypted. The broadcasting companies make you pay for the channels before your dish can pick them up. Today there is AM, FM, long-wave, short-wave and now there is digital radio. You can have thousands of signals and you can receive them all. So you pay money and they give you a decoder to decode the signal and then it passes through your system and comes to your radio or TV.

This is why God, the Exalted, gave us these earlobes. They act as our satellite dishes. It is round like the satellite dishes on our roofs. It receives all kinds of signals. However, you didn't pay for the encrypted channels to be unencrypted. As a result, you only get the basic ones. So the channels go from the outer ear, to the

---

[186] Bukhari, Ahmad.

drum, then to the inner ear. God, the Exalted, grants us certain "free" channels, decodes it and gives us what you are hearing today.

Under certain conditions God, the Exalted, will open more channels. He says, "When My servant approaches Me through voluntary worship, I will love him. When I love him I will give him heavenly hearing." This means that the person hearing has paid his dues, his taxes. He approaches his Lord through voluntary worship; he did more than what is required.

This is the opposite of the common practice today when people do their five daily prayers and then go off to the shopping mall. There is nothing wrong with that: it will get you to Paradise and open up the basic channel of universal broadcasts. But, if you want more, you will need to work hard and earn the money to pay for the more costly channels. Why settle for the cheapest channels? If you are doing well and work hard then you go and get the best, most expensive ones. Your time and effort is the currency in this transaction.

If you are taking the time usually allotted to yourself, and spend it worshipping the Lord and following the way of Sayyidina Muhammad ﷺ, then God, the Exalted, will supply you with the de-encryption codes.

"If he approaches Me with voluntary worship," God says what will happen next? "*Kuntu*" which means "I would be" or "I would have been." The next word is *sama'hu*—his hearing with which he hears. What is the hearing he hears with? That is what Imam Bukhari's students experienced when he addressed the throng of 25,000 people without microphones or speakers. God, the Exalted, gave him the power to make everyone hear.

Extended Vision

To continue with the hadith: "I will be his vision with which he sees," meaning "I will give him heavenly sight, heavenly vision that he can see with." To see what? What then is this heavenly vision? Just as there are audio signals, there are also video signals. When you progress more, God, the Exalted, will grant you vision. This is not something that has no basis in Shariah, quite the contrary, God, the Exalted, is saying it. He said, "I will give them heavenly hearing and vision."

Vision of what? He gave Sayyidina 'Umar ﷺ Allah vision. He gave Sariya hearing. When they were fighting in Sham and Sayyidina 'Umar ﷺ was in Madina Sayyidina 'Umar ﷺ called out, "Ya Sariya! Al-jabal."ᵛ Sayyidina 'Umar ﷺ saw him and sent him the message via the voice channel. Sariyya did not see 'Umar ﷺ but he heard his voice. It depends on the level: one is receiving "audio," the other is receiving "video." But these are not our normal audio and video channels.

They say today there are three dimensions. If you put on 3-D eyeglasses in a theatre, you can see the movie in three dimensions. God, the Exalted, gave this sort of vision to the *awliyaullah* fourteen hundred years ago. Sayyidina 'Umar ﷺ was seeing, feeling and hearing as if he were at the same location as Sariyya.

Contemporary scholars say there is no such thing in Islam. In fact there is. If God, the Exalted, wants to do so, He gives: He is not waiting for anyone's approval.

The hadith continues: "I will be his hearing with which he hears; I will be his eyes with which he sees; I will be the tongue with which he speaks."

How is such a level attainable?

Allah said: *"And remain conscious of Allah and Allah will teach you."*[187] And He said, *"We had taught knowledge from Our own Presence."*[188]

This verse is about Sayyidina Khidr, and it means Allah taught him to understand the meanings behind the verses of the Holy Qur'an. *'Ilmun ladunni* is heavenly knowledge, knowledge from and about the Holy Qur'an to understand what others cannot. That is why we say, wise people or sincere people understand far more than the common person or as God, the Exalted, said in the Qur'an:

> *Behold! verily on the friends of Allah there is no fear, nor shall they grieve;* [189]

Remember the hadith "My saints are under My domes, no one knows them except Me."[190]

When God, the Exalted, wants to give, who or what can stop Him? God, the Exalted, is the Generous One, al-Kareem. Do you think that God, the Exalted, is not giving all sorts of things to us? He is sending gifts to us all the time, but because we are still like children, we don't know the value of these diamonds.

Such valuables are held in trust for children until they become adults. When you become mature you can understand the value of a diamond. Before that, all you want are candies and toys. When you become an adult, you acquire the maturity to understand the importance of faith and prayer. Your heart is opened to the treasures of Islam.

When you pray and say *Allahu Akbar*, you are transported to another place. You might be in this room, facing the Ka'ba, but

---

[187] Suratu 'l-Baqara, (The Heifer), 2:282.
[188] Suratu 'l-Kahf, (The Cave), 18:65.
[189] Suratu 'l-Anbiya, (The Prophets), 10:62.
[190] Al-Ghazali, *Ihya 'Uloom ad-Deen.*

what do you see? If we open our eyes, as in Shari'ah, we must look at the place of prostration, but your gaze must not go farther than that. Look at most people: they look up, down, and sometimes in front. What do they see? They see the wall. Do they see anything else?

Praise of the Prophet

The Prophet said, "The best time for me is when I am praying. I am standing in the Presence of God, the Exalted." His prayer brought him to the Divine Presence.

If God, the Exalted, gave to great gifts to the Prophet ﷺ and the Prophet ﷺ, in turn, asked only on behalf of his Ummah, don't you think that when you say "*Allahu Akbar*" you are not in the Divine Presence? You may only see the surrounding walls, but your prayers can open up all the layers of creation and transport you to a place where God, the Exalted, is observing you and listening to you. This does not mean He does not see you at other times, for He is the All-Seeing, al-Baseer, the All-Hearing, but it means in that station He directs His special care to you. If you reach adulthood, it will be shown to you. If not, this will be granted when you die. That is why Imam Ghazali said, "In *dunya* you are blind and when you die you can see." Now there is a curtain. You have to take that curtain away. There are people who took that curtain away, by Allah's ﷻ grace. God, the Exalted, gave this to them because they gave their life for Islam and for Prophet ﷺ. Allah is not *bakheel*, stingy, He is al-Kareem, the Most Generous.

God, the Exalted, will reward your prayers and lift you to His Divine Presence where you may pray behind the Prophet ﷺ. We are the Ummah of the Prophet ﷺ. This is why we say *Allahuma salli 'ala Muhammad wa 'ala Muhammad.*

Why did God, the Exalted, say:

*Allah and His angels send blessings on the Prophet: O
ye that believe! Send ye blessings on him, and salute him
with all respect?*[191]

God, the Exalted, and His angels are saying *salawaat* on the
Prophet ﷺ. We, in the Ummah, can say *salawaat* on the Prophet ﷺ
as well: this will make him the imam in our prayers. That is why
God, the Exalted, has ordered us to make *salawaat* . *Allahuma salli
'ala Muhammad* ﷺ. Always keep this *salawaat* to show your
dedication and your love to Sayyidina Muhammad ﷺ. God, the
Exalted, wants us to do that. The verse does not say stop. God, the
Exalted, is saying it in the future tense. It means we must repeat
salawaat on the Prophet ﷺ until Judgment Day. *Salloo 'alayhi fa'l
amr. Salloo 'alayh* is a command to praise Him and pray on Him.
And at the same time, the Prophet ﷺ and the angels pray on you:
His prayers on you will bring you peace."

God, the Exalted, is infinitely generous. When we say, "Ya
Rabbee, our prophet is Sayyidina Muhammad ﷺ; our leader is
Sayyidina Muhammad ﷺ; our imam is Sayyidina Muhammad ﷺ,"
and then we say *"Allahu Akbar"* to begin the prayers, who is going
to be the imam standing before us? In truth, the imam for every
Muslim is Sayyidina Muhammad ﷺ.

The Prophet ﷺ said, "I saw Prophet Moses ﷺ in his grave,
praying."[192] If Prophet Moses ﷺ is praying in his grave, what is
Sayyidina Muhammad ﷺ doing? He didn't say "I saw Musa
praying in Paradise." When someone is praying what does it
mean? It means Musa ﷺ is living. They are *anbiyaullah*, God's
prophets. If Prophet Moses ﷺ is praying in his grave, is not
Sayyidina Muhammad ﷺ doing so? If he is praying who is he

---

[191] Suratu 'l-Ahzaab, (The Confederates), 33:56.
[192] Muslim.

praying with? By himself or for himself? He is praying to God, the Exalted and who then is behind him? His Ummah.

So when we say "*Allahu Akbar*," the *'ubudiyya*, worship, is for God, the Exalted. We are servants to God, the Exalted, the Creator. We are prostrating to God, the Exalted and following Imam al-Mursaleen—leader of the messengers and their master. In our physical life there is a veil between us and that reality. When you connect your heart in that fashion, it becomes the reality of what is happening with your prayer. Slowly, over time, that curtain becomes subtle and eventually you can begin to penetrate the veils of darkness. None of us will see as far as Sayyidina 'Umar ﷺ, but we can approach this kind of connection. Why can Sayyidina 'Umar ﷺ see while we cannot? Why would God, the Exalted, give such things to the Companions of the Prophet ﷺ, but to no one else? But at least we have an exemplar, Sayyidina 'Umar ﷺ.

Vision of *Awliya*

After the time of the Prophet ﷺ, the Sahaba scattered across the globe. Everyone went in a different direction: to China, the Middle East, the Far East, even to Europe. They appeared in Portugal and Andalusia even though they didn't know the European languages. They were able to bring Islam to lands far across the planet. They had no oil money, no books, not even a command of the local languages. Instead of all that, God, the Exalted, gave them *haybah*, majesty, and beauty, special traits they inherited from the Prophet ﷺ. If anyone looked at them, they were won over. God, the Exalted, put His power in their voices to sway great masses of people. When they said "*La ilaha illa-Llah*," before a crowd, the people would turn to Islam. This is very different from today when one person takes *shahada* and the whole mosque celebrates for a month.

In those early days the Sahaba were converting entire nations. This is because God, the Exalted, gave them a heavenly language. Observe how an archer aims his arrows to hit the target. He knows the critical point to aim for. If something is just a little out of balance and you push it gently, it will remain standing. But if you push a little harder, its weight will pass its center of gravity and cause it to fall.

Everyone has a center of gravity: a point around which our identity, our sense of self, our spiritual and psychological lives revolve. When a Divinely-inspired archer takes true aim and hits a heart, that target's center of gravity will change. That person can then be transformed from what he was into what he should be. This special kind of aim is made possible by the vision of *awliya*. They can see into a human heart and know when and where to shoot the arrow carrying a Divine and transformative message, a message meant for just that one person.

The *awliya* are supported by a Divine force that flows out to humanity along certain lines. That is why they don't feel sad on the plane of this earthly life: they are given power to change *munkar*, falsehood, to good. Every verse that God, the Exalted, gave to *awliyaullah* carries thousands of meanings. This is not what you read in books. Scholars generally give one or two, sometimes a hundred meanings. In reality, however, a new meaning is revealed each time a verse is read. This new meaning is not created at that time.

Heavenly Steps

The Qur'an is Allah's Ancient Words—*Kalamullah al-qadeemi*. We are limited in understanding; our minds can reach just so far. Some scholars' minds are larger, some smaller. The quality of their interpretations, their *tafseers*, depends on how they see a verse. It would be best to accept all *tafseers*. If you look at the history of *tafseers* of the Qur'an, you can see that Allah can grant insights without restrictions to some interpreters.

In the holy hadith we cited earlier, God said, "I will be his foot with which he walks." That means that wherever he walks, he takes the people behind him to Paradise. People who walk behind him are on *sirat al-mustaqeem*, the straight path, following a proper guide. That is the meaning of guidance. This is an authentic hadith in Bukhari.

God, the Exalted, is the Most Generous. He gives each one of us those things which should make us happy. Different thing make different people happy. Remember, *"Above every knower there is a higher knower."*[193] That is from the Holy Qur'an. It means that if there is someone who has some knowledge, there is someone who has even more. Knowledge and our relationship to it, is in a continuous state of ascension. Don't ever think that you are the topmost expert on a given subject. It would be better to consider ourselves as ants. *"Above every knower there is a higher knower"* means that if you have some knowledge, there will always be others above you with even more.

The Prophet ﷺ said, "The best of generations is my generation, then the one after it, then the one after it."[194]

So how can anyone consider himself an *'alim* when compared to those centuries of the *salaf al-saalih*, the righteous predecessors? But God, the Exalted, is generous. He gives to someone today more than what He gave to another on a different day. That is why the *awliyaullah* have a scope of knowledge which widens and rises with the ascension of the Prophet ﷺ. This is something that they have inherited from him. Prophet Muhammad ﷺ is in

---

[193] Surah Yusuf, (Joseph), 12:76.
[194] Muslim.

continuous *mi'raaj*, because Allah's knowledge grants never stop growing and expanding.

Unlimited Names

God, the Exalted, gives from His Beautiful Names and Attributes through the Divine Attribute *al-'alim*. And yet, from that one Name alone there is enough knowledge to flood the entire universe. *'Ilm* from al-'Alim. All this knowledge and the message of Islam and all that we see in the history of Muslims and non-Muslims, everything that we see as knowledge flows from that single Divine Attribute.

We know the Beautiful Names and Attributes, but what we don't know are their Essences. The reality behind the Divine Names eludes us. The holy hadith Allah says, "I was a hidden Treasure and I wished to be known so I created creation."

In Surat al-Ikhlas, the chapter of Unicity describes the Essence from the view of the Attributes. Allah said: "*Qul Huwa.*" Huwa is the Divine Name describing the Absolute Essence, *al-Huwiyyat al-mutlaqah*. The Divine Essence is the absolute Unknown. God informs us, "No one knows Me! Even you, O Muhammad ﷺ! The One you don't know is Unique, *Ahad*. So the first Divine Name mentioned in that surah is Huwa. It is His first name—the Utterly Unknown One. God, the Exalted, is unknown and unique, Ahad. This succession of attributes leads all the way back to the Essence behind all things, God, the Exalted.

However, for us even these Beautiful Divine Names are just that: only names. God, the Exalted, may be indicated by these names, but never really defined. Al-'Alim, al-Khaliq, al-Qaadir, whatever Name you might consider, there is always another Name behind it emerging, one after the other, like the drops in a fountain. The ascension is continuous and the Beautiful Names keep flowing: the knowledge keeps growing. Nothing is static, the universe is a dynamic system of expanding points and connections. Meaning itself gestates and transforms. If you say al-ʿAlim now, whatever came with that instance in that moment will be superseded in the next instance as each new instance of the name emerges from the absolute unknown. As this process moves forward, each name apprehends more about itself. The fountain flows, the water deepens, the meanings grow richer, and so the universe is woven in ever more intricate and elegant patterns.

Are there really only 99 Divine Names? No, of course not. There are an infinite number of Divine Names because God, the Exalted, cannot be limited. These are deep matters, beyond our ordinary comprehension.

There was no electricity in past centuries, no computers and no telephones. The *awliya* who lived in those times used lamps for light and camels for travel. That was the technology of the civilization in which they lived and functioned. As the centuries go by, each age considers itself "the modern age." Yet Allah ﷻ gives us different things in each age. Even in the Stone Age, people thought of their time as "the modern age." Today our modern life presents us with technologies and inventions undreamed of in past centuries. And yet, the most important aspect of human life in any age can be measured against progress, both individual and general, towards the Lord. This one aspect is the true gauge of humanity's state and station at any given time.

Knowledge: Today and Yesterday

Consider the knowledge and understanding that people had in past centuries. Their knowledge was a million times richer than our knowledge today. Yes, scientific knowledge seems important and advanced, but that sort of knowledge is not going to feed your soul. It can certainly transform your worldly lifestyle, but not your after lifestyle. *Kalaamullah al-qadeem*, Allah's Ancient Words contain that knowledge that was brought out before by the 'ulama. Such knowledge will give you a new afterlife style. In past centuries, knowledge was transmitted from one generation to the next in a very personal fashion. Books were manually transcribed. They were works of love—not mass-produced on printing presses. I have a copy of Sahih al-Bukhari written by hand. I found it in Morocco. It is ten volumes and scripted in different colors. Think how many years it must have taken to inscribe that single copy. Today, if you paid someone a fortune, they could not make a book like that. Such a work displays immense dedication and love to God, the Exalted, and the Prophet ﷺ.

In a way, it is as though today people had bodies and no souls, while in bygone days they had souls with no bodies. Today there are millions of books in print, but they have no ruh—spirit. I found this book copied seven hundred years ago, written originally by Isma'il Bukhari twelve hundred years ago, three hundred years after the Hijra. How did it get all the way from Central Asia to Morocco? How did it pass from one hand to another through Asia to the Middle East, and then to West Africa? The Hanafi Imam al-Marghanini's Kitaab al-hidayah; And Imam Shafi'i's Al-Umm; Imam Ahmad's Musnad. Where are the books of Imam Malik and Abu Hanifa? They followed the Prophet's blessed era by only seventy-five years.

Spirituality is the most important aspect of Islam. That is why the dedication and spirit of these early writers was so important. We don't have that quality today. This is a failure of our modern lifestyle. Spirituality is paramount and that is why the Prophet ﷺ described it as maqaam al-ihsaan—the station of perfection. When he was asked about religion, he described it as consisting of Islam, imaan and ihsaan. He described ihsaan—the perfection of religion— as "to worship God, the Exalted, as if you are seeing Him and if you are not seeing Him, remain conscious that He is seeing you."

Think about the implications of this practice. How are you going to cheat if you are seeing Him, and if you are not seeing Him, realizing that He is seeing you? Either way, your behavior is bound to change for the better when these possibilities become part of your awareness. We are weak: that is the central problem. We ask God, the Exalted, for His support: "O our Lord! Please, don't leave us in the hands of Satan, even for the blink of an eye."

Bi hurmati 'l-Fatihah.

THE CHAPTER OF ABUNDANCE

In the name of God, the Beneficent, the Merciful. God's prayers and peace on Sayyidina Muhammad ﷺ.

Interfaith—Old and New

I would like to explore the connection between the interfaith process and the Prophet's ﷺ in his role as a mercy for all humanity. He is so near the center of creation, surely all faiths were and continue to be touched by His mercy.

I was in London for an event celebrating the birthday of our beloved Prophet ﷺ. There was a parade with about 25,000 people. Following that there was a concert and an interfaith panel discussion including a rabbi and a priest. I followed those speakers with a speech about Islamic Interfaith.

I said that the Prophet brought so much mercy to the Earth that much of his mission was, in effect, an interfaith outreach. He was always open to contacts with other religions. This is an important aspect of the heavenly mercy that God, the Exalted, has given to Sayyidina Muhammad ﷺ as well as to the many prophets who preceded him.

Kawthar Revisited

The Surat al-Kawthar touches on this aspect of the role of the great messengers. In it God, the Exalted, says, *"We have given you a great many things."* Prophetic Tradition says Kawthar is a huge fountain in Paradise. God here is saying that He has given humanity whatever we need to quench our thirst, physical and spiritual. The Prophet said, "All that Allah ﷻ has granted for this universe, for this whole creation of favors and sustenance, are from the Fount of Kawthar."[195]

If we look more deeply into the meaning of Surat al-Kawthar, it indicates that what we have been given can cover everything from the beginning to the end. It follows that the Prophet ﷺ has a lot to give us as well. God, the Exalted, is saying:

> *Verily, We have bestowed upon you (O Muhammad)*
> *good in abundance. So pray unto they Lord, and*
> *sacrifice. Verily it is your insulter (and not you) who is*
> *without posterity.*[196]

So the Prophet is being told *"pray to your Lord and sacrifice."* Sacrifice means to slaughter. Slaughter what? It means "pray to your Lord and give things to your Lord. We have sent you as a mercy for all the worlds." It means "pray as much as you like and don't worry. Pray to us and slaughter the evil that is within people. Eradicate those things in people that cause them to do wrong. You have the power to change things from bad to good. I am giving you that power." That is why God said to the Prophet ﷺ:

> *Your prayers on them will bring them peace.*[197]

An Incomparable Heir

Many scholars today give only the literal interpretation of Surat al-Kawthar, relating it to the Prophet's heritage. It is said that this verse was revealed concerning Abu Lahab, for when one of the Prophet's infant sons died, his chief opponent from his tribe Abu Lahab went to the idolaters and said, "When his sons die, he

---

[195] Isma'il al-Haqqi al-Bursevi, *Ruh al-Bayan.*
[196] Suratu 'l-Kawthar, (Abundance), 108:1-3.
[197] Suratu 't-Tawbah, (The Repentance), 9:103.

228

will no longer be remembered." They interpret *"I have given you abundance"* to mean that God, the Exalted, is saying to the Prophet ﷺ, "I gave you a daughter and a wife," referring to Sayyida Khadija and Sayyida Fatima, "I gave you a daughter whose value is incomparable to anything in this world" as your heir.

When Sayyida Fatima was asked if she would accept marriage to the cousin of the Prophet ﷺ, Sayyidina 'Ali ؏, she said to her father, "Do I have the permission to refuse?" "Yes," he said, "it is up to you." Then she said, "I don't want to marry him."

Never had anyone said something like that to the Prophet ﷺ.

He said, "Why don't you want to marry 'Ali?"

She said, "Do not think my refusal is without reason. I will marry him on one condition."

Consider now the mercy in the heart of this lady and the importance of the family of the Prophet ﷺ. She said, "O my father! When my grandmother was giving birth to you, you came forth and you were saying, "My Community, my Ummah! O my Lord, my Community!" As soon as you came out of the womb of you mother Amina, you were already asking about your community. Let my dowry be the Ummah, the community; then I will accept this marriage."

What does it mean "let my dowry be the Community?" It means that on Judgment Day, when Sayyida Fatima appear in the presence of the Lord, when all are standing for judgment, she will say, "O my Lord! I am requesting that You give me my dowry. Let the whole Community enter Paradise, I will not leave one of them behind!'

Such is the daughter of Sayyidina Muhammad ﷺ, the gifted mercy to humanity—*al-rahmat al-muhda.* Thus the meaning we see in that verse is "O Muhammad ﷺ! We have given you a lot. Your daughter is enough to bring everyone to Paradise."

That is just one of the things that God, the Exalted, gave Sayyidina Muhammad ﷺ.

Interfaith in Heavens

The Prophet ﷺ was always engaged in interfaith activity. He even participated in such dialogues in heaven. When I said that in London, people were surprised. How could the Prophet ﷺ conduct interfaith dialogues in heaven?

The explanation is simple. As you know, he went on the Night Journey and Ascension—Laylat al-Isra wa'l-Mi'raaj about which God said:

> *Glory to He Who did take His servant for a Journey by night from the Sacred Mosque to the farthest Mosque, whose precincts We did bless — in order that We might show him some of Our Signs: for surely He is the Hearing, the Seeing.*[198]

On that night the Prophet ﷺ was invited by the Archangel Gabriel to meet the Lord, reaching the station of *"two bows-length or nearer."* On that night he prayed in heaven with Jesus ئ and Prophet Moses ئ. He was engaged in an interfaith dialogue with Jesus and Moses, discussing the issues of his Community and the people on earth. Then, with the invitation from His Lord, He left that meeting and reached the nearest point to the Divine Presence, the Station of *"two bow's-length or nearer."* Then our Lord ordered Sayyidina Muhammad to oblige his nation to observe fifty prayers every day. Since our Lord ordered us to do fifty daily prayers why are we doing only five? The Prophet ﷺ was happy with that order: fifty prayers had been ordered, and he was happy to do hundreds of prayers if so ordered.

---

[198] Suratu 'l-Isra, (The Night Journey), 17:1.

Then on his return from the Divine meeting, he descended to the fourth heaven where he met Moses, who said to him, "Why are you bringing so many prayers? Fifty is far too much, don't accept them. I am your brother, I have been in heaven a long time; you are just visiting. I know how the people are. The people never listen to a request of this nature."

So Sayyidina Muhammad ﷺ asked, "What do I have to do?" Moses explained, "You must request a reduction."

The Prophet ﷺ said, "How can I go back?"

Moses said, "You don't need to go back. You can ask from here."

So the Prophet ﷺ said, "O my Lord, with the advice of my brother Moses, I am asking to reduce the obligations of fifty prayers." God, the Exalted, said, "I accept, I will reduce it to forty-five."

Then Moses said, "What did your Lord do?" The Prophet ﷺ said, "He gave me a reduction of five prayers." Moses ﷺ said, "No, ask for it to be less. That is not enough." So the Prophet ﷺ went back and asked again. Then Allah reduced it to forty. Each time the Prophet ﷺ was granted a reduction, when he informed Moses, Moses kept insisting on further reductions, and so it went from forty to thirty-five, then thirty and so on. How many are we praying today? As you know, it came down—from fifty to five.

Even then, even when God had reduced the obligation down to five, Moses told the Prophet ﷺ to go back and ask to reduce it to zero. This is because he knew we are very lazy. We try to postpone the prayers as much as we can. This requirement is very heavy for us. The Prophet ﷺ however felt shy about asking his Lord for a reduction from only five daily prayers, but God, the

Exalted, understood and said, "O Muhammad, it is only five, but I will write it down as fifty."

There you have an example of interfaith cooperation between two brothers in heaven. That quality of cooperation should be reflected on earth. This is why God, the Exalted, said:

Verily We have honored the children of Adam.[199]

Allah is telling us: "We have honored them. I have given so many gifts to humankind. I sent Adam 醬, I sent Noah, I sent Abraham, I sent Jesus, and all the other Prophets in between. I sent Muhammad 醬. I have not created all this to generate hate. No—this was something I made to create love."

Witness for Humanity

The whole world is built on love. There is nothing except love. Four letters. Love. In French it is five letters: *amour*, while in Arabic it is two: *hubb*. There you have an Arabic discount.

There is nothing but love. A man loves his wife, and she loves him. You love your children, they love you. You love your grandparents, they love you. If no one loves, then why did He create us? Did He create us to punish us? Did He create us just so that He could say, "You are a bad one, and you are a sinner?" No. He created us to be always feeling the blessings of His manifested love.

Just now they were playing music. Out of their love, their hands and fingers are playing on the strings. Similarly there are strings in the heart. When these strings in the heart work with the strings in the throat, then *dhikrullah* emerges through our voices.

God said:

---

[199] Suratu 'l-Isra, (The Night Journey), 17:70.

And for men and women who engage much in Allah's
praise,- for them has Allah prepared forgiveness and
great reward.[200]

We should remember our Lord in the evening and the morning, for God said:

And celebrate the name or your Lord morning and
evening.[201]

Allah said:

O Prophet! Truly We have sent you as a witness, a
bearer of glad tidings, and warner.[202]

We have sent you *shaahidan*. What is *shaahidan* in Arabic? It means "witness." God has sent him as a witness to what, O Muslims? Witness on what we do daily of good or bad. That is the usual, literal meaning. However, does that go deep enough?

When Allah says, "*O Prophet! Truly We have sent you as a witness,*" it is important that we fully understand what is meant. We, like most of humanity, are not mature. We should seek a firmer grasp of this concept and move beyond common interpretations.

God, the Exalted, sent the Prophet ﷺ as a mercy to humanity; as a means by which we might gain access to the highest levels of Paradise. God, the Exalted, sent the Prophet ﷺ to witness His Beautiful Names and Attributes. He is sending him as a mercy for humanity to witness what God, the Exalted, has prepared on the Day of Promises. Our souls were all together on that day—the day that He gave each of us a pure, living soul. Muhammad ﷺ saw what we were given. The Prophet ﷺ sees all these things because

---

[200] Suratu 'l-Ahzaab, The Confederates, 33:35.
[201] Suratu 'l-Insaan, (Man), 76:25.
[202] Suratu 'l-Ahzaab, (The Confederates), 33:45.

he is the original light—the first light. It is what we call the light of Muhammad ﷺ, *al-nur al-Muhammadi.*

O human beings, God, the Exalted, has sent Muhammad ﷺ as a witness. And then Allah said, "O My Prophet! Tell them what you have seen in My Presence, tell them all about it! Give them good tidings of *'ulum al-awaleen wa 'l-akhireen,* the knowledge you have of all things, the firsts and the lasts."

Then He said, *"and [we sent you O Muhammad] as a warner."* On the Day of Judgment one moment will elapse—after that, everyone will be sent to Paradise. Do not think that God, the Exalted, created us merely to be tortured and punished. Do not worry so much over what wrong you have done. Over the ages, the great prophets, Muhammad ﷺ, Moses, ﷺJesus ﷺ, Ibrahim ﷺ have brought us infinite mercies. In the end, do you really think that anyone will be left standing outside the gates of Paradise? No, on that day we will all be admitted to Paradise by the intercession of our Prophet ﷺ by means of Allah's Infinite Mercy.

ONE SHAYKH

Mawlana Shaykh Nazim

May the station of Mawlana Shaykh Nazim ق ever increase and ride on the waves of the ascending creation. Anyone who gives *baya'*, initiation, to Mawlana Shaykh Nazim ق is, in a sense, authorized as his representative. However, don't consider that person your shaykh. Perhaps he is nearer to the shaykh, more than any other representative, but he is still not the shaykh. The shaykh is Mawlana Shaykh ق. This distinction is echoed at all levels. Even though the Prophet ﷺ was invited by His Lord on the Night Journey and Ascension, Laylat al-Isra wal-Mi'raaj, where he reached the level of *"two bow's-length or nearer."* One must never confuse the Prophet ﷺ with God, the Exalted. Whatever degree of nearness to his Lord He reached, He is happy to be a servant and He is only a servant.

All of us are not true servants. Only Sayyidina Muhammad ﷺ is the true servant and God, the Exalted, is the Creator. Similarly, though the Sahaba were in the presence of the Prophet ﷺ, their status should never be confused with that of the Prophet ﷺ.

Allah gave each of the Sahaba his own particular secret — their inheritance from the Prophet ﷺ. Also *awliyaullah*, their disciples cannot be the shaykh; the representative cannot be the shaykh. However, there are degrees of nearness, and some can be nearer to their shaykh than others. That is why when people practice *muraqabah*, in meditation and in understanding the perception of *taffakur*, contemplation, it is important that they focus on Mawlana Shaykh Nazim ق. The nature of the connection made in meditation rests solely with the shaykh, no matter who officiated your *baya'*, initiation, or introduced you to the practices of the order.

At various times the shaykh has visited different places in the world; some only once. Certain people there may have been assigned to give *dhikr*. Sometimes, even though such individuals are of very low rank, they are the only one in the area deputized to perform specific functions. It is our hope and prayer that such appointees do not become ill with the disease in their hearts which causes them to begin saying, "I am the shaykh."

In officiating the *baya'*, we are only reciting the verse:

> *Verily those who plight their fealty to thee do no less*
> *than plight their fealty to Allah. the Hand of Allah is*
> *over their hands: then any one who violates his oath,*
> *does so to the harm of his own soul, and any one who*
> *fulfils what he has covenanted with Allah,- Allah will*
> *soon grant him a great Reward.*[203]

We know we have nothing in our hand, but Mawlana Shaykh is supporting us. May God, the Exalted, keep that connection with Mawlana and the connection with Sayyidina Muhammad ﷺ strong, and not let us fantasize about being big shaykhs. The shaykh is trying to make you nothing—so don't try to make yourself something.

Wahabi Soup

Today, many people of the Wahabi persuasion have found support in their efforts to deceive and cheat people about the nature of Islam. Even members of government are being deceived by these people. Due to a general lack of understanding about the

---

[203] Suratu 'l-Fath, (The Victory), 48:10.

aims of the Wahabis, not to mention the enormous funds backing them, many people across the globe have come to trust them. Nevertheless, this unfortunate ideology aims for a target that would surprise many of their supporters. Their ultimate aim does not show now, but it will in the end. Those who are on *siraat al-mustaqeem,* the straight path, are pushed out and put on the side. It is always going to be the case, because the Prophet said, "*La rahata fi'd-deen*—There is no rest or relaxation in the way of religion."

There is no ease when you are traveling in the way of God, the Exalted, and of the Prophet ﷺ, and following the right path. That is why, throughout history, most Muslim scholars, and Sufi scholars in particular, were under attack. Today they are the scholars that are being studied: al-Qastalani, Imam Malik, Imam Abu Hanifah, Imam Ghazali, Imam Nawawi. Until today many said that Imam Abu Hanifah didn't have the capacity to memorize hadith and that his knowledge of hadith was deficient. They said that Abu Hanifa's memory was weak and therefore most of the hadith of which he mentioned were weak. And yet, half or a third of the Muslims in the world follow his *madhhab,* school.

Yesterday at a celebration of the Birthday of our beloved Prophet Muhammad ﷺ (Milad an-Nabi ﷺ), the speaker said that the hadith predicting the Ummah would split into seventy and more divisions was fabricated. This is a modern interpretation, entirely unwarranted and uninformed. What else can we expect today, when everything they speak of is modernity and nothing else?

Go the Distance

You would think that there had never been modernity before. And yet, each century developed its own modernity. In past times they were accommodating their modernity through Islam. Islam is able accommodate any time. It even accommodates New Age people. With such people you must exhibit *an-nafas at-taweel*—go the distance. You go along with them ninety-nine steps in order to get them to accompany you one step. That is the meaning of the holy hadith that says, "If My servant approaches Me one handspan, I will approach him one arm's length; if he approaches Me one arm's length, I will approach him by a cubit; if he comes to Me walking, I will come to him running."[204]

We are now, *Alhamdulillah*, with the heavenly sponsor while many of the modern people are with the *dunya* sponsor. Those who are heavenly-sponsored are going to win in the next life, the worldly will win in this life.

We must not look with an eye of hesitation and jealousy. When we are with the Muslims we speak up and say the truth. We are not afraid. The other side is supported by the eminent people of the worldly life. We don't care. We are supported by the next life, from a far more eminent source. When we are with New Age people we speak in the way they understand.

Sincere Follower of Mahdi and Jesus

As Grandshaykh said, and it still rings in my ears, "When Mahdi ☙ and Jesus ☙ come, most of the followers will be New Age people and westerners." That is because today most Muslims do nothing but criticize and complain. When people criticize and complain people get fed up and give them what they want.

When *awliyaullah* criticize and complain they are doing so in a constructive way, not in a destructive way. They criticize and complain to the Prophet ﷺ because that is where they get their power.

---

[204] Bukhari and Muslim.

How much longer Wahabis?

This is why one time Grandshaykh asked the Prophet, in a spiritual meeting, "*Ya sayyidee, ya rahmatan lil-'alameen.* I am becoming old and you know how much damage these Wahabis have done to religion and to you. Why can they not be changed?"

The answer came from the Prophet ﷺ, "When utter ignorance has completely spread everywhere, then revenge comes and following that mercy comes quickly. That is why we are leaving them. O my son, don't think we cannot change them from Wahabis to Sunnis. They are necessary for this time, for they are the dark chunks of dissension and tribulation (*fitna*) that I predicted in the coming night."

They are like the wolf who goes to the flock of sheep and cries, "I am innocent of the accusations of eating the lambs." He shed tears and they believe him and then he jumps on them.

Even after 911 they believe these people, even after what was done. Yet again the flock is under the sway of the wolf. They have learned nothing.

The Prophet ﷺ said, "The *mu'min*, believer, cannot be bitten from the same hole two times."[205]

Consider the hole of a biting animal. You should not be bitten twice. You must know your enemy. 911 came from the Wahabis. The people in control of Islam today are basically the same as those in charge prior to 911. How could so many of these high government officials continue to believe the Wahabis?

The answer lies in what the Prophet ﷺ said to Mawlana Grandshaykh in his vision: these events are necessary in this time, in order for dissension to arise and spread the ignorance the Prophet ﷺ predicted in the Last Days.

---

[205] Bukhari.

So don't feel awkward or discouraged. The troublemakers are supported. *Alhamdulillah,* they are supported for bringing forth tribulation. That is what we are waiting for. Because the corrupt people must go with the other corrupt people, the bad with the bad, the dirty with the dirty. The dirty cannot be with clean. The principle of fiqh, Islamic jurisprudence is *"Al-jins ma' al-jins—* every substance goes along with its like."* Therefore one puts the *khabeeth,* the vile, with the *khabeeth,* as God said:

It is in the nature of things that corrupt women are for corrupt men, and corrupt men, for corrupt women—just as good women are for good men, and good men, for good women. [Since God is aware that] these are innocent of all that evil tongues may impute to them, forgiveness of sins shall be theirs, and a most excellent sustenance![206]

And God said:

Verily, for all men and women who have surrendered themselves unto God, and all believing men and believing women, and all truly devout men and truly devout women, and all men and women who are true to their word, and all men and women who are patient in adversity, and all men and women who humble themselves [before God], and all men and women who give in charity, and all self-denying men and self-denying women, and all men and women who are mindful of their chastity, and all men and women who remember God unceasingly: for [all of] them has God readied forgiveness of sins and a mighty reward.[207]

---

[206] Suratu 'n-Nur, (The Light), 24:26.
[207] Suratu 'l-Ahzaab, (The Confederates), 33:35.

The corrupt females will go with the corrupt among the males while the pure females with go with the pure among the males. God, the Exalted, said, "The believer is with the believer, and those males who remember God are with those females who remember God." The good ones will go with the good ones. So today New Age people are looking for a clean way and pure spiritual leaders. They are looking for the spirituality which many supposedly religious people have already discarded or dishonored. Many of the great Muslim traditions and systems of thought have been flushed down the toilet because there has emerged a new mentality that cannot tolerate cleanliness.

Odors Attract Flies

These Wahabis and their organizations have a rank odor about them—one that attracts flies. People holding similar political views are attracted to this odor. Satan makes these reeking odors attractive to those who swarm like flies to the Wahabi sponsored groups in the West. Satan tells them, "These are delicious delicacies I am giving you on a golden plate, eat them!" The power they derive from such food is Satanic power, and the more they eat the dirtier they become. Once they become crazed with this poisonous food, they attack the *awliyaullah* and those who follow the friends of God, the Exalted. They criticize the saints because they are righteous and pure.

Grandshaykh has said that this is their way and the Prophet ﷺ said that these kinds of people are exactly what is needed to bring about the time of the Mahdi ﷺ and Jesus ﷺ. So Grandshaykh understood the wisdom of this answer and did not ask further. Therefore, realize these evil ones are best catalyst now to stir up confusion and make a soup. Then when people drink the soup they will taste the sourness and recognize it.

Of Sunnis, Sufis and Shia

A speaker yesterday described three major groups within Islam as the Sunnis, the Sufis and the Shia. This is not a correct division. The Sunnis were Sufis. The imams of the four schools of thought were Sufis. Among the twelve Imams were great Sufis and ascetics (*zuhad*). At the same time, Imam Ja'far as-Sadiq is the fifth after the Prophet in the lineage of the Naqshbandi Golden Chain. If you examine the history of this you will see that all Islamic teaching came from these Imams and their schools. These Imams were the Sufis.

Imam Malik explicitly enjoined *tasawwuf*, Sufism, as a duty of scholars in his statement:

He who practices Sufism without learning Sacred Law corrupts his faith, while he who learns Sacred Law without practicing Sufism corrupts himself. Only he who combines the two proves true.[208]

Imam Abu Hanifa said: "If it were not for two years, I would have perished."

This refers to the two years Abu Hanifa accompanied Sayyidina Ja'far al-Sadiq and he acquired the spiritual knowledge that made him a gnostic in the Way. Imam Ja'far as-Sadiq was the great grandson of Sayyidina 'Ali, through al-Husayn on his father's side, and the great grandson of Sayyidina Abu Bakr as-Siddiq ﷺ through his mother.

Imam al-Shafi'i said:

I accompanied the Sufis and received from them but three words: their statement that time is a sword: if you do not cut it, it cuts you; their statement that if you do not keep your ego busy

---

[208] Ali al-Qari, *Sharh 'ayn al-'ilm wa-zayn al-hilm.*

with truth it will keep you busy with falsehood; their statement that deprivation is immunity.[209]

Imam Ahmad said about the Sufis: "I don't know people better than them."[210]

Honey-Seekers

In the time of the Prophet ﷺ those who were looking for spirituality opened their hearts to Him and became Companions. When people open their hearts today they cannot be Companions. Sufis can give westerners some taste of the inner teachings of Islam. The western Sufis are giving a drop from an ocean with the taste of honey. One drop can makes the whole cup of water taste like honey. When New Age people receive even one drop of Sufism, their lives can assume new dimensions. What then do you think of a real Sufi master who is connected to the Prophet ﷺ?

If you want to focus interfaith work on New Age people, it is a good thing, because they are thirsty for knowledge. In every city, there are people who have the connections to arrange programs and lectures on a monthly basis. Each month such programs could rotate among various cities. However, keep in mind that we have to keep up our work with our own Muslim groups. It is these groups that need to have the inner spark of Islam rekindled in their souls. The heart of the teaching lies within the tariqats and Sufism. At the same time, New Age people are genuinely searching for truth. If they are given small doses of Islamic spirituality, they come in huge numbers and the fill up any hall where you have booked an event.

If you look at Mawlana Shaykh's disciples, you will see that they are about evenly split between born Muslims and converts.

---

[209] Suyuti, *Ta'yid al-haqiqa al-'aliyyah.*
[210] al-Saffarini, *Ghidha' al-albab li-sharh manzumat al-adab.*

He speaks to both New Agers and Muslims and both groups find tremendous meaning in his words. We can focus on both sides.

Taste of Straw

Today we drop the political issue if that political issue is creating difficulties for us. We don't need it. Leave it to Wahabis to pursue political intrigue. Politics involves lying and we cannot lie. How many times have we advised the politicians of the truth? And yet they seldom listen, because the professors and academics already have their ears. Many key positions in the universities have been filled with such people: it is very difficult to loosen these knots or combinations. They are everywhere.

For example, yesterday the speaker was talking about modernity: "how to bring Islam into the present day." His words were rigid and dry. While he did say that you have to follow the example of the Prophet ﷺ, most of his talk was more along the lines of the Muslim Brotherhood. He did not seem to have the spirit of the *ruhaniyyat*, spirituality of the Prophet with him. These academics are trying to make everything a political issue. They are creating a stark structure without paint, without decoration, without art, without beauty—only blank walls. Form without spirit. When people look in from the outside, they see that there is house here, but inside they don't know that there is dirt in the hidden corners. There is no spirituality in it. Spirituality fills a place with perfume. There is no spirit in the house of the academics and the political activists.

The New Agers are looking for perfume: they are fed up with the bad odors issuing form the Wahabis camp and their supporters. People want to take spiritual showers to become clean. This will be particularly important when the Mahdi ؏ comes. Such cleansing showers can come from the Sufis alone. The honey will not come from Hizb at-Tahrir or the Muslim

Brotherhood or other Islamist groups—their background is Muslim but they are dirtying it by mixing in the poison of the Wahabis. The extent of their betrayal will become evident when the Mahdi ♐ comes.

Ignorant Scholars

Then be happy that they are in power, because that is a hadith of the Prophet ﷺ that this should be so.

The Prophet ﷺ said:

Allah will not take knowledge from the hearts of the scholars but He takes the scholars (they die). There will be no more scholars to take their place so people will take extremely ignorant leaders. They will be asked questions and will give *fatwas* (legal rulings) without knowledge. They are misguided and they misguide others.[211]

This flood of ignorance heralds important events. In the meantime, the *awliyaullah* prefer to quietly retire to places where few people can meet them. As for us, we have our orders to go and mingle with people. That makes it difficult for all of us but the time is coming when all that will change and knowledge will spread across the globe and whatever happens will take place as foreordained.

That is why Mawlana and Grandshaykh said that if the yearning in heart of Mahdi ♐ were to appear, then this *dunya* would turn into ashes in an instant. The hearts of *awliya* and their followers are bleeding, but there is no permission to use the power God has granted them to effect change through miraculous means. Some of the followers of the shaykh have passed on without reaching the time of Sayyidina al-Mahdi ♐ and Prophet

---

[211] Bukhari and Muslim.

Jesus ﷺ, but by Allah's Favor, we expect they will be resurrected on the intention of awaiting their coming and be rewarded as if they had lived in that golden epoch.

ASCENSION OF THE *AWLIYA*

Irony upon Irony

The American government is sponsoring several Islamic groups giving them money to train the FBI to help identify terrorists. People from such organizations give speeches, but they have nothing to do with Mawlid. If they do, at best it is not fresh material: they only parrot things they have heard or read in books. Mawlana Shaykh on the other hand is taking words from the heart of the Prophet ﷺ in that moment informing people of what they need to hear. There is a big difference between fresh fruit and fruit that is one or two week old or even made of plastic.

The Prophet ﷺ is in continuous ascension. This means that even though the *'ulama* and *awliya* knew much before, the *awliya* of today know still more. As the Prophet ﷺ continues to ascend, it doesn't mean that the living *awliya* know more than *awliya* who have passed away. Those who have passed on are dead in body but still ascending with the Prophet ﷺ in their souls. They possess even more knowledge but the ones who have passed away cannot speak to you. Those who are alive can speak. We can read the words of what the *awliya* said in the past, but that is from centuries ago. In reality they are ascending with the Prophet ﷺ but they cannot transmit that knowledge to the living except through the tongues of the living *awliyaullah*. The *awliya* alive today are also ascending with the Prophet ﷺ and with the other *awliya*. They can relay things back to us, and serve as a communication link between us and the saints of the past.

Generally, these speakers who commonly show up at community events cannot bring you knowledge coming fresh from the heart of one *wali* to another: people who have real connections to the prophets. Such qualities are extremely rare. These saints are scattered around the world and only they can transmit knowledge with the special taste of things that comes directly from the heart of the Prophet ﷺ.

When people go to a Mawlid celebration, they are happier listening to recitation of the poem *al-Burdah* and the celebration than they are with the words of the speakers. They are happier with the music and the spirit of the occasion than with the formal speeches. This is because the usual talks from the podium are the same old recycled material, dry and uninspired. When you bring someone like that to speak, he is speaking from the level of the Muslim Brotherhood.

Knowledge from the Heart of the Prophet

On the other hand, when Mawlana Shaykh comes to speak, he speaks from the heart of the Prophet ﷺ. His connection to the innermost spirit of this faith brings with it an energy and wisdom that can be sensed immediately. One type of speaker gives you a dead body, another brings a living one. It is a waste of time if people don't appreciate living knowledge. So it is finished, it is going to its end. Sometimes I wonder if I should stop doing this because so few people seem interested anymore. Today, it seems, the shaykh is not seen as a source of knowledge. People go to the shaykh only to bring their problems and ask for solutions, for prayers, for protection, but then, that is all they are seeking.

The Prophet ﷺ said, "My Ummah will divide into seventy or more divisions."[212] Now public speakers openly say that this Prophetic Tradition is fabricated! What then, is left of the *Sunnah*?

Kawthar Revisited Again

Verily, We have bestowed upon you (O Muhammad)
good in abundance So pray to your Lord, and sacrifice.
Verily! It is your insulter (and not you) who is without
posterity.[213]

I was praying and we prayed Salat al-ʿAsr before we left. And it came to my heart from Mawlana Shaykh to explain Surat al-Kawthar, with a new emphasis.

The verse says, "*We have given you good in abundance,*" and scholars explain it, "We have given you the heavenly river of Kawthar."

When you are *junub*, in a ritually-impure state, what do you do? You take a shower. If you are near a river, you bathe in it. So the meaning comes, "We gave you that river to clean the Ummah." These meanings came to my heart, so I shall speak of them here.

God said, "O Muhammad ﷺ, We have given you that a lot." When God, the Exalted, says "a lot" to us it means something limitless. So when something has no limit it means you can take whatever you want and you can ask whatever you want and you will get it.

Imam Bukhari relates the hadith in which God, the Exalted, says to the Prophet ﷺ at the scene of the Great Reckoning, "*saʾl tuʿtah*—ask and you will be given."

---

[212] Tirmidhi, Abu Dawud.
[213] Suratu 'l-Kawthar, (Abundance), 108:1-3.

Allah is referring to something in a quantity that cannot be described. It has no beginning and it has no end. It means, "O Muhammad! You will be given all that you request." So when you are given something what do you have to do? Say "*Shukr*, thanks O my Lord." Then *"Pray to your Lord!"* And when you pray you give thank, and when you give thanks He gives more:

When ye are grateful, I will give more (favours) unto you.[214]

There are many meanings here. God, the Exalted, is saying to the Prophet 🌿 the He could take his Ummah under two wings: Paradise of dunya or Paradise of *akhira*. Which one you want? We want both. What is the meaning of:

Our Lord! Give us good in this world and good in the Hereafter?[215]

It means, "O our Lord! Give us *dunya*, worldly, Paradise and give us *akhira*, next life's Paradise." Everyone knows that Paradise, however you may imagine it, is worth more.

This World and the Next

What is the worldly Paradise: to have a yacht in the sea or to have a bank account with billions of dollars? What is its inner meaning? It means give us in *dunya* servanthood and sainthood. He said: *"Verily, We have bestowed upon you (O Muhammad) good in abundance."* It means "We gave you the Paradise of this life and the Paradise of the afterlife."

It means that the Prophet 🌿 will not leave anyone in his Ummah to die without reaching the level of sainthood. When that servant is dying and breathing his last seven breaths, the Prophet 🌿 will put on his or her tongue: *"ashadu anna La ilaha illa-Llah wa ashadu annaka Rasulullah*—I testify that there is no god except

---

[214] Surat Ibrahim, (Abraham), 14:7.
[215] Suratu 'l-Baqara, (The Heifer), 2:201.

Allah and I testify that you, O Muhammad ﷺ, are the Prophet ﷺ of God."

Sayyidina Azraeel, the Angel of Death, cannot take the soul of any member of the Community of Muhammad ﷺ without his permission. The Prophet ﷺ is present with every one of his Ummah at every moment. That is fresh knowledge coming directly from *awliya* sources. It is not dry knowledge coming at the end of a tedious line of quotations and distant references. This is coming from Mawlana's heart. You will never find this in books. We never found that in books and it is not written in them.

When you take *shahada*, the Prophet ﷺ is present, he presents the servant and that servant is clean, for the Prophet ﷺ said, "Islam waives everything that came before it."[216] That is why we become true Muslims at the moment of our death. That is what Imam Ghazali said, "when a someone dies he reaches reality." He did not say what he will see. What he will see is the Prophet ﷺ waiting to take him to Paradise.

Repeat Your Shahada

Whatever a convert did before conversion is erased upon saying the *shahada*. We lifelong Muslims also say *shahada*. Each time we said *shahada* it erases whatever came before. Why should a convert deserve this and not us? Because we are guilty of *shirk*; *shirk al-khafee*—secret or hidden idolatry. In name we are Muslim, but in reality we are *mushrik*, idolaters. For that reason in every *salaat* we say *ashadu an La ilaha illa-Llah wa ashhadu anna Muhammadan Rasulullah*. In effect, we convert back whenever we perform our prayers. The Prophet ﷺ ordered us to do fifty *salaats* a day so that we would be converting at every moment. Even though God, the Exalted, reduced the requirement to five daily

---

[216] Muslim.

prayers, on His scale it is still counted as fifty. Why, as born Muslims do we not have the same rights as converts? *Alhamdulillah*, God, the Exalted, created us Muslim and made us from Ummat an-Nabi. That is why Mawlana ordered us to pray two *raka'ats shukr*.

We are asking, *"Ya Rabbee,* as you forgive the converts, let us have everything erased as well." To that end, Islam erases whatever was before. Therefore, we are saying *shahada* every moment in order to erase what was before. If you have dirty clothes and put them in the washing machine, then they become clean.

The *awliyaullah* understand each letter of the secrets that the Prophet ﷺ reveals to them. That is why when a *wali* speaks, light flows through his words. That light, the *Nur al-Muhammadi,* manifests on that person. So the *awliyaullah* know the meaning of:

We have not sent you except as mercy to all creation.[217]

What is the meaning of *rahmat*? That means that the Prophet ﷺ will not let any soul be taken by the Angel of Death unless he cleanses it from beginning to end. The entire life experience will be cleansed. That means that God, the Exalted, is giving you Paradise in *dunya* and Paradise in *akhira*. If you are clever enough you will be able to taste that level of witnessing before death. That is what the *awliyaullah* are achieving while still alive. Those who don't take the level of *awliya* will take it at death.

Take from Their Wealth!

This is why God, the Exalted, said, *"Pray to your Lord and give sacrifice."* Sacrifice what? God, the Exalted, said:

---

[217] Suratu 'l-Anbiya, (The Prophets), 21:107.

*Of their wealth, take alms, that so you might purify and
sanctify them; and pray on their behalf. Verily your
prayers are a source of security for them: And Allah is
One Who hears and knows.*[218]

God is ordering the Prophet ﷺ, "Take donations from their money by force. Don't leave without taking their money. They are lazy and their hands shake." It is in the form *fa'l amr*—a commanding action to take from their wealth a donation. Why? *Li-yutahirahum*—to purify them. And after he purifies them what does he do? *"Fa-salli 'alayhim—pray on their behalf."*

What is prayer of the Prophet ﷺ? Allah said:

*Allah and His angels send blessings on the Prophet: O
ye that believe! Send ye blessings on him, and salute him
with all respect.*[219]

So when you pray on him he prays on you and that gives you *sakinah*, tranquility. What do people love above all things? Their money. Take their money in order to change them into *awliyaullah*. Do you know how much the Prophet ﷺ took when that verse was revealed? From some Sahaba he took one third of their wealth and he purified them. What are people paying today? Are they paying one-third?

Blood's Significance

In Surat al-Kawthar, "pray to your Lord and sacrifice." We don't say slaughter, rather "sacrifice." *Nahar*, is to take the knife and to put it to the neck of the lamb, cow, sheep or camel and say *"Bismillah Allahu Akbar."* You then present the sacrifice to your Lord. Before the time of Sayyidina Muhammad ﷺ, the prophets

---

[218] Suratu 't-Tawbah, (The Repentance), 9:103.
[219] Suratu 'l-Ahzaab, (The Confederates), 33:56.

used to give *qarabeen*, putting their offerings on altars. Fire would then come from heaven and take the sacrifice.

What is the significance of slaughter and blood? Blood is what carries the oxygen throughout the body. The dirt of sin is flushed by the movement of blood through the body. This circulation cleans the body and rejuvenates it. The action of the heart and the blood takes the poison out of the body. This is the symbolism behind the slaughter of the lambs. When blood comes out of the sheep it is as though the sins and negative energy and poisons were flowing away as well.

"Pray to your Lord and sacrifice," or "slaughter". This is the meaning here: "let the blood carry away the sins." The Prophet ﷺ is being told to cut the neck of the Ummah by taking Satan from their hearts; to slaughter the Satan that is in their hearts. After you purify them and bring them to tranquility then take Satan out.

Someone accused the Prophet ﷺ of having no children. They were referring to the fact that he had no sons. The implication was that his line was cut off without any male heirs, bringing only daughters. The *tafsir* of that surah is that the accuser himself was the one who was cut off.

The Prophet's ﷺ inheritance is a spiritual one. Sayyidina Muhammad ﷺ is always there for us. His reality is everywhere, at every time. *"Know that the Messenger of God is within you."*[220] It means the Prophet ﷺ is in you, manifesting in you and taking over your very self. That is the meaning and function of the Nur al-Muhammadiyya. This light connects all the way back to Prophet Adam ﷺ. *"Lo! It is your insulter (and not you) who is without posterity."*[221]

---

[220] Suratu 'l-Hujuraat, (The Private Apartments), 49:7.
[221] Suratu 'l-Kawthar, (Abundance), 108:3

Prophetic Inheritances

In truth, the one who accused the Prophet ﷺ of having no inheritors was wrong: the Prophet ﷺ has inheritors both through blood, knowledge and through the spirit. His physical descendants are the children of his daughter. For that reason in the last days, that will appear in the person of Mahdi ؏, for the Prophet described the Mahdi ؏ as: "from my family, from the progeny of Fatimah."[222] His inheritors in knowledge are the scholars, where he said, "The scholars are the inheritors of the prophets."

His inheritors in spirituality are the *awliya*. That is why the Prophet said in a hadith, "Whatever Allah poured into my heart, I poured into the heart of Abu Bakr."[223] God, the Exalted, said of His perfect Messenger, "You have been raised," which means "I raised your name with My Name."

This came to me from Mawlana Shaykh when I prayed 'Asr today. Some things you hide and some things you share.

Islamic Leadership

It is very strange to see Muslims here in this area going to the Dalai Lama, a Buddhist leader, to ask him to defend and support Islam. The Dalai Lama is a kind and gentle man, but he usually seems to repeat the same advice, like a greeting card. You know the sort of thing: show kindness, compassion, and so forth. There is nothing wrong with what he is saying. But this is essentially what everyone's mother would have told them from a young age.

We are asking a non-Muslim to be the defender of Islam. They might as well ask him to go to Saudi Arabia to defend Islam from there. As for the speaker we heard the other day, such speakers

---

[222] Abu Dawud, Ibn Majah.
[223] As-Suyuti, *al-Hawi li-l-fatawi.*

255

tend to focus on social issues, like the colonization of Muslim nations. They drag Islam into their speeches almost as an afterthought. They have no love for Sayyidina Muhammad ﷺ and no love for the *awliyaullah*.

Oddly enough, Muslims from this areas approached a Buddhist leader and asked him for support in the defense of Islam. The idea seemed to be that the spirituality of Buddhism could in some way be transferred and improve the image of Islam. Five hundred people from local Islamic organizations and mosques, even one local scholar, went to hear him speak. One time when our staff suggested they invite us to one of their functions and they said, "No, he shines too brightly."

Why would they ask a Buddhist for support through spirituality? Can support not be found through the spirituality of Islam? *Subhanallah*, they are bankrupt! They have lost the living symbol of Islam and can no longer receive things directly from the heart of the Prophet ﷺ.

GLOSSARY

'Abd (pl. *'Ibaad*)—lit. slave, servant of the Lord.

Abu Bakr as-Siddiq ﷺ—one the closest Companions to the Prophet ﷺ, his father-in-law, who shared the Hijrah with him. After the Prophet's death, he was elected as the first caliph (successor) to the Prophet ﷺ. He is known as one of the most saintly of the Prophet's Companions.

Abu Yazid/Bayazid Bistami—A great ninth century *wali* and master in the Naqshbandi Golden Chain.

Adab—good manners, proper etiquette.

'Ali ibn Abi Talib ﷺ—the cousin of the Prophet ﷺ, married to his daughter Fatimah and fourth caliph of the Prophet ﷺ.

Alhamdulillah—Praise God.

Allah—proper name for God in Arabic.

Allahu Akbar—God is the Greater.

Amir (pl., *umara*)—chief, leader, head of a nation or people.

'Arafat—a plain near Mecca where pilgrims gather for the principal rite of Hajj.

'Arif—knower, gnostic; in the present context, one who has reached spiritual knowledge of his Lord.

Ar-Raheem—the Mercy-Giving, Merciful, Munificent, one of Allah's ninety-nine Holy Names

Ar-Rahman—the Most Merciful, Compassionate, Beneficent, the most often repeated of Allah's Holy Names.

Astaghfirullah—lit. "I seek Allah's forgiveness."

Awliyaullah, Awliya (sing., *wali*)—the "friends" of Allah, Muslim saints.

Ayah/Ayat (pl. Ayaat)—a verse of the Holy Qur'an.

Bayt al-Maqdis— the Sacred Mosque in Jerusalem, built at the site where Solomon's Temple was later erected.

Baya'—pledge; in the context of this book, the pledge of initiation of a disciple (*murid*) to a shaykh.

Dajjal—the False Messiah (Antichrist) whom the Prophet ﷺ foretold as coming at the end-time of this world, who will deceive mankind with pretensions of being divine.

Dhikr—literally, "remembrance" (of Allah) through repetition of His Holy Names or various phrases of glorification.

Du'a—supplication.

Dunya—worldly life.

'Eid—festival; the two major festivals of Islam are 'Eid al-Fitr, marking the completion of Ramadan, and 'Eid al-Adha, the Festival of Sacrifice during the time of Hajj.

Fard—obligatory worship.

Fatihah—Suratu 'l-Fatihah; the opening surah of the Qur'an.

Ghawth—lit. "Helper"; the highest ranking saint the in hierarchy of saints.

Ghusl—full shower/bath obligated by a state of ritual impurity prior to worship.

Grandshaykh—generally, a *wali* of great stature. In this text, where spelled with a capital G, "Grandshaykh" refers to Mawlana 'Abd Allah ad-Daghestani, Mawlana Shaykh Nazim's shaykh, to whom he was closely attached for forty years up to the time of Grandshaykh's death in 1973.

Hadith (pl., ahadith)—reports of the Prophet's ﷺ sayings, contained in the collections of early hadith scholars.

Hadith Qudsee—God's Words relayed on the tongue of the Prophet ﷺ, but which are not part of the Qur'an.

Hajj—the sacred pilgrimage of Islam obligatory on every mature Muslim once in his/her life.

Halaal—permitted, lawful according to the Islamic Shari'ah.

Haqq—truth, reality.

Haraam—forbidden, unlawful.

Haasha—God forbid!

Haqq—truth, reality.

Hijrah—emigration.

Imam—religious leader; specifically, the leader of a congregational prayer. Also an advanced scholar followed by a large community.

Imaan—faith, belief.

Ihsaan—perfected character.

Iraadatullah—the Will of God.

258

Jinn—an invisible order of beings created by Allah from fire.

Jumu'ah—Friday congregational prayer, held in a large mosque.

K'abah—the first House of God, located in Mecca, Saudi Arabia to which pilgrimage is made and which is faced in the five daily prayers.

Kalaamullah al-Qadeem—lit. Allah's Ancient Words, viz. the Holy Qur'an.

La ilaha illa-Llah, Muhammadun rasul-Allah—there is no deity except Allah, Muhammad is the Messenger of Allah.

Maqaam—spiritual level of attainment, station.

Mawlana—lit. "our master" or "our patron," referring to an esteemed person.

Meezaan—the Scale which weighs the actions of human beings on Judgment Day.

Mi'raaj—the Prophet's ascension to the Heavens and the Divine Presence.

Mu'min—a believer.

Murid—disciple, student, follower.

Murshid—spiritual guide, *pir*.

Nafs—lower self, ego.

Nur—light.

Qiblah—direction, specifically, the direction faced by Muslims during prayer and other worship towards the Sacred House in Mecca.

Qiyamah—(the Day of) Resurrection or Judgment.

Ramadan—the ninth month of the Islamic lunar calendar, the month of fasting.

Rasulullah—the Prophet of God, Muhammad ﷺ.

Rawhaaniyya—*spirituality, spiritual essence of something.*

Ruh—spirit. Ar-Ruh is the name of a great angel.

Sahabah (sing., sahabi)—the Companions of the Prophet, the first Muslims.

Sajda (pl. *sujud*)—prostration.

Salaat—prayer, one of the five obligatory pillars of Islam. Also to invoke blessing on the Prophet ﷺ.

Salawaat (sing. *salaat*)—invoking blessings and peace upon the Prophet ﷺ.

Sawm—fasting.

Sayyid—leader; also, a descendant of Prophet Muhammad ﷺ.

Sayyidina—our chief, master.

Sayyidina 'Umar—'Umar ibn al-Khattab ﷺ, an eminent Companion of the Prophet ﷺ and second caliph of Islam.

Shahadah—the Islamic testification of faith, *"Ash-shadu an la ilaha illa-Llah wa ashhadu anna Muhammadan rasulullah*—I bear witness that there is no deity except Allah and I bear witness that Muhammad is His Prophet."

Shah Naqshband—Grandshaykh Muhammad Bahauddin Shah-Naqshband, a great eighth century *wali*, the founder of the Naqshbandi Tariqah.

Shari'at/Shari'ah—the Divine Law of Islam, based on the Qur'an and the Sunnah of the Prophet .

Shaykh—lit. "old man," a religious guide, teacher; master of spiritual discipline.

Shirk—polythism, ascribing divinity or divine attributes to anything other than God.

Sohbet (Arabic, *suhbah*)—the assembly (Association) or discourse of a shaykh.

Subhanallah—glory be to God.

Sultan/sultana—ruler, monarch.

Sultan al-Awliya—lit., "the king of the *awliya*,"; the highest-ranking saint.

Sunnah—the practice of the Prophet ﷺ; that is, what he did, said, recommended or approved of in his Companions.

Surah—a chapter of the Holy Qur'an

Takbir—the pronouncement of *"Allahu Akbar*—God is Greater."

Taraweeh—the special nightly prayers of Ramadan.

Tariqat/tariqah—literally, way, road or path. An Islamic order or path of discipline and devotion under a guide or shaykh; Islamic Sufism.

Tasbeeh—recitation glorifying or praising God.

'Ubudiyyah—state of worshipfulness.

'Ulama (sing. *'Alim*)—scholars.

Tawaaf—the rite of circumambulating the K'abah while glorifying God during Hajj and 'Umrah.

Ummah—faith community, nation.

'Umrah—the minor pilgrimage to Mecca, which can be performed at any time of the year.

Wali (pl. *awliya*)—saint; "friend" of God.

Wudu—the minor ablution that precedes prayers and other acts of worship.

Zakat/zakah—the obligatgory charity of Islam, one of its five "pillars" or acts of worship.

Zakat al-Fitr—the obligatory charity of 'Eid al-Fitr, the festival marking the completion of Ramadan.

ENDNOTES

[i] Narrated from Anas by al-Bayhaqi in *Shu'ab al-Imaan* and *al-Madkhal*, Ibn 'Abd al-Barr in *Jami' Bayaan al-'Ilm*, and al-Khatib in *al-Rihla fi Talab al-Hadith*.

[ii] From at least the time of 'Ali al-Hujwiri (d. c. 1075 CE) the word *ghawth* had become a Sufi technical term indicative of the head of the ... one occupying an important position in the hierarchy of Sufi saints, the "Men of the Unseen" (*ahl al-ghayb*). In his *Kashf al-mahjūb* (*The Unveiling of the Secret Things* written c. 1050) Hujwri wrote:
Of those who have power to loose and bind are the officers of the Divine court there are three hundred called Akhyaar ["Choice Ones"], and forty called Abdaal ["Substitutes"], and seven called Abrār ["Pious Ones"], and four called Awtad ["Pillars"], and three called Nuqabaa' ["Directors"], and one called *qutb* ["Pivot" or "Axis"] or Ghawth ["Helper"] (Tr. Nicholson, R.A.: 1921 *Studies in Islamic Mysticism* . Cambridge University Press: Cambridge : 214)

[iii] Amru ibn Hisham (d. March 17, 624) better known as Abu Jahl, was one of the Meccan leaders, known for his hostility against the Muslims. He was known as Abu al-Hakam (meaning father of wisdom) but was later renamed Abu Jahl, meaning father of folly/ignorance by Prophet Muhammad himself. Abu Jahl was killed in the Battle of Badr.

[iv] A hadith with similar purport is found in Ibn Majah, "Verily to God belong receptacles from the people of the earth; and the receptacles of your Lord are the hearts of His sincere servants, and

the most beloved of them to him are the most lenient and the most soft."

ᵛ Ibn 'Umar 🌸 said that his father, Sayyidina 'Umar 🌸, was delivering a sermon on Friday. In the middle of his sermon, he shouted, "*Ya Sariyya, al-jabal*—O Sariyya! [look towards] the mountain!" Then he resumed his sermon and said, "He who stole a wolf, he oppressed," which means, "He who fed and watered the enemy, he committed an act of oppression."

Some people looked at each other in dismay. Sayyidina 'Ali 🌸 said to them, "He will likely say (something) about this statement."

When the people had finished the prayer, they asked Sayyidina 'Umar 🌸 about the incident. He said, "The idea crossed my mind that the enemy aggressors had defeated our brethren and they would run towards the mountain. Thus, if the Muslims moved towards the mountain, they would have to fight on one side only, while if they advanced, they would be destroyed. So those words escaped my mouth."

After a month, a messenger came with good news. He said, "The people of the army heard Sayyidina 'Umar's 🌸 voice on that day. We all went towards the mountain and God made us victorious."

It is reported from his son 'Abd Allah 🌸 that his father Sayyidina 'Umar 🌸 [who was caliph at the time] dispatched an army, designating one man named Sariyya 🌸 leader (*amir*) over it. It is said that one day Sayyidina 'Umar 🌸 was delivering the Friday sermon [in Madinah]. During the sermon he said loudly "*Ya Sariyya al-jabal*—O Sariyya! [towards] the mountain." Then [later] a courier came from the army and said, "O Commander of the Faithful! We were on the verge of being defeated when we heard a voice thrice: '*Ya Sariyya al-jabal!*' So we moved the back of our army near the mountain and Allah Most Holy defeated them." Ibn

'Umar ﷺ says that Sayyidina 'Umar ﷺ was told that it was he who was shouting in that voice.

It says in one tradition that the people said to Sayyidina 'Ali ﷺ "Did not you hear Sayyidina 'Umar that while delivering the sermon from the pulpit he said, *'Ya Sariyya al-jabal!'*? Sayyidina 'Ali ﷺ said, "A thousand pities for you! Leave Sayyidina 'Umar ﷺ alone! Whenever he has entered anything, he has surely acquitted himself well."

Both narrations are in *Life of the Companions*, by Shaykh Zakariyya Kandhalvi.

CPSIA information can be obtained at www.ICGtesting.com
233583LV00006B/71/A